ONLY ANGELS HAVE WINGS?

To Ali.

With Best Wishes.

John H Evans.

Oct 20/17.

Only Angels Have Wings?

J.H. Evans

Library of Congress Control Number:		2011917079
ISBN:	Hardcover	978-1-4653-5967-4
	Softcover	978-1-4653-5966-7
	Ebook	978-1-4653-5965-0

This book was printed in the United States of America.

To order additional copies of this book, contact:
Xlibris Corporation
0-800-644-6988
www.xlibrispublishing.co.uk
Orders@xlibrispublishing.co.uk
302798

In memory of, and my everlasting gratitude to my parents,
Ruby, and William John Evans.

Contents

Foreword

Sitting on my bookshelf I have a textbook of Qualitative Chemical Analysis given to me in February 1964 by one John H Evans, ex-school teacher, pilot, flying instructor, company director and entrepreneur. He had abandoned school-teaching, while I was in the throes of studying for my advanced level school exams. I had spent, and would continue to spend, my weekends and school holidays being the general dogsbody for the fledgling Cormorant Air Services, as John and his colleague Paul Weeks struggled to persuade the great British public in Swansea and Ramsgate that they wanted to fly with Cormorant.

Indeed, I had turned down the chance of playing my violin in the Welsh National Youth Orchestra rather than forego the opportunity of devoting the summer holiday to selling pleasure flight tickets to the bemused holidaymakers of Ramsgate. (I am relieved to see that nowhere in his book does John mention the occasion I reversed the company's new Minivan into a Ramsgate lamppost.)

My father at that time managed Swansea Airport and I had inherited his enthusiasm for aeroplanes and things aeronautical. Like so many of my generation, I would cadge free flights in anything that flew in return for washing airframes, cutting the grass round the hangar, refuelling aircraft or selling tickets for pleasure flights.

I couldn't believe my good fortune when this larger-than-life ebullient Welshman appeared on the scene and actually encouraged me to get involved with aeroplanes and aviation. However, John's enthusiasm was tempered with wisdom. When he gave me that textbook, he cautioned that if I wanted security and certainty in life, I should not enter commercial aviation without the benefit of some other profession behind me (to make a small fortune in aviation, you start with a large one).

Wise words, which led me into a medical career. But only in parallel with a career as a military jet pilot, test pilot and flying instructor, and later as a commercial pilot.

Other words I remember include the statement that John's ambition was to make sufficient money from aviation to afford a house where it was warm enough to shave in the nude.

John's infectious enthusiasm springs from every page of this book. I began by intending to have a preliminary cursory skim through the volume, but found that I just could not put it down. He has the skill to bring the situation to life in glorious literary Technicolor, and you cannot wait to turn the page to find out what happens next.

I have sat in the cockpit of that Aero 145 and marvelled while John cursed the idiosyncratic electric control of the propeller pitch.

I have marvelled as the Tripacer appeared from nowhere out of the low stratus and kissed the wet concrete with its (ahem!) bald tyres.

I would wonder how these guys survived, and yet retained their sanity and above all, their enthusiasm. Retain it they did, and the stories pour forth as you read through this book.

As you follow the amazing story of John's aviation life, you are on occasions tempted to suspend belief. But I can assure you that everything recounted in this book really did happen, as indeed did more.

John's entrepreneurial skills and powers of persuasion enabled him to establish aviation companies which have become household names, such as Brymon and Air Wales. John has the vision and provides the catalytic spark, and then eventually moves on to some other achievement. Yet despite being an entrepreneur, he has remained a thoroughly nice man who cares for the feelings of others and is immensely proud of his family.

John H Evans was a major influence in my life, and I am delighted to provide this foreword. You acquired this book to read about John Evans and not about me, so I will hold you back no longer from the treat which awaits you in these pages. Enjoy it!

Dr Michael Bagshaw
Head of Medical Services, British Airways

Preface

Early in 2003 my cousin, Colin Evans, having spent considerable time researching the family tree, sent me a copy of his work. This led me to thinking of how little I knew of my antecedents. In fact, my grandparents were barely known to me, and my great-grandparents remain a mystery. Coincident with this my daughter, Sian, gave birth to little Katy, and I became a grandfather for the first time. This made me realise that Katy would only ever know me in part, and her children not at all. This loss of family history is not untypical however, and so much personal history becomes tragically lost forever. Consequently the writing of this book was initially conceived merely as a manuscript for family consumption. However in addition, over the years a number of my friends strongly suggested that I set out in print some of my experiences, recounted in drinking sessions and at various dinner parties, the result is this book!

Following an early skirmish with the desire to be an engine driver, aviation became my focus of endeavour, more precisely, to be a pilot. This book is therefore a personal memoir of some of my flying activities, and the perpetual adversary, the weather, which despite the best efforts of man remains shrouded in mystery and danger. The airline business too is not without its unwelcome possibilities, and although no blood is spilt, on some occasions it certainly felt as if it had. Apart therefore, from one of my excursions into the field of pedagogy, the events depicted are largely aviation related.

All the people, companies and events that follow are as real as my imperfect memory has allowed, and I have toned down rather than exaggerated them. Sometimes however, I have deemed it necessary to use false names, in order to protect their anonymity. In writing this book I have been gratefully helped by my flying log book, and some ill kept diaries. No career is so carefully documented as that of a professional pilot, whose personal log book, (kept by law), records the day, hours and minutes of each flight from the origin to the destination airport. Many years later, just one look at one line can usually invoke the memory of that moment as nothing else can. Girls and flying are more often than not inextricably linked in civil aviation. I cannot therefore pretend to have eliminated all the girls I have known from the following pages, and the careful reader will notice that from time to time, that the odd girl does indeed crop up.

Finally I would like to pay homage to the many pilots, who shared the skies with me in the latter part of the twentieth century. Almost without exception, they were among the best of their generation, and I was privileged to have known some of them.

J. H. Evans
Butleigh, Somerset
March 2004

CHAPTER 1

FIRST DAY ON THE SCILLIES

It was the evening of Thursday 1st April 1965. The shrill note of the telephone silenced the babble of voices in the flight office. I picked up the telephone to hear the pleasant West Country voice of Andy the commercial manager of West Point Airlines of Exeter.

"Hi John," he said, "do you have any availability on your Aero 145 this weekend? Unfortunately our Rapides are unserviceable, and we need you to operate a number of services for us to the Isles of Scilly."

"Hang on, I'll check the movements board," I said knowing full well that there was nothing booked. I waited a few moments picked up the telephone and said "Andy, you're in luck the aircraft is free on Saturday and Sunday this weekend."

"Great, I'll meet you at Plymouth airport at whatever time you can make it, and brief you on the Saturday programme. Then, I suppose, you'll need a couple of rooms, so I'll book them at the George, as no doubt you will be bringing company." Clearly, Andy seemed to know me all too well. I put the telephone down in a mood of excitement with this apparent success, as West Point was an established airline at that time, and our company 'Cormorant Aviation' was but a fledgling business, largely operating on the proverbial shoestring. Seven to eight flying hours at £35 per hour represented a small fortune to us, and although it was April fools day this was for real.

Fate would have it that the next morning we took a charter to pick up a group of people at Plymouth and fly them to Swansea. As a result I didn't land back at Plymouth until later in the evening where Andy and his wife were there to meet me as planned in the wooden shack that passed as a Terminal Building. Seated around a small table in the airport lounge, Andy spelt out the programme for the following day. I remember the sequence of flights as if it were yesterday. It was as follows:

"You will fly: Plymouth to Scillies, Scillies to Plymouth, Plymouth to Scillies, Scillies to Bristol, Bristol to Scillies, Scillies to Newquay, Newquay to Scillies and finally Scillies to Plymouth." I casually asked him, what he wanted me to do in the afternoon. At this he fell into a paroxysm of uncontrollable laughter. When the mirth subsided, he asked how well I knew the Scillies. When I answered that I had never landed there in my life, he looked at me like a headmaster addressing his favourite pupil and said solemnly, "It's a difficult airfield John, but at least the weather forecast looks good for tomorrow, so you should be ok!"

I had arrived in Plymouth that evening together with an entourage of three girls, one of which was the belle of Cormorant, our very attractive eighteen-year-old secretary Valerie. In addition the ever present Dick Rosser had once more cadged a ride with me. Dick was an incorrigible eighteen year old from Llanelli whose main purpose in life, it seemed, was to be in, or near aeroplanes. He habitually took in all the Air shows around the country, hitch hiking and sleeping rough as the needs arose. I was his flight instructor back at Swansea, and he had, to date, completed about twelve hours instruction. His full time occupation was that of a trainee chemist at the Trostre Steel Works in Llanelli, but how he ever retained his job, remained a mystery to me in view of his many travels.

In the short time available to me from Andy's telephone call and my arrival at Plymouth I had of course briefed myself as well as I could on the West Country in general, and the Isles of Scilly in particular. The island group consisted of five inhabited islands in addition to over a hundred smaller uninhabited islands 25 nautical miles southwest of Lands End. My Air Navigation chart indicated that the longest runway, at just over 600 metres, was the second smallest in the country and was sited on St. Mary's. This was the largest of the many islands, but was less than three miles across with a coastline somewhat short of ten miles. But it was the weather that created an ever-present hazard for the aviator. The large moist Atlantic air masses hits the West Country first, creating airport conditions of low cloud, poor visibility in mist and fog and at other times would generate fierce winds and turbulence. These conditions could change almost in minutes, with cloud lifting and visibility improving, convincing the pilot he could pull-off a successful landing, only to be thwarted a short time later when the cloud descended once more with a corresponding fall away in visibility.

Had all the airfields in the West Country been adequately equipped with runways and good navigational aids then one would have felt that the odds against you had somewhat diminished, unfortunately this was not the case. In retrospect, and after many years flying the West Country routes I had no doubt that Land's End Airport was the worst in terms of weather, closely followed by Plymouth. The latter is situated almost 500 feet above sea level, and was at that time an all grass airfield. At night without proper runway electric lighting the pilot depended only on gooseneck flares, which were pots of oil with a wick shaped like a gooseneck and which, sometimes, blew out, giving a sporting chance only of landing safely. It did possess a basic direction finder which was not automatic, and to use it the controller had to leave the tower, jump on his bicycle and travel a hundred yards or so to a wooden shack (often confused as an outside loo), to use this antique piece of machinery. To increase the odds against the pilot, the high ground of Dartmoor stood to the north and west, not to mention the BBC Television mast at North Hessary Tor, standing as an obstacle to flying at an elevation of 2400 feet above sea level.

Land's End airfield was not on the schedule service route, but in the event of problems aloft, could be used as a suitable diversionary airfield, weather permitting. Once again it was a grass field, standing almost 400 feet above sea level. It had no navigational facilities at all, and on future occasions I would stand on the airfield watching the cloud and visibility rise then fall with monotonous regularity. In autumn and winter there could be quite fearsome and dense fogs, which would suddenly descend and envelop the airfield for days on end, preventing any flying activity. The weather on Scillies could be very treacherous, but in my view infinitely better than that of Land's End. In the years ahead, my agent on the islands described it as the only place in the UK where you could experience the four seasons in one day. Certainly the flower growers on the islands knew this, and their fields of daffodils, which bloom early in the year, were well protected by stone walls.

The one serious 'bolt hole' for the pilot in the area was, and presumably still is, the RAF master aerodrome at St. Mawgan, now named Newquay Civil Airport. Perched on the north facing Cornish cliffs, it is bordered to the north east by Padstow and in the south west by the town of Newquay. This airfield was superbly equipped with all the up-to-date navigational equipment as befitted a North Atlantic diversion airfield. Here a pilot could be talked-down by precision radar in the vilest of weather the West Country had to offer.

The least affected airport in warm front conditions, which plagued all the others, was Exeter, which was sheltered in such conditions by the mass of Dartmoor to the West. Although equipped with concrete runways and electric lighting, it nevertheless lacked any precision navigational let-down equipment, having only a voice direction finder (VDF).

The next morning I arrived at the airfield to find an anxious looking Andy waiting to meet me.

"You did say last night that you'd never been to the Scillies before."

"Quite right," I said, inwardly smiling.

"Well you know it's a difficult airfield, don't you?" he said.

"Andy," I said, "the trouble with you is that you worry too much. Remember my motto, 'fly with us and you'll never walk again'." The required smile did not appear on his face.

"I'll be here when you get back," he said and stalked off. Andy was understandably worried, as he was aware that the correct procedure prior to visiting a category 'C' airfield, would have entailed a pre-visit with an experienced line check captain. Little Cormorant however could stretch to no such luxury.

My four happy smiling passengers suitably briefed and strapped in their seats were clearly deluded into thinking that they had a competent pilot up front. I shuddered to think what they would have said or done, had they known that I knew little of the islands, and had never landed there before. The weather forecast that morning looked reasonably good, with no recorded cloud and above three kilometres of flight visibility in thick haze. At 0845 hours I opened the throttles on the Aero, registered as GASWS (Golf Alpha Sierra Whiskey Sierra), and rolled down runway 24 at Plymouth. I climbed initially to three thousand feet, but forward visibility was so poor that I continued the climb to flight level 60 (six thousand feet), hoping things would improve. Nothing changed however, so I slid the aircraft in a shallow descent back to three thousand feet. I was now comfortably settled on instruments which, for me, was never a chore. In fact I rather enjoyed instrument flying simply as recognition of necessity, and my own keen instinct to survive. Locked on to instruments you learned to completely disregard any bodily indications that your inert sense of balance gave you, otherwise the fluid in the semi-circular canals of the ears would surely lead you astray. These were fine for standing or walking in the normal earthly environment, but in the cockpit at night or in cloud, the only indications as to which way up you were rested on those little dials which stared at you from the instrument panel.

Although forward visibility was poor, looking directly downwards I could see we were now crossing St. Austell bay bang on track. Forty minutes after take-off Whisky Sierra (WS) was crossing Land's End, although the peninsula was barely visible below. Now for the fist time I changed the radio frequency and called the Scillies.

"Good morning Scillies this is GASWS. Whiskey Sierra is crossing Land's End at 25 level 3000 feet estimating you at 35." (Time is always reported as minutes after the hour). The controller's voice, later identified as Tom Ashby, answered in a friendly relaxed manner.

"Good morning Whiskey Sierra, the weather here is good, we have no cloud and visibility is three kilometres in haze. The wind is calm and the runway in use is 28, and QFE 1010." (QFE is the pressure setting at aerodrome level). "Call passing the Eastern Isles, there is no conflicting traffic."

I confirmed the instructions and reset the altimeter to the Scillies pressure setting and descended to 1000 feet. Now to spot the Eastern Isles, I thought, as I peered out for my first glimpse of the islands.

Nothing I had ever seen or read could have prepared me for the next few moments. Suddenly as if a curtain had been opened, in front of me were the islands. They were glistening like jewels in a sea of blue and green as though in welcome. I gasped with pleasure and shouted to the passengers.

"There they are! There they are! What a sight." Like a kid glimpsing the sea for the first time on his summer holidays, I heard myself reciting

"Earth has not anything to show more fair dull would he be of soul who could pass by a sight so touching in its majesty." It was a shame that old Wordsworth wasn't sitting alongside me that morning, as even he would have been stretched to find words to match the occasion. My reverie was soon shattered when the controller called again.

"Whisky Sierra, have you been to the Scillies before?"

"Negative Scillies," I answered.

"Then I suggest you fly overhead the field and have a good look at it before landing."

"Roger," I answered. "I think that would be a good idea." This was not the time or place to engage in false pride. Visibility had marginally improved, and now overhead I looked intently, searching for the airfield. Suddenly I saw it, and stiffened in my seat. It looked just like a postage stamp from 1000 feet, and was certainly the smallest airfield I had ever seen. The runway extended down to the rocks, and only the first 280 metres of it was tarmacadam, and the remainder 243 metres grass. I slowly turned on a three mile final for runway 28, and then for the first time realised that the runway was in fact nothing more than a steep gradient. I descended to fifty feet over the sea and flew directly at the hill with the far end of the runway stretching before me. With undercarriage and flaps down, I made the approach at ninety knots with a large helping of power. I had never landed up a hill before, so this required a new technique. I skimmed over the rocks, and across the threshold of the runway, and rotated the aircraft upwards, at the same time closing the throttles. The wheels kissed the tarmac gently in greeting and the steep gradient soon slowed the aircraft to a stop. I had completed my first ever landing on the Isles of Scilly, and was suitably gratified. I turned right and parked the aircraft in front of the control tower as directed. The time was 0940 hours a flight time of 55 minutes. I climbed out of the aircraft and made my way to the tower to meet the friendly controller. From that vantage point the runway approach seemed almost impossible, and I marvelled at my own ability to land there. However the day's work had hardly begun.

Later I was to find out that the land between Scillies and the mainland was known historically as Lyonesse, where in long gone days sailors claimed to hear bells of engulfed churches. In the next twenty years or so I was to complete almost five hundred landings on the Scillies, but apart from flying in the most beautiful of weather, the islands rarely advertised themselves. In fact, many times I was taken aback by their sudden and magical appearance, even when they coincided with my ETA (Expected Time of Arrival). Often a mysterious veil seemed present, and once through it, the aircraft and passengers seemed to enter a time warp. I always felt a profound sense of pleasure on arrival, and without doubt a spell was cast, which endured. Landings on the most exotic of Caribbean islands never induced the same effect.

The flight back to Plymouth was uneventful, and Andy was there to greet me, now with a large smile on his face. I was sure he expected me back early, having not completed the flight, or perhaps not at all.

"Every thing OK then?" he asked.

"Sure," I said, "piece of cake." This was perhaps the greatest understatement of my flying career, but that morning I felt positively 'god like'.

"I'm off to Exeter now," said Andy, clearly confident that I could complete the flying programme without difficulty, "if you have any problem just tell the staff, and they will contact me."

"Thank you Andy, see you next week," said I hopefully as he disappeared into the Terminal Building.

I now discovered that for the remainder of the day I had a maximum of three passengers per flight, so I turned to Dick and asked him would he like to accompany me, knowing his answer before he replied. At least I felt he could hold my clipboard with the paperwork, and even hold the controls from time to time, thus giving me a bit of a rest. I had learned my basic instrument flying with Mike Conry at Biggin Hill airfield in Kent. I doubt that Mike ever held an instrument rating in his life, but his ability to teach 'flight on instruments' in my view would be difficult to beat. For the uninitiated, instrument flying meant simply flying without reference to mother earth i.e. flight which precluded the pilot's ability to refer to the ground or natural horizon. Most flying schools in the UK still initiate their pupils into visual flying and do not fly at all unless the natural horizon can be seen, when the aircraft can be flown clear of all cloud. Mike's first words to me, unfailingly, were, "Let's go find some cloud," which in the UK is not too difficult to find most of the time. So I would climb the aircraft into the thickest cloud, usually over East Anglia, and there in order, descend, climb, turn and attempt to recover from the unusual attitudes that Mike would leave the aircraft. He also had the rather nasty habit of covering up some of the instruments, leaving me on a very limited panel to perform my tasks. In this way I came to achieve a familiarity and proficiency on instruments that became second nature. When I started a flying school at Swansea later, my pupils were taught on the same principle, learning to fly in cloud. In this way I was confident that Dick could at least maintain level flight in the goldfish bowl conditions prevailing that Saturday.

I had become aware during the course of the day that fog had gradually formed over the sea on both sides of the Cornish and Devon coasts. Fog that forms in this manner is commonly known as "advection fog", and is caused by warm air passing over a colder sea. Fortunately this had not spread over the land, so I could not imagine any impending threat from it, and my flight to Bristol and Newquay back to Scillies were completed without any problems.

At 1710 hours I slowly taxied down the hill that was runway 28 on Scillies and gunned up the engines for my last flight of the day to Plymouth. Prior to departure I had checked the meteorological actuals and forecasts for Plymouth and Exeter airports, and both were excellent. Fifteen minutes after take off Whisky Sierra crossed Land's End and I changed frequency to Plymouth approach. Apart from Dick my only two passengers were Finnish doctors; a husband and wife team both in their late seventies or early eighties. I looked back and saw that they were relaxing contentedly, so I began my contact with Plymouth approach.

"Plymouth this is Golf Alpha Sierra Whisky Sierra good afternoon." (Lew Byatt was the controller on duty and he cut out the preliminaries.)

"Good afternoon Whisky Sierra. Here is the Plymouth weather. We have eight octas of cloud on the surface with the sky obscured!"

This was impossible I thought, how could it all have changed in so short a time. I looked downwards and saw the earth was choking in a miasma of clinging fog. Everything was blanked out and there seemed no escape from it. My mouth suddenly became dry as I knew that landing under such circumstances was nigh impossible, yet the unrelenting fuel quantity gauges told me that soon I would be forced to land, or gravity would take over when the engines stopped. A full VDF (Voice Direction Finding) approach was too time consuming, and even then would only take the aircraft down to 200 feet or so, with the hope that the runway was some where ahead. The alternative would be to spiral down when overhead with the great possibility that I would eventually fly into the ground. I sought a solution, but no solution offered itself.

I had filled both tanks to the brim at Bristol, but since then had flown almost three hours, and with no refuelling facilities either at Newquay or on Scillies, I had calculated that I had sufficient left in the tanks, with a little left over, to make a safe landing at Exeter. My eyes were now drawn inexorably to the fuel gauges, and I felt rather than saw, Dick looking at me anxiously. An atmosphere of fear now permeated the cockpit. Homing onto a series of QDMs (course to steer to reach the airfield in conditions of no wind) I flew directly overhead Plymouth airport, confirming the time and my position when the bearings changed. I was about to change frequency to Exeter when I saw what is called in the business a 'sucker hole', and below it the greenery of Dartmoor. Without hesitation I dived into it like a drowning man clawing for the surface. Sweeping Whiskey Sierra on to a reciprocal heading. I quickly informed Plymouth of my approach from the east, and Lew, the Air Traffic Controller, started firing yellow flares into the sky to help me line up with the runway. I slowed up the aircraft slammed down the flaps and undercarriage and peered ahead. Suddenly the hanger and the tower appeared in the murk. Unfortunately I was slightly too high, and about 100 yards to the north of the centre line. I had no choice now but to overshoot and climb back into the fog, and set course for Exeter.

My fuel was reading lower on the gauges than I had ever seen them before, and I now realised that I could only have one shot at landing at Exeter. My radio call to them confirmed my worst fears, the fog off the coast during the day had, as the temperature dropped, rolled in up the river Exe completely covering the airfield. My body was now stiff with the tension, my eyes ached, and I fought hard to control my thoughts and find some sort of rational solution. I took stock of the position. Exeter was about ten minutes away, and by my reckoning, I had between 15 to 20 minutes of flight left before there would be an overwhelming silence. Fog, the blasted fog covered everything. My mouth was drier than I ever remembered it, and fear was now tearing at my guts. If I followed the prescribed VDF approach (there being no radar), the chances were that my fuel would run out somewhere on my inbound leg. The next few minutes would decide my actions, and our collective future. As I approached the airport fate intervened yet again, when in a divine fashion, a second 'sucker hole' appeared directly in front of me. This time it was different however, as at the bottom of the hole I spotted the figures 09 painted on the western end of the main Exeter runway. No invitation was needed, and I dived through the hole levelling out at 100 feet, tore across the airfield passing the tower and took Whisky Sierra into a pulsating turn to the left. Exeter unlike Plymouth was at least equipped with proper runway lights, and like a godsend these were glowing brightly. I had overshot in the turn, but picked up the lights on my left. Flaps down, undercarriage down, landing checks completed. Whisky Sierra's main wheels touched concrete about half way down the main runway at 1830 hours.

Dick gazed at me with a strange look in his eyes, probably still suffering from shock. For my part, I felt a huge surge of relief, as I knew that fate had been kind to me that day. A rather subdued and tired pilot taxied the aircraft in towards the terminal, and parked. I felt very stiff and 'all-in', having flown eight and a half hours, all on instruments. The aircraft had no auto-pilot, but having Dick alongside had helped some. I had completed eight landings, four of them on the Scillies. Now I was interested to find out how much fuel remained in the tanks, so I stood by and watched the refueller fill the tanks. Six gallons only had remained after landing, and some of those unusable, confirming my earlier calculations. Had I performed the standard VDF approach it was clear that the engines would have died on me, somewhere on the inbound leg, so how could I account for that hole appearing directly over the runway end when it did? It was a question that could never be resolved.

Dick and my two passengers were enjoying a coffee when I entered the airport lounge. Something of the challenge had clearly passed to them, and they showered me with their grateful thanks. How little they really knew!

As soon as our taxi driver approached us I felt rather sorry for him. Perhaps it was his odd ball looks and strange eyes. May be it was all in my imagination, as understandably, I didn't feel my normal self. I sat alongside him in the car almost mesmerised by his peaked cap, which almost fell over his eyes. The term 'Simple Simon' came to mind but for no good reason. Dick and the two Finnish doctors sat behind, as off we went back to Plymouth and the George Hotel. I stretched out in my seat, my hat over my face, and tried unsuccessfully to relax and sleep. My senses were too taut, and I felt that I should at least be sociable and talk to the driver. Sleep was impossible, and roughly fifteen minutes had passed since we had left Exeter. I sat bolt upright, and as I looked across towards him I saw what appeared to be a large church set on the hill above. I looked at he driver and asked him.

"What is that church up on the hill?"

"That be Buckfastleigh Abbey, that be. They make carpets up there, they do."

Again in conversation making mode, I asked.

"Is it Benedictine or Cistercian?"

"Oh, any sort of carpets." he answered. At this Dick became hysterical with laughter, in the back seat, and I stated shaking uncontrollably in the front. I collapsed into the seat, all conversation over, and pulled my hat back over my eyes. It had been one hell of a day, and I fell into a deep sleep, with Dick's laughter still ringing in my ears.

Note: The weather for 3rd April 1965 is set out below and on the following page.

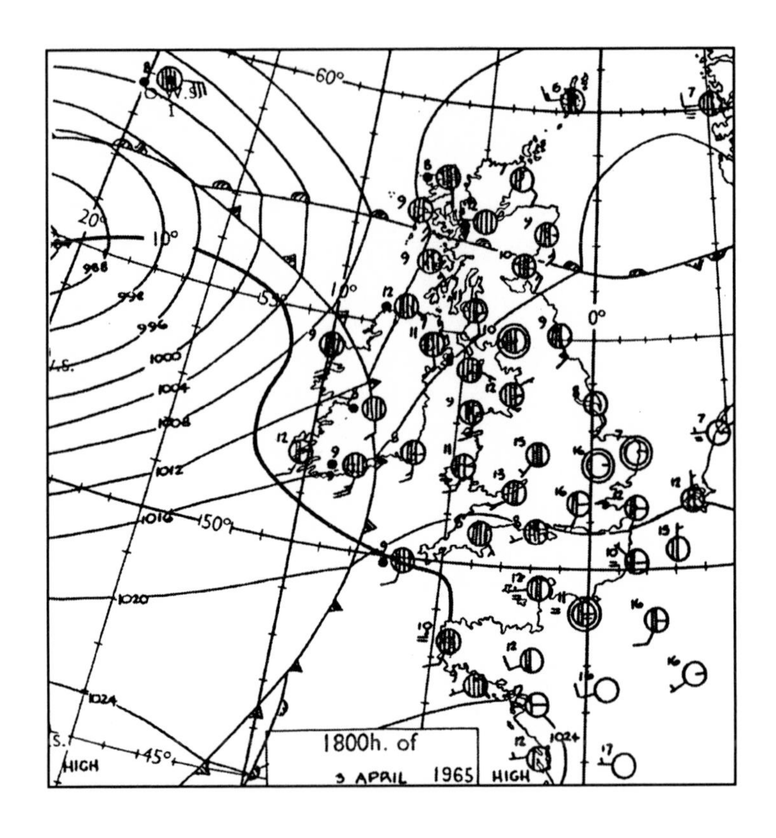

PLYMOUTH, MOUNT BATTEN
NGR: 2492E 0527N
ALT: 50 Metres AMSL
DATE: 3rd April 1965

Day	Month	Year	Hour (GMT)	Mean wind direction (deg true)	Mean wind speed (KT)	Dry bulb temp (°C)	Wet bulb temp (°C)	Present weather
3	4	1965	0	0	0	6.1	3.0	haze
3	4	1965	1	0	0	5.6	1.7	haze
3	4	1965	2	0	0	4.6	1.9	haze
3	4	1965	3	0	0	5.2	3.8	haze
3	4	1965	4	0	0	5.0	3.4	haze
3	4	1965	5	170	2	4.0	3.0	haze
3	4	1965	6	0	0	3.7	2.5	fog patches

3	4	1965	7	0	0	3.7	3.0	smoke haze
3	4	1965	8	0	0	5.1	3.0	smoke haze
3	4	1965	9	0	0	7.5	4.5	fog patches
3	4	1965	10	210	5	8.7	6.8	fog patches
3	4	1965	11	230	5	8.0	6.8	fog patches
3	4	1965	12	230	9	7.2	6.2	fog patches
3	4	1965	13	220	10	8.1	6.8	fog patches
3	4	1965	14	210	9	8.8	7.3	fog patches
3	4	1965	15	200	7	7.7	7.0	fog
3	4	1965	16	200	7	8.1	7.0	fog
3	4	1965	17	200	4	7.4	7.2	fog
3	4	1965	18	0	0	7.4	7.0	fog
3	4	1965	19	210	4	7.1	7.1	fog
3	4	1965	20	220	9	7.6	7.6	fog
3	4	1965	21	220	7	8.0	8.0	recent fog
3	4	1965	22	220	7	8.3	8.3	slight drizzle
3	4	1965	23	200	9	8.3	8.3	slight drizzle

(It was a Saturday evening in my home during the summer of 2003. I had just completed writing the above chapter, when my telephone rang and I heard the mature voice of Dick Rosser for the first time in 37 years—what could be more coincidental? He was speaking from Sakhalin Island off the East Coast of Russia, lying between the sea of Okhotsk and the Sea of Japan. He confirmed the events of the above chapter, saying "That I had bloody well nearly killed him." We both roared with laughter as once more we recounted the story of Buckfastleigh Abbey, and it's carpets. Being fluent in Russian Dick now holds the position of Project Logistics Coordinator for ABB Lumps Global L.L.C.).

CHAPTER 2

SUCCESS, FAILURE AND A NEW REALITY

When I entered the club house the dancing had already begun, and the place was fairly full of club members and their partners. I had spent the previous eight months gaining my Commercial pilots licence, which had involved trekking around the country, like a trappist monk, seeking the cheapest digs I could find, and gaining my flying experience, largely at Biggin Hill, Shoreham, Southend and Cardiff. Once I had successfully passed the hurdles of the flying tests at Stansted, I returned home hibernating in my father's shed, where I grappled with the intricacies of Air Law, Navigation, Plotting and Meteorology, and most demanding for me, the Morse Code. In the examination you were asked to take down Morse at about three to four words a minute and interpret flashing and occulting lights. My father, a hospital engineer, had brilliantly conceived a system of lights, which could be operated through a tape on my recorder. In this way I learned the necessary skills sufficient to pass the examination. Little did I know then that this knowledge would save my life, and that of my companions, not in the air as one might expect, but at sea, which was an environment just as dangerous.

With all this safely in the past, and now released, at least temporarily, from the bondage of examinations and tests, I now sought fun in any shape or form, which inevitably meant booze and girls, and not necessarily in that order. I had finally realised that girls were not just objects that went backwards in a dance, and it appeared that they seemed keen enough to attach themselves to a chap who could, with some justification, call himself a pilot. However I was still a pilot without a job, not an unknown phenomenon in the 1960s. Furthermore, having spent all my meagre savings on flying, I was very much broke; depending on my parents for free board and lodgings. However with what little I had, I was hell bent on living it up in the best way I could.

From the edge of the dance floor, suitably fuelled with a couple of cognacs, I spied a rather attractive female who appeared alone, and dressed like a million dollars. In my moral way I sought unattached females first, which was the necessary precursor to wading in to the attack. Several dances and drinks later I realised that with her clasped firmly in my arms, I had become a very skilful practitioner of the South American Tango as couples had begun to move away and watch us perform. Undoubtedly the Tango needed a high degree of limb co-ordination, and this level of skill had clearly annoyed some of the other dancers, who glared in my direction. Eventually, exhausted by my effort, I left my erstwhile partner and repaired to the bar to rest and refuel. After a few more drinks I took in some of the faces around the room and didn't like what I saw. Faces looked mean, eyes small and hard, and then I realised that they were all men's faces. Where were all the women? Even my erstwhile partner seemed to have disappeared. I emptied my glass and was about to seek a refill, when a voice behind disturbed my planning process.

"Hello," said the voice, "haven't seen you here before, what's your name?" I looked at the source, and found somebody who appeared to like me. He was exceedingly well dressed, a good looking, middle age chap holding a glass of larger in his hand.

"John Evans," I replied. "Here by yourself?" I asked.

"No," said the voice, "I came with my wife."

"Oh, where is she?" I asked trying to make polite conversation.

"You ought to bloody know, you've been dancing with her all evening." So it came to pass that Stan Edwards entered my life. The flying club had taken on a commercial pilot that summer ostensibly to fly charters as and when required. His name was Paul Weeks and he was to play a pivotal part in my life the next few years. Paul was a tall good looking guy, who had arrived from Canada. He had left Toronto for Dublin hoping to join Aer Lingus as a co-pilot on the DC3 Dakota. Unsuccessful at obtaining employment, he had arrived at Cardiff for a job at the club, which paid him the princely sum of eight pounds per week, and twenty pence per hour flown on charter, in other words penury. The early sixties were one of the worst periods for pilot employment, the industry being in serious contraction, and I was one of the many commercial pilots with little experience, on the market seeking a job at that time. I had answered the few jobs advertised with no success, and then I met Jim Callan, the operations manager of Cambrian Airways. He seemed a kindly sort of chap with a splendid sense of humour, who spent a great deal of time at the flying club. So one night I took my courage in both hands and asked him about a job with the airline. A few days later I visited him at his office where he offered me a trainee pilot position with the company whilst I obtained my instrument rating, which they would pay for. In the meantime I would also be in receipt of a small salary.

In the early sixties the headquarters of the Civil Aviation Flying Unit was Stansted Airport in Essex. To the average "joe pilot" like myself Stansted represented the ultimate 'Temple of Doom'. I had passed my day and night Commercial Flying Test there successfully at the first attempt. However, by the time of the test, I was fully conversant with the Chipmunk aircraft used, having flown the type for many hours at the Surrey and Kent flying club at Biggin Hill, the famous Second World War airfield. The instructors there, Tiny Marshal and Peter Chinn, were fine practitioners of their art and helped me a great deal. So on the 30th June 1961 I trundled around Norfolk and Essex in Chipmunk GANWB (Golf Alpha November Whisky Bravo) with Captain Westgate of the flying unit aboard, who proved quite happy with my performance. I had all of ten hours at night registered in my log book, when I again presented myself to CAFU (Civil Aviation Flying Unit), for the commercial night test on the twin engine Dove aircraft, which I had never flown before. My lack of preparedness was due to the lack of a suitable Dove to practice on, and the prohibitive cost of hiring one, at fifty pounds per flying hour. The test consisted of a take off, circuit followed by an overshoot, a further circuit and landing. Somehow I managed to please Captain Hale, the examiner, although I was never absolutely sure as to which of us finally landed the aircraft. It seemed quite a pointless exercise at the time, an opinion I still hold today.

In order to prepare for the more exacting instrument rating, one first had to attend for a prior test of procedures in one of the rooms at Shell Mex House in the Strand, where a D4 link trainer was installed. This consisted of nothing but a box which was able to move on all axis, and rested on a bed of compressed air which made strange puffing sounds when the contraption changed direction. In this machine you could replicate a flight on instruments between virtually any two airports once the examiner had set it up on his large plotting, glass-topped table in front of him. Sitting there he communicated with you as per Air Traffic Control, issuing instructions as to height, direction and speed, whilst all the time a pen arm plotted the progress of your flight on the glass top table. I had trained at Oxford airfield, on the D4 link trainer, and was confident that I could fly all the procedures. However I had not allowed for the personalities, and idiosyncrasies of the link instructors. For one small thing or other they found fault, and repeatedly you found yourself trekking back to Shell Mex House. It was to be my fourth shot at the test, when I caught the night sleeper from Cardiff to Paddington. I was troubled by a mild dose of influenza, so I did not take kindly at being asked to vacate the train at 0530 hours. Fortunately a few coffee bars were open, and after a few hot drinks and a couple of paracetamols I began my purposeful walk towards Shell Mex House. It had been snowing when I left home and I was wearing my fur lined boots, hardly the appropriate apparel for the test, but that morning I felt somewhat truculent, a feeling probably reinforced by my flu symptoms!

When I entered the room I saw John A Terras, who was certainly not my favourite person, he had already failed me twice on what appeared to be trivial points. I put all my charts on the table and prepared the airways route as directed. He busied himself with my checklists, turned to me and said.

"You don't seem to have your aircraft external check lists with you." Belligerently I told him that this was not a bloody aeroplane, but a D4 link trainer.

"Nevertheless." he said. "You must always carry all your charts in the future." The bastard, I thought, he's bound to fail me for that. In the link, with the hood closed, I accepted his instructions and took off. Pretty convinced I had already failed the test I burst into the song 'Oh Sir Jasper do not touch me', making sure I left the transmit switch on so that he could hear. Contrary to my expectations I performed pretty well that morning, and on completion I stood in front of his table to see and hear the results of my efforts. Acting like the gentleman he undoubtedly was, he said.

"Mr Evans, that was an almost perfect test, but remember when you get to Stansted please watch your attitude." I had passed the first part of the instrument rating test. The flying section would prove however to be considerably more difficult. Sometime later I was to meet a very experienced former Royal Canadian Air Force pilot, who recounted his first experience at Shell Mex House with Mr Terras. He had been suitably trained in the procedures, and with his overall experience felt very confident as to the result. Within five minutes of the start of the test the lid opened and John Terras's head appeared.

"Mr Dorman." he said, "I feel we are both wasting our time this morning." It was a severely chastened pilot who left the building!

The CAFU Dove aircraft was fitted with oblique screens allowing the examiner to see the outside world but not the candidate sitting in the left seat. However there was a small aperture about 8" by 4" which was left open for take off, and closed when the aircraft reached 200 feet. It was best therefore if the candidate established himself directly on instruments on leaving the ground as this would remain his condition until the examiner opened the shutter shortly prior to landing. The test flight usually took the form of a Stansted to Gatwick return flight with two candidates on board, each of them flying one sector, alternatively a flight down the airway to Clacton VOR (VHF omni directional radio range), and a return Stansted would be operated for a single candidate. On reaching the Stansted NDB (non directional beacon) the aircraft would be put into the holding pattern of four minutes plus or minus 15 seconds (outside these parameters you failed the test), followed by an approach to land using the ILS (instrument landing system). At the decision height, usually about 200 feet, you called out overshooting, and within seconds the examiner would reach behind your seat and cut off the fuel to one of the engines. At that moment you had to effectively control the aircraft in the climb, identify the failed engine and call for the appropriate propeller feather drill. The engine was then restarted and you returned to the beacon before commencing a non-precision approach with the ILS switched off. At the decision height the examiner would open the shutter, and hopefully the runway would appear directly in front of you. Throughout the test the aircraft had to be flown at plus or minus 100 feet of the cleared height except at the decision height, where you could stray up to 50 feet too high, but suffer an automatic fail if you descended below that level. Additionally the tolerance on tracks between the beacons on the airway was five degrees. To accomplish such a task on an aircraft you barely knew, and never really flown, was an almost impossible task, particularly when you couldn't practice on the beast between tests. In fact the CAFU test was subsidised, and at £25 a test was much the cheapest Dove available in the country, so you went to Stansted for test flights as much as to practice as for any other reason. People who had little trouble with the test tended to be military pilots, mostly from Royal Navy Communications, who regularly flew Doves or 'Devon' as they called them. In 1962 the pass rate took an average of 6.2 attempts. One poor chap, clearly under enormous family and financial pressure, had failed on his fourteenth attempt, after which he killed himself in his car a short distance from the airport. In that year also, the Ministry of Aviation issued a report on pilot licensing and introduced the five-year licence. It stated that candidates of adequate calibre were few and far between. Mike Conry, my instrument flight instructor, was also the editor of the 'Aviation' magazine. He of the acid tongue was not a man to mince his words, and was simply damning in his criticism of the Ministry, and CAFU in particular:

> "They state," he said, "that the proportion of candidates passing flying tests on the first attempt is very low, and yet they themselves (i.e. CAFU) are of such inadequate calibre, that to avoid doing circuits at night on single engined aircraft, the subject candidates have to perform this test (and the instrument rating test) on a twin engined and fairly heavy light-plane a Dove. Invariably the candidate has not even flown a Dove in daylight let alone at night. Yet these wizards, clamouring for 'calibre' are prepared to put these candidates to a ridiculously pointless test in an aeroplane to suit the examiner's complex and not the candidates needs or finances."

By the end of my fourth attempt at the rating, I had passed all the relevant parts of the test, but unfortunately had been unable to couple them together to achieve a pass, or partial pass. My next attempt could be the last in which the company would pay and so the pressure was on to succeed. Captain Picken was the examiner, and he was accompanied by an examiner from a British airline who was renewing his rating. The latter briefed me before the flight and when I had landed he winked at me conspiratorially, and I really felt the test had gone well. I was debriefed and passed by the Airline Examiner, but to my chagrin Captain Picken felt it necessary to over rule him and suggested I needed further training on the aircraft. It was the last straw and I left Stansted feeling very bitter, convinced that I was now out of a job. This proved to be the case, and once more I joined the mass of the unemployed.

As there were no flying jobs available anywhere, I applied for a teaching post at a new school in Buckinghamshire, where I would face an entirely new challenge, teaching Educationally Subnormal Children (called today Special Needs) in a mixed boarding school administering to the needs of the senior boys as their residential house master. What had I let myself in for?

During the remainder of the summer of 1962, prior to taking up my teaching appointment in September, I flew any aircraft available on charter, aerial photography, pleasure flying and more often than not with Paul. We both felt that possibilities existed for this type of work, which could point to a full time occupation away from the shackles and bureaucracy of an airline. We agreed that by early 1963 we would eventually embark on our own business by hiring an aircraft and plying for work countrywide. We had already acquired some contacts in the business who could, perhaps, at a pinch, provide us with some work and keep us busy. My inability to acquire an instrument rating, although disappointing at the time, proved to be a blessing in disguise, and I would soon learn more about the aviation business in the ventures ahead, than I ever would as a lowly co-pilot with an airline. Additionally Paul and I got on pretty well and shared many of the same views and aspirations, and although we had minimal experience, we had a great enthusiasm and a total commitment to making our project succeed.

My last day of freedom was a September Sunday, and I enjoyed it, having lunch with many of my flying friends at the "Old Pyed Bull", a pub in Woodstock near Oxford. I would soon come to miss such people with their wonderful appetite for life, and their unbounded love of the freedom of flying. Woodstock would be a happy meeting place for us pilots for some years ahead, having the great advantage of being geographically adjacent to the female nursing homes in Oxford, and the famous Radcliffe Infirmary. The girls were inevitably an attractive high class intelligent bunch, who were ever ready to take part in our high jinx and wild parties with gusto, and sometimes a great deal more!

I remember well that drive to Bletchley that that fateful Sunday afternoon. I was giving up the freedom that I always associated with flying, for a semi-institutionalised life among people who, at that moment, I could only regard as alien. I drove fifty miles or so via Bicester in a sombre and contemplative mood. A return to school teaching particularly in this type of school would be a far cry from the flying life I craved and loved so much. My libertine ways, stupidly acted out in front of the very airline people who had chosen to help me, had been an act of supreme folly, and I had paid the price, particularly when I had also failed to acquire an instrument rating. I now shut off these thoughts from my mind as I entered the main drive to the school. I parked in front of the building and pressed the bell on the large glass front door. A rather plump lady, who looked as if she could take care of herself in the front row of a scrum, opened the door and led me to the staff room for tea and biscuits. I deemed it inappropriate to ask for a large scotch and water, which I badly needed then, as I had a strong urge to turn about and flee. My only comrade in arms was the master in-charge of the junior boys, Tony. Nobody, it appeared, had ever taught ESN children before, other than the head master and deputy head, a straight speaking northern lady. The head lived on the premises with his family, and apart from the daily pleasantries, never questioned what I taught or how I taught it. It appeared to me that providing I prevented the children from killing or raping one another, or absconding at night, then I was fulfilling the terms of my contract.

The staff room was the nerve centre of the school, shared by the teachers, house mothers and the matron, where the subjects of conversation ranged from the colours of curtains in the bedrooms to the enduring rash on little Jimmy's dick! For some reason or other the word 'penis' was never used. All the women on the staff seemed to have a particular affection for Tony, who appeared to have a predilection for all things feminine. Had they been physically attractive, and of a younger age, then I would have certainly joined in the fray. Sadly however, that was not the case, and I was left somewhere outside in the wilderness. I often tried to turn the conversation to politics, economics or sport, with totally negative results. It appeared that the happenings and events of the outside world would never succeed in intruding into the inner sanctums of the school. To maintain a sort of sanity, I ran a football pools sweepstake weekly for all the staff, but felt reluctant to ask the headmaster to take part. I even persuaded some of them to join my girl friend and me to take a flight one weekend from nearby Sywell Airport in Northamptonshire. I flew the Cessna at 7000 feet in beautiful weather over Boston, the Wash and Kings Lynn before returning them safely back to Sywell. In such ways I increased my low standing in the school, at least marginally, and even the cook, who had shown no love for me hitherto, now indicated a greater respect the following Monday, by gracing my plate with an extra large portion of pudding! In reality however, little had changed, and I resorted to sitting in the staff room on my off moments sucking on an orange and spitting the pips across the room into the metal waste paper basket. This usually brought a halt to the banal conversation, until at last the deputy head, in a fit of pique, removed the orange bowl to the dining room, where the kids usually ate them.

What saved my sanity was the presence of my girl friend Jenny in nearby Oxford, where I tended to spend most weekends. Woodstock was the desired venue, and there at the George Hotel, I would meet up with Stan and Paul and some of Jenny's friends; mostly nurses from the Radcliffe. We were always received with open arms by Mrs Roberts, who just ignored our wild goings on and the multitude of females who tumbled in and out of the various bedrooms. A Lord of the Realm was the landlord at the nearby Savoy Hotel, and he was truly a wonderful character. He would enter the breakfast room and see us sitting there, usually in a room crowded with American visitors, and shout. "Hello you fuckers, back again I see!" The Americans would look stunned at this as we rolled around in amusement. His lady joined us for breakfast one morning dressed in a fur coat. When she reached across the table for the sugar the coat slipped off her leg revealing a bare body underneath. She seemed totally unconcerned, but Stan, who was sitting alongside and saw the whole works, managed to pour his cup of coffee down his leg.

Our arrival at the George was always marked with a short ceremony, when a well used condom of substantial length was hoisted on a stick out of the front window over Woodstock's main street. This was greeted with great hilarity, particularly by all our female companions, who entered the spirit of things by saluting as they passed underneath. It was these simple pleasures that allowed me to escape from the 'Trappist' existence of school life.

Sheila Scott had a room opposite mine at the George, and shared in many of our wild parties there. Later she became famous for flying solo around the world, a distance of 31,000 miles in 33 days. In 1971 she made a solo flight from the equator to equator over the North Pole in a light aircraft. Some years later I met her at Halfpenny Green airfield near Bobbington west of Birmingham. I had flown-in a group of people interested in the King's Cup air race, and saw Sheila standing in conversation with Sir Douglas Badar, the legless fighter ace of World War II. I stood close by until Sheila was forced to acknowledge my presence, and was duly introduced to the great man. Beset by many admirers I was unable to ask him any of the questions that came to mind about his wartime exploits. However I did notice his look of firm resolve and the self-assurance of the man. Sadly, I was never to meet either person again, Badar dying in 1982 and Sheila Scott in 1988.

Back at school, the children presented me with a great dilemma of how and what to teach them, assuming of course that I could teach them anything. My class was fifteen in number, of mixed sex and it seemed of varying ages. What was constant was the low level of intelligence, which confirmed to me that the teacher needed to be of a high intelligence and capable of lateral thinking to achieve any level of success. I asked the class on one occasion to write a short story of just one side of paper describing what and whom they saw on their way to school on the Monday morning. In my ignorance I thought that such an exercise would keep them quiet the rest of the morning. Within fifteen minutes however young Billy, not known for his literary talents, had his hand up indicating he had completed the task. He stood next to my desk while I attempted to read his essay, but apart from the articles 'a' and 'the', nothing that made sense was discernible. I felt very much like Ventris the first time he attempted to decipher the Linear B Minoan Script. I turned to Billy and asked him to read his story for me. This he did with ease, and could do so three days later when I asked him. A week later however I tried him again, and this time the poor lad just stood there and looked completely blank.

It now fell to me to introduce the boys to outdoor activities, starting with athletics. The sprints and distance running passed with no problems, but I looked hard at the head, when he suggested that I introduce the boys to javelin and discus throwing. Having shown them how to hold, carry, walk and throw the javelin. I spaced them out behind a long drawn line from which they threw one at a time. I insisted that nobody retrieved their own javelin until everybody else had completed their throw. This seemed to work quite well until I saw Matron walking across the playing field to talk to me. I told the boys to hold fire and walked a short distance to meet her. The ensuing conversation only lasted a minute or so before Matron, looking over my shoulder, broke into a loud scream. Shocked, I turned to see a re-enactment of the fight at Rorke's Drift with javelins flashing about in all directions, with great whoops of joy. I sprinted back, niftily dodging a missile en-route, and quickly brought things under control. Amazingly none of the boys had a javelin through their heads or bodies, a minor miracle in itself. Use of the discus was even more dangerous as you couldn't be sure what direction it would take after leaving the thrower's hand. After Willie was hit on the head with one whilst running around the track, I put an end to all uses of these weapons of mass destruction. Willie's head appeared to be undamaged, but I did observe a slight dent in the discus. In accordance therefore with the head's unwritten law of not allowing the children to kill one another, the implements were returned to the lockup, and remained there for the rest of my time at the school. Cricket, at this level, would appear innocuous enough, but when young Jimmy was struck on the back of his head by a ball thrown from the deep, I resorted ultimately to cross country running, and in the evening took the boys on long walks across the Bedfordshire country side.

The inadequacies of my boys had been well documented, but nevertheless they still retained the ability to surprise. During walks I was simply amazed at their knowledge of the countryside. It was as if such knowledge were ingrained in their genes. They taught me the names of trees, of birds and insects, and how to climb trees and identify the various speckled and coloured eggs, replacing them once they had demonstrated their easy knowledge. Flowers too, and their Latin names, came easily to many of their lips, and left me floundering and humble. 'By your children you'll be taught', was the phrase that came to mind. After such walks I would marvel at their knowledge, with a certain humility and realisation of my own inadequacies. Clearly even the lowliest and dullest of children could make a contribution to humanity in the great scheme of things. This was the most significant lesson I learned whilst teaching at White Spire School.

Despite their relatively low intelligence, two basic instincts were clearly evident i.e. the instinct of self-preservation and the sexual instinct. Sometimes on our walks we would play at soldiers or their adventure games, which the boys loved. We would lash wooden planks together and place them across some deep drainage ditches being constructed near the school. I would then see fear in the eyes of even the bigger boys as they faced this obstacle. Freddie, a well-built lad, burst into tears just at the thought. The bottom of the ditch was a mixture of mud and water, and from head high looked a long way down. Freddie, was the last of the boys, and had refused to cross. I eventually persuaded him to cross on my back, but the combined weight caused the planks to break and Freddie and I disappeared into the glutinous mess below. At that Freddie burst into hysterical laughter, probably at his relief in being unhurt, and also realising he wouldn't have to perform the stunt again. The children were generally well supervised at all times, in and out of lessons, and this was just as well. One day, when such supervision was momentarily relaxed, one girl in the corner of the hall was quickly surrounded by four boys and her clothes were magically shed like wrapping paper. The girls generally were well shorn of inhibitions, and were quite willing. The boys on the other hand would act like demented rabbits chasing a doe. Fortunately this little incident was stopped before any real damage was caused, but it ensured that vigilance was the 'name of the game'!

Breaking out of school seemed to be a pre-occupation of a few of the senior boys. They would cunningly slip away after supper and their absence would inevitably be discovered at bedtime. One rather senior boy was the established leader in this event, but as he fell into a low-level category of brainpower, he was not too difficult to find. I would drive into the centre of the town and always find him and his fellow escapees in the same shop doorway looking very sad and miserable. I would drive them back to the school with only the mildest of reproaches. There was no physical punishment in the school and that standard was adhered to by all members of staff. This was certainly in accordance with my view and feelings, particularly when one considered the nature of the children under our care.

Stan visited me at the school just once during my stay, as he said he had an aversion to all types of boarding schools having been incarcerated for years as a child at Taunton Public School. He arrived in a very large Bentley, which created a huge stir. It was almost as if God himself had arrived. Even the head master was seen walking around the Bentley with envious eyes, but he had agreed to find a bed for Stan, particularly when I told him that Stan had been one of my more senior airline captains. At breakfast I took the morning prayers. Later Stan told me he had been truly amazed, as he had no idea I knew any. Young James, a small junior boy at my table, looked unwell and had a greenish colour, he assured me he was quite well, and he was until he began eating his porridge. Suddenly in a most dramatic manner he threw-up, the vomit describing a superb parabolic curve directly into the sugar bowl adjacent to Stan. Later I told him that such a performance was strictly limited for special guests. Stan left the school early that morning unable to understand how I could ever stay in such a place. But then I too was full of surprises!

Unusually, a number of weeks passed and no word from Stan, we inevitably spoke for a few minutes on the telephone every week, but now a strange and unusual silence reigned. I decided therefore to motor westward on a free weekend to determine what was amiss. A few weeks previously Paul had picked Stan up at London Heathrow on his return from his skiing trip to Zermatt in Switzerland. He had looked exceedingly bronzed, fit and healthy and we spent a marvellous weekend at Woodstock—then silence!

I arrived outside his home in Cardiff at about 1900 hours to find his curtains drawn, and no sign of life. The front door was locked, so I made my way around the back and clambered through on open window.

"Any body home." I shouted loudly. Hearing no response I quietly opened the door to the huge lounge and switched on the lights. Stan was stretched out on one of the large settees clearly having been asleep. When he saw me he shouted.

"Get out. Get out. I've got typhoid!" He had been diagnosed with the disease a short time after his return from Zermatt and had been left to fend for himself, and his wife similarly diagnosed, had been taken to the local isolation hospital. Stan then told me, after he had calmed down, that his only meagre support had been his brother, who would leave groceries at the end of the drive and then flee. That same evening I arranged a visit to a local doctor, explained the position and was given a booster injection of typhoid and para typhoid. I stayed with Stan for two weeks having explained to the school that I was suffering from a bad dose of influenza. Shortly afterwards Stan was admitted to the isolation hospital and I returned to school suffering no ill effects from either influenza or typhoid.

I spent the next few weeks reading up all I could on typhoid in the town library, its history and symptoms, sending Stan a synopsis of all my findings. The typhoid germs seemed to rest-up in the gall bladder and in serious cases it would become necessary to remove the organ. Following such an operation, if the typhoid bug still remained, then the chances were that the patient would become a permanent carrier. Some weeks later I visited the hospital after Stan had had his gall bladder removed and was now well into recovery. He was in bed, totally immobile being connected to machines with drips and a variety of tubes. I took out a magazine I had purchased for him in a shady bookseller in Cardiff with the salacious title 'Busty'. This I opened and placed at the bottom of his bed, the picture revealed a woman with enormous tits, certainly the largest that I had ever seen.

"You can't leave that there," Stan moaned, "the Matron will be visiting here soon."

"Don't worry," I said, "she'll probably confiscate it for her own use," and with that I left the room. When I saw him next he was well recovered and I asked him how had the visit gone with the Matron.

"Very well," said Stan, "she took one look at the picture looked at me, and said, it appears Mr Edwards that you are made a remarkable recovery!"

CHAPTER 3

CORMORANT CLIMBING

I have great admiration for teachers who, for year after year, ply their pedagogic skills with abused children, partially sighted children and (ESN) educationally sub normal children. But by the summer of 1963 I had used up my bank of goodwill, patience or whatever it took to continue in this type of work. Make no mistake I loved kids, but I had grown weary in the seemingly uphill task of trying to teach them anything at all. Believe me, I had tried most of the methods known to man without the minutest responses. The headmaster, who was trained in this type of teaching, helped me not one iota. He walked around the school inevitably carrying his youngest child in his arms, and seemed quite content with my efforts. The children however had taught me a knowledge of trees, flowers, birds and birds eggs, and I had tried desperately to redress the balance, without success. My learning took place on the long evening walks across the fields of Bedfordshire with senior boys. But my efforts in the classroom were palsied in comparison. In my class I had about 15 children of IQs ranging from 70 to 90. We made paper mache balls of varying sizes and strung them across the classroom as a permanent feature. These represented the planets in our solar system (not to scale of course), and every morning I would have the children recite them as a liturgy. The headmaster was quite thrilled by that effort. He was less thrilled when I played the top 20 musical hits every Friday afternoon, on my tape recorder. It was noticeable that few, if any, feet moved in time with the music. Years later when I flew John Lennon, he turned to me one day and asked me what I thought of his music. Thinking back to the lack of inspiration it had raised with my former class, I told him, "Not much". At this remark, to his credit, he burst into loud laughter. I have always had a genuine love of poetry and thought that by reciting some better known lines and some nonsense poetry to my class it would at least raise a smile of two. Sadly not a glimmer illuminated the classroom. I made valiant efforts to teach them how to use the public telephone system. I used my car as a taxi taking a group of children up the road to the nearest telephone kiosk, and showed them, each in turn, how to dial the school number, and then insert the four coins, and press button A when the voice sounded the other end. This exercise, not only drove me half-mad, but succeeded in blocking the school line for hours on end. Even this exercise was only partially successful, and some of the children never mastered this simple skill. It was for me the last straw, and I felt that the sooner I returned to the world of flying the better.

Paul arrived at the school the day the summer holidays started, and together we drove across London to Biggin Hill Airport in Kent. I had arranged to do a twin engine rating with the Vendair flying club, and to hire a Cessna 172, and fly it the following day to Culdrose in Cornwall, where we had been contracted to carry out the pleasure flying at the Royal Naval Air Station's open day.

A twin rating with Vendair was the cheapest available in the country at the time, flying the all wooden Miles Gemini aircraft, which at a push could carry four people including the pilot. With only 100 horse power, Gypsy Major engines, its performance could only be described as marginal. With a reasonable load and an engine out the aircraft went one way; that was down, and thus was known as a 'field of your choice aircraft'. You could choose a field to land in, but you certainly would have little time to find one. Paul climbed bravely into the back seat and I sat in the left-hand seat to fly the aircraft. The only set of brakes were on my side and Mr Harris, the instructor, sat alongside. Over the Weald of Kent, after a few medium turns Harris told me to return and complete a landing. He seemed reluctant to allow any harsh manoeuvres in his aircraft. On landing he quickly got out, allowing Paul and I to defy the sky together. I was a little high on the approach when I returned to the field, so I closed the throttle to loose height. Immediately a horn blew loudly, frightening the hell out of the both of us. Paul, in fact, left his seat and crashed his head against the cockpit canopy. This had occurred when you closed the throttles with the undercarriage locked up, a good feature, if only we'd been told about it. I would never have described the Gemini as my most favoured aircraft, and sadly the one I flew that morning GAJWE (Golf Alpha Juliet Whisky Echo) crashed at Biggin a short time later, killing all on board. The aircraft type was eventually consigned, by the Ministry of Aviation, to the dustbin of aviation history. At least I had obtained my twin rating flying one, which in itself proved a popular talking point with pilots on future occasions.

I had seen my first Gemini two years previously parked at Cardiff Airport. I climbed onto the wing and saw the captain dozing in the cockpit. In this way I met Captain Philip Cleife, who a short time later started a new airline called Mayflower Air Services, out of Plymouth Airport, operating to the Isles of Scilly. That day he showed me around his Gemini with some pride. Indeed it was this aircraft, registered as GAKHW (Golf Alpha Kilo Hotel Whisky), which achieved a certain notoriety some time later. While taxiing down the steep slope, that was runway 28 at Scillies, the brakes failed. Despite all efforts to stop the beast and change direction he was ultimately faced to jump out to save his own skin. The final indignity was to be smacked in the back by the tail section of the aircraft, which left him prone on the runway, whilst the runaway aircraft ploughed on to crash on the rocks below.

That night Paul and I stayed at Ken Fenn's Oak Lodge Country Club near Westerham in Kent, a place we were both to frequent many times in the future. Alas it no longer remains, and dear Ken yet another reminder of the past. But in the 1960s' it was very much alive, particularly at weekends, when it was host to the wildest of parties. The weather was our main worry for the morrow, and I certainly slept uneasily as the next day could be the beginning of a partnership which we both hoped would create a degree of permanency in the crazy world of aviation.

Next morning the sun shone and the weather was set fair for the next few days. We took off from Biggin at 1240 hours, landed at Culdrose in Cornwall at 1435 hours. We flew without deviation, as if on rails, across the south and west of England in the most beautiful of flying conditions imaginable Nobody bugged us that morning and even Air Traffic Control left us very much to ourselves. In the early 1960s' light aircraft were equipped only with a single radio, and visual navigation was undertaken by drawing a straight line on the topographical map and then attempting to fly along it by checking the terrain below. Railway lines were a good source of safe navigation, but Mr Beeching had already been charged by the Government to remove many miles of track, thereby making our work that much more difficult. When the weather deteriorated, with low cloud and poor visibility, map reading became more difficult, if not impossible, and then one resorted to using the radio to obtain QDMs from any airfield on route. Map reading the best of times was uncertain, and after a short time into the flight we would generally become uncertain of our position, a general euphemism for 'being lost'.

On this morning however we had no such worries and arrived at Culdrose on schedule. At 1600 hours we commenced our pleasure flights, and continued for over three hours until the crowds dispersed. It was an established maxim when pleasure flying to shorten the time aloft the greater the number of people waiting to fly. So although flights were a nominal ten to fifteen minutes, their duration could be cut in half at a busy air show. Mr Lucas, the show's organiser, was also the chief flying instructor at Plymouth Airport, and that evening we followed him there, where in exchange for the tickets we had collected, he paid us the vast sum of £64 and ten shillings for our day's work. That night we flew to Cardiff, where for the next few days we carried out more pleasure flying, charging 15 shillings for adults and 10 shillings for children. In this way we had almost trebled our money in the space of three days. We also convinced ourselves that there was business aplenty in our chosen field, but the need now arose for us to choose a permanent base, and find an answer to the question 'What do we do during the winter months?' In January 1961 I had landed at Swansea in an old Auster, the place seemingly completely deserted with a marked absence of other aircraft. What struck me then, was the nearness of the airfield 'Fairwood Common', to the beautiful beaches of Gower. The knowledge that these beaches were the nearest to the people from the Midlands (give or take a few miles) added to the potential for our summer flying. This, of course, was before the advent of jet flights to the sun resorts of the Mediterranean.

Mr Bagshaw, the then manager at Swansea Airport, was very friendly and amenable to our suggestion that we set up a permanent camp there. There was little air traffic at the airfield at the time, but Cambrian Airways and Derby Airways (later British Midland Airways) did operate DC3 charter flights, mostly on weekends to Jersey in the Channel Islands. There was also a once a day flight to and from Gatwick Airport by the Morton Air Service's Dove or Heron aircraft. The old Swansea Flying Club was then largely a social club owning just one old Auster Aircraft, which rarely flew. It was on Saturday 3rd August 1963 that we set up our store at Swansea. We parked the aircraft alongside runway 26 right against the perimeter fence, which was the main parking area for sightseers, on their way to and from the beaches. We hoisted our pleasure flying banner, opened the fence, wide enough for passengers to come through, and with our small desk and supply of tickets we anxiously waited. Inclement weather often acted in our favour, as it diverted people from the beaches, in search of alternative pleasure activities. This our first day was subject to such weather, and our little Piper Tripacer GARCB (Golf Alpha Romeo Charlie Bravo) looked quite forlorn in the dripping rain. But our efforts were thwarted by the very low cloud-base, and we only completed 40 minutes flying all day, which amounted to six flights. The take was a meagre £12—fifteen shillings, which we blew that night on a first class meal with champagne at the Blackhills Grill near the airfield. The next day was a bonanza, in the most god-awful conditions and even the Cambrian Airways flight was forced to divert to Cardiff. We completed thirty-four flights with a cloud-base never higher than 200 feet all day. I had stuck the back of a cigarette packet behind the compass in front of me in the aircraft. On this I marked out the tracks and timings which would hopefully bring us out of the cloud with the runway appearing directly in front of the aircraft. It miraculously worked, and Paul and I flew five flights each before swapping for a rest, a sandwich or for a bar of chocolate. In the hotel, that night, we took all the money out of our flying jackets throwing the notes on our beds. We then jumped prostrate on the mattresses and watched with great delight as the notes flew high into the air. We had taken a further £68, but by golly we had really earned it. That night we slept the sleep of the dead!

It seems standard procedure in the UK, that when somebody creates a scheme benefiting themselves and the public at large, and show any sort of entrepreneurial spirit then, as sure as God made little apples, somebody finds a way to hamper, or stop it. Our difficulties commenced almost at once. The Gower and Fairwood common was, and still remains, common land, and a group of Gower commoners, who remained nameless, put the 'boot in' through the redoubtable Gower Warden. Dressed in a brown uniform with brightly polished breeches he looked a formidable figure reminiscent of a pre-war Automobile Association motorbike and side-car representative. But as Lloyd George said of Field Marshal Haig, "he was brilliant only to the top of his boots". Complaints about us breaching the fence had already reached Swansea Borough Council, and apparently, we had with Mr Bagshaw's approval, broken an antiquated bye-law. The fence therefore was duly, and firmly, closed. In furtherance of our efforts to take flying to the public it was necessary for us to remain with our aircraft parked at the airport boundary. In this way the public could talk to, pay and subsequently fly with those two brave young pilots trying to make a living. Our first efforts were to carry and lift passengers over the fence, but a very fat lady nearly did for Paul's back, so an alternative method was sought. Young Bagshaw, son of the airport manager, found the answer, obtaining a large double ladder which could span the fence quite easily. Still the Gower Warden was unhappy, and claimed that the flights attracted more cars, and thus reduced the grazing land for the horses. Also that crowds frightened the horses, and then in complete contradiction, that the people were feeding stray ponies. Finally, in desperation, he claimed that our customers were scattering their used condoms on the common and choking the sheep!

By the 17th August we began attracting the attention of the media, and the Herald of Wales led with the banner headline 'Ground to—Air Problem'. The article said that "unless a group of Gower Commoners and a company running pleasure flights from an edge of Fairwood Aerodrome settle differences soon, two professional pilots will spend much of their time lifting passengers over a fence on to the runway". This article clearly preceded the advent of the ladder. "The pilots came to Swansea," the article continued, "on a three week trial. Now they want to stay, organise charter flights and make their headquarters at the airport. The manager of the airport welcomes the idea, 'A great boon' he says."

By this time we had carried out more than 600 flights and flown almost 2000 passengers. We had acquired the enthusiastic assistance of a group of local boys, about eleven years of age, who distributed leaflets to the parked cars, and engaged in their first attempts at selling. Donald and Philip were great kids, and whenever we had a spare seat on the aircraft, they jumped in and flew with us. When we had a shortage of passengers Philip would perform a cabaret on the grass indulging in some freak acrobatics of his own. When people gathered around, his 'piece de resistance' was to push a long pin through his hand between thumb and forefinger without any apparent distress. This may have shocked some people into buying tickets, but I had my doubts. A few days later the Western Mail (the National Daily Newspaper of Wales), took up our case. They coined a new phrase for the pleasure flight calling it the 'flip trip', offering ten-minute flights that covered the Gower coast and included the Mumbles, Caswell Bay and Oxwich. They said nothing of our bad weather flights, when our passengers saw absolutely nothing at all until they landed.

Glamorgan County Council now got involved and their spokesman stated. "We are anxious to settle these differences amicably. When we have a report from the Gower Warden we shall be getting in touch with Swansea Borough Council. Between us we should sort it out." For the remainder of August and into early September, when the kids returned to school, we remained at the perimeter fence plying or trade. Then suddenly and as quickly as it started the supply of passengers dried up, and we retired to our office in the airport. We had certainly put Swansea Airport on the map that summer, and some of the passenger reaction was quite amusing. One woman asked Paul if the airport was bigger than the main one at Swansea. Another said, that she didn't know that Swansea had an airport. Both these ladies actually lived in the town. One night during the month of August Paul and I had been searching for a name for our company. Clearly with the monies we were taking, it seemed necessary to put the operation on a more business like footing. We flipped various names around, but none seemed suitable, or had already been taken up by other companies. Suddenly I remembered one of the nonsense poems I had tried to interest my class in at the White Spire School. It went as follows:—

The Common Cormorant or Shag
Lays eggs inside a paper bag
The reason you will see no doubt
It is to keep the lightening out
But what these unobservant birds have never noticed
Is that wandering herds of bears may come with buns
And steal the bags to hold the crumbs

Anon.

So we called the company Cormorant, and registered it as Cormorant Aviation Services Ltd. We felt that a major hurdle had been overcome. Now came the requirement to keep our financial accounts in order. For this we used Deloitte Plender and Griffiths in Swansea. With greater knowledge of business affairs our demands could have been met by a simple book-keeper, and at a lower cost. Clearly we were feeling our way in business and certainly making our own mistakes.

We were still leasing our aircraft from Flairavia at Biggin Hill. I remember the disbelief on the face of the owner when we had paid him £200 in cash after the first four days or so of operating. I also remember the amazement on his face when he saw the tyres of the aircraft, which had very little rubber left. They were not used to flying their aircraft at that intensity at Biggin for sure. It was on our first positioning flight to that airport that we first ran into trouble. The engine on Charlie Bravo clearly decided that it had had enough. Paul was flying the aircraft and we were within five minutes or so flying time from Biggin, when the engine started seizing up and the propeller slowing up. Just as fate would have it, we spotted a large expanse of grass on our left hand side and without further ado Paul landed and ran up to, what looked like, an aircraft hanger. No sooner had we come to rest when a man dressed in overalls came towards us shouting. "You can't land here!" Very politely I informed him that we had in fact landed here. "The manager will go bloody mad," he said. "Well where are we?" I asked him politely. "It's the old Croydon Airport, and we've been closed for years. We now build and repair Rollason aircraft, that's all we do." he concluded. Paul remained with the aircraft, as he was more technically minded than I was, and I made my way to the large building, which had clearly been the Air Terminal in a more leisurely age.

The airport had first been used in 1916, but became the prime London Airport from 1920, only ending when war became imminent in September 1939. In 1946 civil flying returned, but the airport finally closed in September 1959. Many of the buildings however remained in commercial use, including the unique terminal and the central tower. It took little imagination, on my part, to see the Imperial Airways' Short L17s parked outside, with the Junkers 52 of Lufthansa and the Douglas DC2s of KLM.

Confronting me as I entered the terminal was the grand sweeping staircase, which had featured many times in scenes from old British films. As I climbed the stairs I heard an angry voice bellowing out, "He can't land here, nobody is allowed to land here, and get the pilot and bring him up here to me!" On the landing I could see that this voice emanated from a half open office door, which I now approached with some apprehension. I knocked on the door and an angry voice shouted a very unwelcoming, "Come in." A rather red faced bellicose aircraft manager looked at me as if I were some dog's faeces found on the green of his favourite golf hole. "I'm the pilot who just landed here," said I in a rather week voice. "You can't land here," he said, "you have no right, The airfield is not open to

Air Traffic. You can't land here, who gave you permission?" The tirade continued and as I opened my mouth to explain, he seemed to repeat himself ad infinitum. Standing in front of his desk I eventually got out the word 'Emergency'. This seemed to slow him up a bit, but he ranted on that I had caused absolute chaos to the traffic system in the London area, and that I was personally responsible for it, and a disgrace to the aviation business. At last however, I was able to explain the reason for our landing on his sacred plot. Somewhat mollified, he consented to us leaving, and with Paul having sorted out our fuel problem, we continued to Biggin Hill in high spirits.

After our first season we were flushed with success, and sought methods of increasing the scope of our business. In early 1964 the first opportunity arose at Morecambe Bay in Lancashire. Here the Blackpool Air Navigation and Trading Company held the pleasure flying franchise for the local Pontin's Holiday Camp. Russell Whyham, the Managing Director of the Blackpool company, flew Paul and I up to Morecambe Bay in a Jackeroo aircraft, which in essence was a modified Tiger Moth, having a cabin for four people. Take-offs and landings were made off the beach at Morecambe. But when we arrived, the beach itself was covered by the incoming tide. I fully expected Russell to point out the area for landing and then return to Blackpool. We were astonished when he lined up with the beach and carried out a landing in about a foot of water. The result would have done credit to the water shoot at the fairground. The sand was rock hard, and the landing was accomplished without difficulty apart from the spray effect. "Russell," I said, "how do you get the passengers out to the aircraft in these conditions?" "No problem, you simply carry them," was the matter of fact answer. Apart from the pleasure flying franchise, the deal was to include the purchase of the aircraft, which on landing back at Blackpool we found to be covered in a white crust of salt. We were wise enough to turn down this opportunity for all the obvious reasons, and we returned down south somewhat chastened by the experience. I somehow couldn't visualise Paul or myself carrying passengers to the aircraft knee deep in water. Attractive females may be, but our experience showed that they tended to be in the minority among our passengers. The aircraft too, would have fallen apart with salt corrosion. All in all, Blackpool had been a 'bum steer', and we were soon looking elsewhere for suitable opportunities. Russell had not finished with us however, and he soon contacted us with the news that he had obtained the sales rights, in the UK, for the Aeromacchi, an Italian built aircraft. This had six seats, which for pleasure flying could be increased to eight. Unfortunately however it was under powered and was very reluctant to leave the ground with even the lightest of loads. Paul and I flew the aircraft GARZG (Golf Alpha Romeo Zulu Golf) at Biggin in March and considered it only a marginal asset for pleasure flying, but reasonable for airfields like Ramsgate which was close to sea level.

We now had our attention drawn to Ramsgate, which sported an all grass airfield, close to Manston Airport. It was there that we met Wing Commander Hugh Kennard, a one-time squadron leader in the famous Eagle Squadron. At that time he was the Managing Director of a relatively new airline called Air Ferry. Previously he told us he had owned and operated pleasure flights from Ramsgate airfield, and was proud to show us pictures of seemingly endless numbers of happy trippers at Ramsgate and Margate, queuing up at their kiosks on the water front to buy tickets for their pleasure flights. At that time they had used a number of small buses to move the passengers to and from the airport.

A kiosk already existed on the front at Ramsgate, and we soon arranged for the construction of a second one for Margate. This was octagonal in shape with a central wooden shaft, which we would use to fly our flag. This kiosk was soon put in place on the sun deck in Margate, where it fell to me to carry out the painting. This was the period of the Mods and Rockers, a strange bunch of kids clearly seeking their way in life. On the day I began the paint job a riot took place on the beech, and a large fight developed between these rival groups. From my vantage point, on the top of the kiosk, suitably equipped with brush and paint pot in hand, I watched with interest this great black swirling mass swarm in my direction. They swept onto the sun deck carrying the kiosk and me along with them, eventually depositing us, stranded, on the main coast road immobilising the traffic. This caused great hilarity among the passers by, who with some persuasion picked us up once more, and returned us to the sun deck.

In retrospect this was a very funny episode, but it certainly didn't seem very funny at the time. That night on the main television network it was reported that a young man had been knifed on the beach during the fight, and had subsequently died of his wounds. Mods and Rockers apart, these were the days of Radio Caroline, the first break away popular radio station in the country, and some of our pleasure flyers paid an extra premium to fly over the ship, sitting well off-shore. Sadly however the pleasure flying at Ramsgate turned out to be disappointing, and although we had temporarily employed an additional pilot, to help us out, the passenger numbers never reached the numbers that Kennard had projected.

The most interesting charter enquiries tended generally to be illegal. An official from Ramsgate harbour approached me and asked if I would be prepared to fly a Chihuahua dog into the area of Thanet from a field near Calais. The dog belonged to that famous, and beautiful, French film actress Martine Carol, who was filming near London. I turned down this offer particularly when a paltry payment of six hundred pounds was suggested. My licence was worth considerably more than that.

I now considered the idea of flying groups of school children from a variety of schools for aerial geography and geology lessons, flying over their local area in the Isle of Thanet. With this in mind I spoke to a Mrs G. Alston at the Ministry of Education, who appeared to be the person responsible for this type of activity. Such an idea, at that time, seemed far too advanced for the Ministry to sanction, particularly as I was seeking a type approval on a countrywide basis. The letter I sent her encapsulated my ideas at that time and can be seen on the following page.

CORMORANT AVIATION SERVICES LIMITED
CHARTER — AIR PHOTOGRAPHY — PLEASURE FLIGHTS

Swansea Airport,
Fairwood Common,
Swansea, South Wales
Telephone: Swansea 24063

125, Shenley Road,
Bletchley,
Bucks.

Mrs. H. G. Alston,
Her Majesty's Inspector of Schools,
Rest Harrow, Ickwell,
BIGGLESWADE, Beds.

24th January, 1964.

Dear Madam,

The above company is keen to begin a country wide scheme of aerial classes for children of school age. Some years ago a Company based at Swansea conducted flights for school children in elementary map reading. These, I believe, were quite successful and ended only when the company left the Swansea area.

We have given much thought to this project, and our plans envisage the following.

1) The Aircraft. Type-Lockheed-Macchi A.L. 60. This has individual seats for six children, plus one teacher who can sit facing the class.

2) The Situation. The aircraft can be positioned at any aerodrome for any length of time. The schools in the surrounding areas can then avail themselves of the service, in a time table prepared beforehand with the Local Education Authority.

3) Scope of Lessons. These will depend on the school and the teacher concerned. Certain topics in Geography, Geology, Meteorology and History seemingly would prove ideal subjects for this type of lesson. The pilot would fly under the directions of the teacher, so as to comply with the general structure of the lesson.

4) Duration of Lessons. A 30 minute lesson is envisaged, but lessons of longer or shorter duration could be arranged if so desired.

continued.

Directors: J. H. EVANS, P. F. WEEKS

CORMORANT AVIATION SERVICES LIMITED
CHARTER — AIR PHOTOGRAPHY — PLEASURE FLIGHTS

Swansea Airport,
Fairwood Common,
Swansea, South Wales
Telephone: Swansea 24063

Her Majesty's Inspector for Schools. 24th January, 1964.

- 2 -

5) Cost. It is considered that for a 30 minute lesson £1 per child, the teacher free, is a reasonable charge. Pro rata charges for longer or shorter periods.

6) In addition to this we could offer short flight familiarisation trips at six shillings per child, again the teacher free.

I have considered the bare essentials of the scheme above, and therefore offer it to you for your consideration. I should be grateful for any ideas and advice you may have to offer on the subject.

Yours faithfully,

J H Evans

J.H. Evans.

Directors: J. H. EVANS, P. F. WEEKS

At that stage in my life I had no idea who Mrs G. Alston was, merely picturing her as a senior bureaucrat in the Ministry of Education. Gwen Alston, it turned out, was far removed from that perception, but it was many years later before I learned the full story of this remarkable lady. She had gained her private pilot's licence in 1929, adding to that a degree in mathematics at Liverpool University. In 1932 she was awarded a MSc in aerodynamics. She worked at the Royal Aircraft Establishment (RAE) at Farnborough, notably on aircraft stability. She flew as an observer on many hazardous test flights. After the war she became an assistant inspector to schools and advised on all aeronautical matters, including sport and recreational flying and air education. Certainly then I had approached the correct person to further my scheme. What I really sought was the Ministry's sanction to bless this scheme on a countrywide basis, an altogether over ambitious plan at that time, particularly in view of our financial structure and constraints. Mrs Alston in theory approved our initiative, but that was as far as it went. However it didn't prevent me testing the idea on the local schools.

A visit to a large Grammar school followed, where an appointment had been made to meet the headmaster. I was shown into a large book lined study, where the head sat across from me behind a huge desk dressed in his dusty chalk marked gown. I used my best sales techniques to encourage him to buy the idea of lessons from the air. As I spoke however I could see his eyes beginning to glaze over, and it was only his good manners that allowed me to continue. When I ultimately stopped my chatter to breathe, he intervened indicating his complete disinterest in the subject, and effectively terminating the interview. Suddenly his name Rieu struck a cord, and in desperation I asked him if he was the person who had translated 'the Iliad' and 'the Odyssey' into English. At this he suddenly came to life, stared at me, his demeanour completely changed. "That was my father," he said, his face lighting up. "Have you read the books then?" he asked. "Yes, of course, I once taught ancient history at a school in Sussex." I said enthusiastically. "Now then," he said, "what were you saying about flying lessons?" Mr Rieu's school was the first in the area to send children, complete with maps and clipboards, to enjoy this new form of learning. What price the value of education?

Despite our best efforts Ramsgate proved to be a great and costly disappointment, and by the end of May 64 Paul and I were back at Swansea, the Ramsgate base well and truly closed. Unbeknown to us Monique Agarazarian, a famous aviatrix, who had delivered Spitfires to the squadrons during the war for the Air Transport Auxiliary had also operated pleasure flights from Ramsgate in the 1950s. She had previously operated similar flights from Northolt and London Heathrow. We would have all agreed that Ramsgate was an airfield too far. Monique had also flown charters in a single engine Proctor aircraft from airfields in the south east to the Isles of Scilly, a brave lady indeed. In retrospect it appeared that many of our aviation experiences mirrored hers of an earlier age.

CHAPTER 4

CORMORANT CRUISING

Despite our disappointment at the failure of the Ramsgate base the year 1964 began to look very promising. However the more we tangled with the weather, technical problems, not to mention the dreaded Gower Warden, the more our plans could change with detrimental effects on our meagre finances. Pleasure flying still provided our main source of revenue, spiced up a little by the occasional charter flight. The pleasure flights, or flip trips as the newspaper called them, tended on the whole to be uneventful, but a few turned out to be more exciting than Paul or I bargained for. I boarded a family one day where the young son, in his twenties, appeared to be unduly nervous and insisted on sitting next to me in the cockpit. As a queue of passengers was waiting, to save time, I took off from the runway intersection thus reducing the available distance for the take-off run. I had almost reached rotation speed, when without warning the young man leapt across the cockpit onto my lap with his arms around my neck. The aircraft was fast approaching the fence and only with the greatest effort could I stop, whilst, at the same time, striking the young man in the throat with my right elbow. This at least saved the situation, and I was able to taxy the aircraft back and give the family the benefit of my opinion. The poor boy was clearly epileptic and had suffered some sort of fit brought on by his fear of flying. The family now changed seats and the flight took place without any further problems. We never turned passengers away—we just couldn't afford to do so! Paul too had his moments, and on a flight with a mother and daughter, safely tied into the rear seats and the aircraft firmly established in the climb the trouble started. The woman suddenly, in sheer terror, grabbed the back of Paul's hair, yanking his head backwards. Even today he blames the woman for his premature hair loss.

Charter flights, although few and far between, enlivened our existence from the tedium of constant and repetitive pleasure flights, even when they produced some unwanted and unforeseen excitement. It was the morning of November 4th 1963 when Paul took three businessmen to Sheffield in the singled-engined Piper Tripacer GARET (Golf Alpha Romeo Echo Tango). The morning flight from Swansea was uneventful, but as no refuelling facilities were available at the little airport of Netherthorpe, Paul was forced to make an intermediate stop at Tollerton Airfield to refuel on his return flight that evening. The events that then occurred were best described by one of his passengers. He started with the words: "No hostess and no engine." An account of an unscheduled air stop. "Suddenly at 1500 feet there was silence, broken only by the whistling of the wind past the fuselage. Somewhere below in the fading light the Nottinghamshire countryside waited . . ." Earlier that day the three passengers had been content as the Piper Tripacer winged its way North to Sheffield. True the comfort of the little single engined aircraft was not up to Viscount standards—for one thing there was no air hostess, but what matter, anything was better than making the journey to Sheffield and back by road. When the business at Sheffield was concluded, the three passengers expected a similar care free ride back home. At about 1615 hours in fading light things began to go wrong. Suddenly without warning the engine began to cough and splutter, and the cabin filled with smoke. The engine was finally shut down to avoid fire, and an ominous silence prevailed. Suppressing an impulse to get out and look under the bonnet, the passengers sat tight and viewed the ground with some apprehension and hoped the pilot knew what to do. Paul revealed later he had only a minute or so to glide the aircraft down over a wooded hill, over a ditch and under the National Grid wires, to make a good landing in the middle of a field of crops. Realising that further flying that day was out of the question, and fearing assassination, by some irate farmer, the travellers decided to evacuate the scene and make for a nearby road. There was just enough time and light, to photograph, with trembling fingers, the dejected aircraft. A chance lift took them to Nottingham Station just in time to catch a train to Swansea. While obtaining their tickets mention was made of the forced landing. The railway clerk remarked, "it's a good job for some people the British Rail is still running!" Under the circumstances the passengers agreed most heartily. Forthright praise was heaped on Paul but for whose skill and composure this tale would not have been told. Later he told me that in the poor light it was only at the last minute that he was able to see the high-tension wires and dive underneath. The engine of course could have failed at any time, over a built-up area for example, or later in the flight in complete darkness. These were risks common to the business however, which we took on an almost daily basis. Before he left the aircraft Paul had locked the doors and fitted the external locks to the aircraft controls. Finally he and the passengers had pushed the aircraft into the prevailing wind. Unfortunately within the next forty-eight hours an autumnal gale of unusual severity blew the aircraft on to its back from which position the farmer dragged it across his field into a yard. The aircraft insurance fortunately covered all the exigencies, and apart from losing the temporary use of the aircraft our company escaped scot-free.

To maintain our professional licence it was necessary every six months to undergo a medical check with a Civil Aviation approved examiner. They were spread around the country, and on this occasion I decided to use the RAF doctor based at the RAF station at Chivenor in North Devon. I took the little Cessna aircraft across the twenty miles or so of water having made a £5 bet with the Swansea Air Traffic Controller, that I could land back at Swansea without him spotting me, until my wheels were firmly on the runway. As Swansea was equipped with radar at that time, it meant to escape discovery I would have to fly at not more than fifty feet above the sea to avoid detection. This I did until approaching the coast when I dropped even lower, whilst at the same time listening-out on the Swansea frequency to check the presence of any conflicting aircraft. Satisfied that there was no other traffic I cleared the cliffs and landed on Runway 04 and called up for taxi clearance thus winning my bet. The next day while being flown by one of our trainee pilots the engine of the same Cessna aircraft failed. Fortunately this incident occurred directly above the airfield and the pilot held his nerve and landed safely. Had this failure occurred one hour earlier it would have caught me skimming the waves of the Bristol Channel. It was a chilling thought to realise that none of our aircraft were equipped with life jackets, and me one of the world's heavy sinkers.

On the 26th June 1964 Paul and I took the rebuilt GARET to the disused airfield of Angle in West Wales carrying a very distressed young lady on a largely humanitarian flight. The aircraft had barely come to a stop when another irate farmer parked his truck across the nose of the aircraft. As I stepped out I heard him say.

"Caught you at last you bastards. Every time I've driven up before you have fucking well flown-off before I could catch you!" I faced him with the maximum gravitas and authority I could muster my uniform clearly helping in this. "Control your language." I said. "We have a lady on board." The farmer seemed somewhat embarrassed, and as he muttered an apology I continued. "Now be good enough to give her a lift into town, that's a good chap." Unused to such authority he quickly loaded the lady and her bags into his truck and drove off. Without doubt Cormorant did provide a first class service! Neither Paul or I had ever visited Angle airfield before, and we objected to farmers who acted like little dictators, protecting their strips of concrete which had been laid and paid for during World War II at the taxpayers expense.

Stan Edwards had now fully recovered from typhoid and had benefited financially by the Swiss Court settlement. With some of the proceeds he had purchased a cabin cruiser and a magnificent Bentley car reminiscent of the ones used by the gangsters of the 1930s' and 1940s' films. From its neat rear long rectangular windows I thought of all the fun I could have with a Tommy gun particularly when visiting the farmers of West Wales. A few days after the Angle affair, I arranged to meet Stan near another World War II airfield, this time Carew Cheriton. He kept his boat on the river nearby, so once more it meant landing on a disused runway, which undoubtedly would be owned by another miserable farmer. Attempts were made, as always, to determine the owner and obtain permission to land, but very rarely was this possible for whatever reasons. In this case I decided to go anyway, and Paul accompanied me to fly the aircraft back to Swansea. A low run over the runway showed that to prevent landings the farmer had placed a wire fence across the runway approximately halfway along its length. He had not reckoned with the short field performance of the aircraft however. The approach was difficult with the surrounding hills preventing a direct approach to land. After two failed approaches I made it on the third attempt landing just clear of the wire fence. I taxied back to the end of the available runway and jumped out with my suitcase, I watched Paul take-off and at the same time attempted to step over the thick barbed wire fence into the field beyond. I had spotted Stan and Bentley parked in a small lane on the opposite side of the field, where he was leaning on a five barred gate. In my haste the barbed wire had torn my trousers upwards from the turn-up to well above my knee taking a chunk of skin and flesh with it in the process. Now hobbling and bleeding I made my way towards Stan. Suddenly I heard him shout, "Bull!" and on my left about sixty yards or so distance I saw this animal take a direct interest in my presence, and began its take off run. My hobbling quickly developed into a very good imitation of a sprint of which Forest Gump would have been proud. Stan was enjoying the spectacle and shouting, "You'll never make it," which served the purpose of generating more adrenaline and quickening my running action. A few yards from the gate I lobbed my bag in Stan's direction and then performed the finest thief vault of my life. My Physical Education teacher would have been thrilled at my efforts. The bull passed by at a rate of knots clearly disappointed at not taking me with him. Certainly landing on disused runways with all their hazards clearly posed a risk to one's health, and I resolved to give them a miss in the future. The weekend on the boat at Lawrenny and the beautiful river, and scenery running down to Milford Haven, soon repaired my damaged ego not to say my injured leg.

There was no flying training available to the general public at Swansea Airport when we arrived, with the old Swansea flying club completely defunct. Paul and I had been asked by a number of visitors why we were not offering the facility of flying training. After some deliberation it was decided that I would attend an instructors course, largely because of my previous training as a teacher. I selected Cranfield as the most desirable venue, predominantly as the Air Centre there had Ron Campbell as its Chief Instructor. Ron had been a wartime bomber command Halifax pilot, who had completed a tour of operations, and more, and was the holder of the DFC. He was also the author of the definitive book on flying training in the UK. I started on the course at Cranfield on the 22nd July 1964, which was to last two weeks, culminating in a flying test and written examination. Here you acted as the instructor flying from the right hand seat with the dumb pupil (i.e. Ron) occupying the other seat. Here you first learned to brief your pupil on the air lessons, illuminating the talk with your exhilarating knowledge of aerodynamics (in my case sadly lacking). It became readily evident to me, during to course, that you learned more about basic flight from your students when instructing than you ever had when you learned yourself. Ron was not just a fine pilot, but the best instructor I had, or would ever encounter, in my aviation career. I desperately sought and worked hard at the techniques that were so obviously second nature to him. After fourteen days and 27 hours of flight training, I successfully passed the ground/flight tests with Bert Russell a resident examiner at the Cranfield Aeronautical College. One of my colleagues on the course happened to be a very wealthy young man, who shortly before had started an aircraft company, leasing light aircraft. I confided in him the story of Cormorant and our desire to start a flying training establishment at Swansea. My ideas seemingly coincided with his own, and I was able to conclude a deal with him to lease two Cessna aircraft, a Cessna 150 and Cessna 172, on what were at that time very low leasing rates. On the 9th of August, shortly after completing the course, I had proudly flown the first of these aircraft a Cessna 150 GASLB (Golf Alpha Sierra Lima Bravo) from Biggin Hill to Swansea. Life was indeed looking up. My time was now largely taken up with instructing the steady flow of students who came my way. The age group ranged from eighteen to sixty five years, but my pattern of instruction remained largely the same. In order to teach students, most UK flight instructors found it necessary to wait for conditions where it was possible to see the visual horizon, and anything remotely approaching cloudy conditions was avoided like the plague. Fatalities often occurred among private pilots when they encountered conditions of low cloud and poor visibility on cross-country flights, as sadly they had never been trained to cope for such eventualities in their basic training. My philosophy therefore was the one taught me by Mike Conry at Biggin Hill some years earlier, when his opening words were, “let’s find some cloud”. Our two seat Cessna training aircraft was fitted with a full blind flying panel, so I had no hesitation in teaching my pupils how to use these instruments from the very start of their flight training. Effect of controls, climbing and descending were all taught in cloud until the student felt completely at home in this new environment. I completed almost forty hours of instruction in the first month and the demand grew.

When a Rolls Royce car drew up outside the terminal building our lives were about to change inexorably. Minutes later three expensively suited businessmen entered our offices with an instant requirement to fly them to London Gatwick airport. Mr Goddard seemed the leader of the group, and he and his colleagues were described as 'Jobbers', a new term to add to my vocabulary. Some weeks earlier John Bloom's empire had collapsed making headline news throughout the country. The press steel factory, a part of Bloom's empire, on the Jersey Marine at Swansea had been taken over by Goddard and company. This factory was a part of the Rolls Razor company's assets, which had produced refrigerators and washing machines. Goddard and Co. would remain in Swansea for some time while they sold-off these assets in job lots. However with their company base in East London it was logical that they turned to us to satisfy their transportation needs. This clearly pointed to a new and rich source of revenue from a large number of repeat flights, and so it proved.

Young Donald was a young twelve year old boy who helped us throughout the holiday period assisting with the pleasure flying. He asked me one day whether he could fly to Gatwick when a seat was free. I readily agreed to this request, and on the Friday morning Paul took him along for a ride to Gatwick, returning around 1430 in the afternoon. Donald lived in the nearby village of Killay and it was his habit to return home for lunch each day, later that afternoon he reappeared in my office with tears in his eyes. "What's the matter Donald?" I asked. "I got home late for dinner, sir, and my mother was angry because I was late. She asked me where I had been, and when I told her London I received a beating for lying to her." Poor Donald had never ventured with his parents further east than Cardiff, so his mother's behaviour was understandable under the circumstances. That evening I wrote a short note, and gave it to Donald to hand to his parents explaining the events of the day. Donald had no further trouble that summer.

Goddard walked into our office one day, faced Paul and myself and suggested that he took a majority equity position in Cormorant. Paul and I were somewhat taken aback by this proposal as nothing had been suggested before hand. Next came the 'punch-line' and an explicit threat 'If you are not prepared to take me on board then I will start a charter company at this airport and see you both out of business'. If we agreed to his proposal however he would provide us with a new twin engined aircraft, free of charge, which we knew would greatly extend the scope of our operation. The decision to accept the offer was almost instinctive on our part. We were not well versed in the whiles of business then, and we could clearly see the advantages that association with Goddard could bring, the disadvantages being less clear at the time. In the short term there were immediate benefits, but ultimately this relationship had disastrous consequences for the company, and by implication for Paul and myself.

It became necessary now to look the part of professional pilots, but had little idea where we could purchase a small number of uniforms. Silvers in Cardiff Docks had been selling naval uniforms for the merchant marine for many years, and it was towards this outfitter I turned to supply ours. My confidence temporarily deserted me when I faced this tall imposing man across his shop counter. "Mr Silver," I said in as important voice as I could muster, "I am starting a new airline and would like to place a initial order for twenty uniforms, caps and shirts." Clearly I had made a hit, and Mr Silver, short of licking his lips, was immensely impressed. "You will understand Mr Silver," I continued, "that I must test the product first, so perhaps we will start with just two uniforms, but the price will of course be based on the larger quantity." He began to haggle so I put on my disinterested look, the haggling stopped forthwith, and the deal concluded. Paul and I felt, with our fairly low level of experience as professional pilots, that just two gold rings on our sleeves would suffice, confident that no passenger would question this rank. Stan purchased the third uniform with our permission largely as a visual aid to attract the ladies, also as an accessory to his Bentley car. When he next appeared at Swansea Airport he created a near riot. Certainly I was stunned when I saw him, as his uniform was reminiscent of Goering's. Not only did he have five gold rings on his sleeve (a non-existent rank to my knowledge in any man's airforce), but also he wore, with a certain elan, a Wilkinson sword hanging from his belt and gleaming in its magnificence. Not bad I thought for somebody who owned a couple of super markets in Cardiff, and who was not a professional pilot. The attention he drew to himself was quite incredible, and in future years I was greatly amused to see RAF Wing Commanders and Airport Managers spring to attention in his presence. Stan was clearly a sublime actor and was nobly aided and abetted by us all in our adventures.

Stan and I had left the Copper Grill, a Swansea restaurant, together, crossed the road, and saw a large and magnificent Daimler car flying the Mayor's flag stationary at he traffic lights on the Kingsway. I opened the rear door and Stan stepped inside. We sat one each side of a little man who appeared to be totally perplexed. Undoubtedly this was either the Mayor or Lord Lieutenant of the County, either way silence prevailed. Stan and I, had had a first class lunch plus a significant amount of wine, so were quite happy to share a car with any sympathetic soul. At the next traffic lights we alighted and thanked the little man for his kindness. To our surprise he thanked us in return, clearly Stan's uniform and our collective presence had a hypnotising effect. This illusion, which we created, was a constant source of amusement to us, and without doubt our appearance en-masse opened many doors. We arrived, very late, at the Randolph Hotel, Oxford one night, Paul Stan and myself accompanied by five girls, all nurses at the nearby Radcliffe Infirmary. Stan took immediate charge and ordered coffee and sandwiches in the lounge and booked two bedrooms for the eight of us. I seemed to have benefited from the company of three nurses that night, but have no recollection worthy of recall. An early breakfast was demanded as the girls were on the morning shift. With a certain solemnity the manager on duty brought in the daily papers with the news that a Britannia Aircraft of Cunard Eagle Airlines had crashed into the mountains near Innsbruck in Austria killing all on board. A former airline captain I had previously flown with, had been a passenger on that aircraft with his wife and daughter on their first skiing trip. Needless to say our conversation became somewhat muted at the news, and the manager approached Stan, with his salutations, clearly taking us as belonging to Cunard Eagle. "I won't bother you with the bill Sir, I'll send it direct to the company. I am sure you have enough to think about this morning." He clearly thought that the CAS embroidered on our wings sufficiently identified us. We didn't have the heart that morning to put him straight.

Cormorant however was not all fun and games, and just as Paul had come close to extinction, now it was my turn to meet with fear as never before. I had already completed two flights to St. Merryn, an old Royal Naval Air Station, now disused. It was situated on the North Cornish coast three miles south west of Padstow. The airfield had been commissioned as HMS Vulture in August 1940 and closed in January 1956. Goddard was building and renovating a cottage close by, so we flew back and fore almost on a weekly basis. I had three passengers to pick-up so alone I flew Tripacer GARET on a direct route to the North Devon Coast with the incipient threat of a South Easterly gale. My judgement of the weather that day was absurdly optimistic, and I was not enchanted by the colour of the sky as I approached the Devon coastline. The air now livened up somewhat, and as I progressed Westwards the turbulence became severe. The aircraft now began to show a marked disinclination to fly at all, in fact it exhibited a passion to return to earth. The turbulence over the land now became intolerable, and I wrestled the aircraft back offshore where I hoped the turbulence would be less severe. I was now at 1500 or so feet crossing Boscastle bay, suddenly I looked up to see mountainous white topped waves almost beckoning me, but I had no recollection of how the aircraft had become inverted. My throat had become dry with fear, the sweat poured off my face. The aircraft was certainly spinning in an inverted position and seemed in imminent danger of smashing into the waves below. To this day I still don't know how the aircraft righted itself, and although I felt like a little boy, I struggled for survival like a man. In this Tripacer the elevators and the rudder were inter-connected and the aircraft had never been cleared for aerobatics, but that day divine providence guided the aircraft back to level flight and safety. I was now running on pure adrenaline, but my first approach to the Westerly runway at St. Merryn failed in torrential rain and severe turbulence. At 600 feet I saw Goddard and two helpers attempting to put a windsock into position, which by the time I turned on final approach had blown away into the distance. As I rolled to a stop willing hands were hanging onto the aircraft struts. The cockpit door opened and Goddard stared at me. "My God," he said, "you've certainly seen it today." Well he would have known, as he was a Burma war veteran, who had fought the Japanese across a tennis court at the battle of Kohima. I was still in a state of shock as later I wrung the sweat from my stained uniform. Such was my shocked condition that I forgot to telephone Paul in Swansea to confirm my arrival. To his eternal credit he had jumped into the other Cessna and scoured the Channel for any sight of me. I returned to Swansea next day in good weather, the storm having abated. Paul was not at all pleased when he saw me and treated me to a range of expletives I had no idea he knew, even less understood. He was fully justified, of course!

A few days later Stan hired an aircraft and me, to fly to Bournemouth Hurn Airport. We stayed at Boscombe in a rather splendid hotel, where it was his intention on the morrow to buy a large motor yacht. The dinning room was full the next morning as we entered, with the silence deafening as we made our way to our table. After all it was a rare sight to see a full-blown admiral and his aide. Stan a usual ordered a full English breakfast and I the usual kippers. Our waiter clearly had an attitude problem and regarded us with a certain disdain, but I became somewhat annoyed when he managed to drop my plate and kipper on the table without any resemblance of an apology. Somewhat aroused I waited for him to walk some distance away and then roared. "Waiter come back here." Once again silence descended and all heads turned in our direction. Pointing to the kipper I said very loudly. "This kipper was not caught, it gave itself up. Get me another kipper that has lived for a few years." This time the waiter almost run down the dining room moved by the loud laughter that followed him. Stan in the meantime was shaking uncontrollably unable to eat his breakfast. Now I am a firm believer in good service, and in the airline business it is absolutely vital. I had of course flown aircraft over a number of years, but I had also greeted passengers at the check in desk, written the tickets, pushed baggage trolleys and loaded the aircraft. Such was the level of service in a small regional charter and schedule airline. In America they grow up on this ethic of service. In the UK however many people believe that to serve is also to demean. I am therefore very hard on any employee who behaves this way, as good service is the only sure guarantee that passengers will return another day, and that in essence guarantees you livelihood. I should have reported the waiter to the manager, but my better nature prevailed, and we were in a happy mood that morning when we took-off for the short flight to Southampton Eastleigh Airport. The staff at both airports treated us like royalty, well Stan anyway, and on arrival some important looking chap escorted us to the Terminal Building. Isn't it just amazing what a uniform can do, particularly when nobody knows what rank and to what service the uniform relates. It was commonplace for Stan and I to act the fool when together, except of course in the cockpit. We acted like a pair of idiots when this rather pleasant ex-merchant navy captain, the owner of the boat, arrived to drive us to the boatyard to view the motor yacht. Moored offshore it was necessary to row out in the tender, in what could only be described as placid harbour conditions. About halfway out I saw a small ripple on the water and called out. "Watch out Stan there's a large wave approaching." Stan turned to the owner and said in a high pitch voice. "Oh, my God, is it always as rough as this?" The owner's face was a picture, and clearly hadn't met any body quite like us before.

The Sancta Maria was absolutely splendid even to my unpractised eye. Almost fifty feet in length, ten feet six inch beam, and equipped with two Perkin diesel engines. The interior positively glistened and clearly indicated that the owner had really looked after her, and bestowed his labour with great care and affection. The three of us sat around the table in the main cabin and Stan looked at me and said. "Well what do you think." Still in a playful mood I said. "Buy it Stan, it's got a double bed." The deal was consummated at that moment and a price of £10,000 agreed. It was only at that moment that the owner tumbled to the fact that we had only been playing the fool. The brandy was then brought out, and we all convulsed with laughter at our silly antics.

The Sancta Maria became our weekend home for almost four years, and we had great fun in her, and when at sea she never let us down, although there were times when perhaps she had every reason to. On the 5th of July 1941 SS Anselm a troopship was in convoy 300 miles North of the Azores when she was torpedoed by the German submarine U96. Stan had been one of those on board. He had climbed a rope out of the hold and dived off the stern of the ship as it was sinking. His lasting recollection of the ship was of the many troops standing at the rail too frightened to jump. Some of course went down with the ship, and Stan spent a considerable time in a lifeboat before being rescued by a British destroyer. Incredibly U-boat

96 lasted almost to the end of the war when, in fact on the 30th March 1945, she was sunk in Wilhelmshaven Harbour by American aircraft. For many years he kept this story from me, probably in the belief that I would scoff at him, as certainly like me, his stories were sometimes wild or weird. Improbably the truth was confirmed some years later when one day at Yarmouth on the Isle of White a fellow yachtsman tied up alongside the Sancta Maria. At a drinks party that evening the owner of the yacht, a retired commander in the Royal Navy, was recognised by Stan as one of the officers on board the British destroyer which had picked him up out of the water that day in the North Atlantic. They both remembered the day, and after a number of drinks embraced like brothers.

In the meantime Paul got himself into trouble once more on a flight carrying Goddard and two other passengers from Swansea to Belfast. Having passed Dublin he called Belfast and Aldergrove Airport for a QDM (a magnetic heading to steer) to arrive over the airport. Having no other method of navigation Paul was shocked to be told that their VDF system was unavailable. Now unsure of his exact position he let down through cloud, and with his fuel low, spotted an almost deserted beach and landed. A local tourist took Paul and his passengers to a local garage where a number of fuel containers were filled with petrol and transported back to the airport. Having now fixed his position he then took-off and proceeded to Belfast Airport and landed safely. The Belfast Telegraph somehow obtained the story, and printed it with the following leader: 'Belfast Bound Plane Ditched on Beach. A plane bound for Aldergrove with three people on board had to make an emergency landing on a North Donegal beach. The Piper Tripacer aircraft was on its way from Dublin to Aldergrove, but in low cloud failed to make contact with the airport and flew west heading for the Atlantic. With fuel supplies running short the pilot decided to make a landing on the White Strand near Lisfannon on the shores of the Swilly. The pilot and his two passengers are believed to be from the Manchester area. They walked to a nearby garage, bought 10 gallons of petrol to refuel, and took off again. The aircraft landed safely at Aldergrove. The aircraft remained at Aldergrove for over five hours before taking off for Swansea.' On his return Paul gleefully admitted he needed retraining, and both of us realised that one should never believe what they write in the newspapers.

Things had now come to a head with the dreaded Gower Warden, the local council and now the Airport Manager. It had been finally decided that car parking on the approached to the runway bordering the main road had to stop. This effectively ended our pleasure flight revenue. It had been recognised, a long time ago, that despite our advertising signs adjacent to the main road people were loath to enter the airport and ask for pleasure flights. The main attraction had been the fact that car parkers could see the happy people getting off our aircraft and wanted to join in the fun. A new source of activity would have to be found, and here we both chased Goddard to deliver the new free twin engine aircraft he had promised. It was soon established that Paul would go to Czechoslovakia to negotiate the purchase of the aircraft, and the preliminary date of delivery would be February 1965. We were still ignorant of the type of aircraft we were to get, and much would depend on Paul's negotiating skills. In the meantime, the council sent earth-moving machinery to dig up the approaches of the road near the airfield boundary fence. As for food, in the future, the ponies on the common would have to make their own arrangements. Nearby a group of Irish gypsy travellers had decided to make camp, at least for a short while. They were soon accosted by the red faced Gower Warden who declared that the Common was a place of outstanding natural beauty. The gypsies nearly caused him apoplexy when they declared that in Ireland they'd call this a bog. They were soon hustled away, and were last seen scurrying westwards back towards Ireland.

It is quite an amazing phenomenon in aviation that companies come and go at a seemingly alarming rate. It is particularly evident at the airline level, even companies once considered sacrosanct like Pan American, Eastern Airlines and British Caledonian folded their wings and disappeared forever from the world's skies. During our residence at Swansea Airport much to our chagrin another small company arrived which threatened our very existence. Bardock Aviation was an amalgam of the names Barfield and Docker. Lord Docker was a famous name in manufacturing circles in the UK, with his British Small Arms Company in Birmingham. Indeed pre World War II BSA motorbikes were a feature both on the racing tracks and the British roads, and such a name was, in our view, redolent of money and power, qualities that we singularly lacked. Our anxiety was further exacerbated when the airfield manager now seemed to spend an excessive amount of time in their presence. Their grandiose schemes involved the building of a large motel with swimming pool on the airport premises to be quickly followed by a new Terminal Building, which they of course would operate on the airport's behalf. We felt now very much the poor relations, and when three aircraft, brightly painted in their name, appeared on the airfield an unavoidable depression set in. It seemed only a matter of weeks when a glimpse of sunlight penetrated the gloom. It was learned from a secretary at the airport that Mr Barfield had not/could not pay the milkman for his daily supply of milk. His aircraft, a four engine Heron, a Dove and a single engined Piper, now dominated the hanger, squeezing our poor offerings into a smaller and smaller space. It was early one morning, before the airport officially opened, when a Dove aircraft landed unannounced on the westerly runway, a group of men ran to the hanger doors and wheeled out the three aircraft. One by one they taxied out took-off and disappeared into the early morning mist. Later I learned that Bardock had rented the aircraft from Transworld Leasing, a company owned by the redoubtable Mike Keegan. Mike was a very tough character, and had set up BKS Air Transport after World War II, operating Douglas DC3s on charter and the Berlin Airlift. Later he owned both Transmeridian Air Cargo (the largest Air Cargo Company in Europe) and British Air Ferries, where he opened the door to woman pilots. Mike advertised his leasing company regularly in Flight International, at that time, and his aircraft were usually shown draped in attractive semi-naked women, probably his stewardesses, accompanied by the punch line 'Everything I have I own' I had no doubt of that myself. Some years later he flew down to Malta from Italy to meet me, and we discussed, among many things, that morning at Swansea. He had also been taken-in by the Bardock Company, albeit only for a few weeks, and when they defaulted on their payment schedule immediately took action, thus ending what we considered to be our main challenge at that time, but others were soon to follow.

One of the great characters in light aviation during this period was one Noel Husband. He was a local surveyor and estate agent, who loved flying like no other. He had soloed in an old Auster and had gloried in the fact that the local undertaker had swung the propeller for him that very morning. Shortly after obtaining his private pilot's licence he had flown to Nice in the South of France breaking every rule in the book. When they had shot up multiple red flares at him to warn him off he had taken this as a sign of welcome and landed. He had taken part in a number of air races including the King's Cup and had performed quite well in these. On one occasion he had departed from Dinard to land at the old Pengam Moors airfield just to the East of Cardiff. He described his flight as follows: 'I saw this cloud over the English Channel and as I had never flown above cloud before decided to try it. The cloud began rising so I climbed the Auster to remain above it. On ETA (expected time of arrival) I let down through the cloud which seemed to persist until I suddenly looked out under my left wing and saw a couple of running sheep. A bump followed and I found I had come to a stop on the top of a mountain just North of Cardiff.' Such was Noel's luck, and his stories told in a laid back manner wrought hysterics in his audience. He later purchased Mike Hawthorn's (the racing driver) aircraft, and had the engine fail above Liverpool. He made a successful landing on a school's Rugby field and walked away completely unscathed. He was in his fifties when he approached me to teach him instrument flying. Under normal conditions this would have been difficult, but Noel's eyesight and hearing were not of the highest order, and when you are unable to hear the instructions of the radar controller things can quickly get out of hand. I had been in the tower when Noel was cleared to land on Runway 26 to see him blithely land on another runway. How he had lived through his many experiences in flight frankly amazed me and many others who understood the business. In a moment of utter madness he went out and purchased a Falco with the most apt registration of TAROT. This was a fully aerobatic, fast single engined aircraft, and its acquisition was, in my view, like asking a 90 year old man to drive a Ferrari over difficult terrain at speed. He had asked me to fly with him in his new aircraft on a number of occasions and I had always been able to offer a realistic excuse. One night having returned from a cross country flight with a student, and having put the aircraft to bed in the hanger, found my exit blocked by Noel and his infernal Falco. "John," he cried, "I've been waiting for you to check me out at night in the circuit." Well not only was I suffering from a heavy cold but my evasiveness over the proceeding weeks had precluded me even sitting in the aircraft and studying its systems. Why I relented I shall never know, but the dear chap had plagued me for so long that I almost felt I owed him a little of my time. A cup of tea and a couple of paracetemols later, I found Noel already strapped into the left-hand seat. I struggled into my seat in a dark cockpit. "OK Noel," I said, "you can now put on the cockpit lights." "I have them on," he said, and only then did I notice a few pinpricks of light on the left hand side panel. "Don't worry," he said, "I have a torch you can hold". At that point my courage, which had never been at a very high level, deserted me completely. "I'm sorry, Noel," I said, "but if I am to fly this aeroplane at night, then we must swap seats, you can observe or hold the torch." Noel reluctantly conceded to my request. He appeared to have no ideas of take-off or landing speeds, so I flew the aircraft at a much higher speed than was really necessary. On landing he then startled me further by telling me it was now OK and I could get out. Reluctantly I stood on the runway and watched the aircraft climb back into the night sky and complete the circuit successfully. I was one among many who marvelled at his foolhardiness, or was it just courage. Later I took sweet revenge on Noel, who generally appeared at our Saturday night parties carrying no more than two small bottles of larger, which he drank himself. As was the custom, he stood with his back to the fireplace and tried the sweet talk on any girl present. From my usual seat at the side of the fireplace I had valiantly striven that evening to generate some semblance of flame without success. Exasperated by this failure I threw a small amount of paraffin on the reluctant coal with no apparent effect. Noel was deep in conversation with a few of our local beauties and had no eye for me. The fire remained dormant so in desperation I threw on the remaining paraffin. It was like a jet starting-up. There was a sudden muffled roar and an explosion. A searing flame shot out hitting poor Noel directly on his arse. He leapt into the air like a frightened gazelle, his trousers badly singed. It proved to be the highlight of the evening, which I must say he took in good part.

CHAPTER 5

CORMORANT DIVING

It was in January 1965 that we were informed that our new Aero 145 from Czechoslovakia would be available for delivery at Oxford Kidlington Airfield on the 21st February. Dick Rosser once more accompanied me on my travels, and we travelled to Oxford by train on the preceding day, and night stopped at the George Hotel at Woodstock. Peter Clifford Aviation was the official UK distributor for Omnipol Aircraft of Czechoslovakia. It was Peter himself who was to check me out on the aircraft at 0830 that Sunday morning. We arrived at the airfield at 0800 with no sign of Peter. Despite a telephone call to his home he didn't arrive until 1030, and seemed unapologetic about it. Peter climbed into the left-hand seat of the aircraft, explaining that the only set of brakes were on his side. During take-off he broke into song as he pressed the various buttons on the panel in front of him, offering me no explanation at all. After the first landing he taxied in, shut down the engines, when I expected to swap seats and commence my instruction. Instead he climbed out of the aircraft and from the luggage hold, pulled out a brown sack, normally used to carry potatoes. "Here's the aircraft's documents," he said, with a certain flamboyance, "if you want me for anything I'll be at home after lunch." I stared at his back in disbelief as he walked away, too shocked to say anything. Dick too shared my amazement as I sat in the cockpit and stared at the instruments. The buttons had strange hieroglyphics printed on them, which meant nothing to me, and to add to the confusion the artificial horizon was coloured blue on the lower half and brown on the upper half, surely, the instrument had been installed the wrong way up? How in hell was I going to deliver this contraption to Swansea in one piece, I asked myself. I now delved into the sack to examine the documents, and here again I was confronted by documents written in Czech of which I had no knowledge. Some however had been translated literally into English, which in other circumstances would have been highly amusing, but not today. Dick with a great aptitude for the obvious asked me, "What are you going to do?" "Bloody well fly the heap to Swansea," I answered with a far greater confidence then I felt. I tormented the engines on the first few take-offs I undertook simply by pressing the wrong buttons the engines being electronically operated. My third take-off was better and we seemed to achieve a certain balance of agreement, so I turned the aircraft on to a southwesterly heading, in the general direction of Swansea. As I approached the long runway of Brize Norton I decided to switch fuel tanks by using the selector between the seats. As I moved the selector to wing tanks both engines reached an immediate and unanimous agreement and quit in the most audible and sudden fashion. To see two stationery propellers was not at all to my liking and in a flash I turned the selector leaver back to main. Almost instantaneously both engines resumed their wild song and my heart, which had almost stopped in sympathy, now resumed its original rhythm. Dick, white in face, was truly explicit. "Jesus Christ," he said, "don't do that again!" I had concentrated so much on flying the beast that I hadn't even had time to check out the radio, so we flew the rest of the way home in relative silence landing at 1535. Paul and a small crowd were on the tarmac to greet our arrival, and I felt like Lindbergh must have done when he landed in Paris after his solo Atlantic flight. Paul never known to use two words when one would do rather excelled himself that day, when he said, "Well done!"

During my instructor's course at Cranfield Ron Campbell, my instructor, on one flight asked me to look down the right hand side of the aircraft to spot what proved to be an illusory chicken farm. In the meantime acting as the 'dumb' student he pulled the mixture leaver and stopped the engine. He had of course carried out this action at 1000 feet half way along the down wind leg close to the runway. From that position I had no trouble gliding the aircraft to a safe landing in what is known in the trade as a 'dead stick' landing. Some months later I thought to try this out with one of my best trainee pilots, David Thomas, a most unflappable sort. Similarly placed on the down wind leg I asked David to look down and see if there was a car on the runway, thus occupied I pulled the mixture leaver and stopped the engine. The consequences were completely unpredictable as David grasped the starting handle in panic and pulled it completely out of the panel his right elbow smashing into my chin, clattering my head on the side of the cabin. All logic seemed to have disappeared in seconds and I was in a semi-conscious state. By the time I shouted, "I have control." The aircraft had almost passed the point where I could have confidently expected to land back on any runway. Fortunately I just managed to miss the approach lights and fence, landing heavily on the first few feet of runway. I never repeated this experiment, as it was evident that people varied in their reaction to an emergency and to subject an inexperienced trainee pilot to such treatment was perhaps asking too much.

A few days later Paul and I took the Aero 145 on a charter to Boston in Lincolnshire. We had no information on the field, and no approach or let down charts were listed for it. The two passengers reassured us however that such a field existed and we took them at their word, not the smartest thing to do really. Despite the good weather we spent almost an hour over Boston and the Wash until Paul spotted a windsock on what appeared to be nothing more than a Rugby field. I took the aircraft down for a slow run and the passengers confirmed that this was indeed our destination. Some airfield I thought as we bumped and bounced down the uneven surface coming to a stop just short of a cabbage plot. Never again would I take the word of a passenger on the subject of airfields.

At this time I was staying with a Mr and Mrs Mackrill in the village of Murton on the beautiful Gower peninsula. They both treated me like a son and attributed almost god like qualities to those of us who flew aeroplanes. Indeed it appeared that not only was I highly intelligent but very brave as well. There were times when I attempted to disabuse them of their views but without avail however. I had taxied the Aero down to the airfield perimeter one Sunday evening before a positioning flight to Exeter. A group of Cormorant supporters and pilots were gathered there including Mr Mackrill. Later he recounted how he had watched my take-off and had followed the flashing light of my anti-collision beacon until it disappeared in cloud over the Channel. This sort of idolatry was great but embarrassed me in the presence of strangers. It appeared that even I was not beyond blushing! He himself chartered the Aero one day and flew with me to pick up his ninety year old mother-in-law, Mrs Cruse, from Weston-Super-Mare. This would save him and the family the tedium of a long car journey. It was Mrs Cruse's very first flight and she was quoted as saying. "It was far less fuss than coming by bus, and I'm looking forward to my next flight." On the return flight from Weston I smelt smoke, and sniffed around the cockpit, like a bloodhound, setting and resetting the circuit breakers and fuses. It was then I saw a puff of smoke above Mr Mackrill's head. I turned to look at Mrs Cruse on the back seat; she was stretched out with a blissful look on her face while contentedly puffing away at a very fat cigar, completely contented. I always knew the Mackrills were very special, but sadly I was working in America when they both died within a short space of time. Years later when I returned to Swansea, I went looking for them and was shocked when I heard the news. I parked the car near the fence where Mr

Mackrill had stood on that Sunday night many years before and said a little prayer. I was sure that they heard it!

My next wheeze was to examine to possibilities of operating flights to Lundy Island eleven miles off Hartland Point in Devon and twixt the Atlantic Ocean and the Bristol Channel. Martin Coles Harman had bought the 1000-acre isle for £16,000 in 1925 and claimed that it was a separate state not subject to the Crown. He had started his career in London as an office boy and by 1930 had risen to the position where he controlled companies worth fifteen million pounds. The inhabitants of Lundy, about fifty in number at that time, paid no rates or taxes and Harman took the title of 'King of Lundy'. In 1930 he was charged under the Coinage Act for issuing coins with his name engraved on them, clearly no shortage of ego there. The coins were known as puffins and half puffins. He also produced his own special stamp also known as puffins. In the subsequent hearing in London he lost his case and was fined five pounds with fifteen guineas costs, and lost the subsequent appeal. When he died in 1954 his son, Albion Pennington Harman, took over the duty of running the island. Prior to World War II Lundy and the Atlantic Cost Airlines operated a service from Barnstaple to the island using Scion and Mona Spar aircraft charging seventeen shillings and sixpence per return flight. After the war Devon air Travel Ltd operated Rapide and Auster Autocrat aircraft from Chivenor until 1955 when the Auster crashed into the sea en-route to the island, the pilot Maurice Lucker, an excellent swimmer, saved the only woman passenger and her two children. I was in total ignorance of all this information when I made contact with Albion Pennington Harman in early April 1965. There were no landline telephones on the island at that time, and contact was made through the short wave transmitter at Hartland Point. A meeting was arranged, and Paul and I flew a Cessna 172 GARWP to the island on the 5th of April. Albion used a number of Austrian Tyrolean students to clear stones off the landing strip, such as it was, and then lit a large bonfire to indicate the wind direction. Paul flew the outbound leg, and although his landing was as competent as ever, we both thought the undercarriage had collapsed. Indeed the landing run was like riding a wild horse and we really thought that the aircraft had been irretrievably damaged, but our luck held and on examination seemed to be in one piece. The Estate Agent, Mr Felix Gade, showed us around the buildings, and strongly made the point that 'certain types of visitors, like the candy floss and ice cream types, were not welcome on Lundy'. I hastened to reassure him on this point, but he was certainly jumping the gun a bit. Albion Pennington Harman appeared to be a very pleasant type of person, and we felt a ready empathy and ease in his presence. We were entertained in the Manor House, which later became a hotel. We sat down for lunch at a table, which seemed to be the length of a cricket pitch, served by waitresses dressed in the old fashioned style. The food appeared on large covered silver platters and was served in a most respectful manner clearly indicating that if Albion was not a king he was certainly the Lord of the Manor. Before we left we were taken on a tour of the island by Albion and Mr Gade, the agent, who had been on the island since the 1930s', and who presented Paul and me with certificates signed by him, which stated that we had visited the Island of Lundy between the Severn Sea and the Atlantic Ocean on the 5th of April 1965. To the best of our knowledge we were the first public transport fixed wing aircraft to land on the island for ten years.

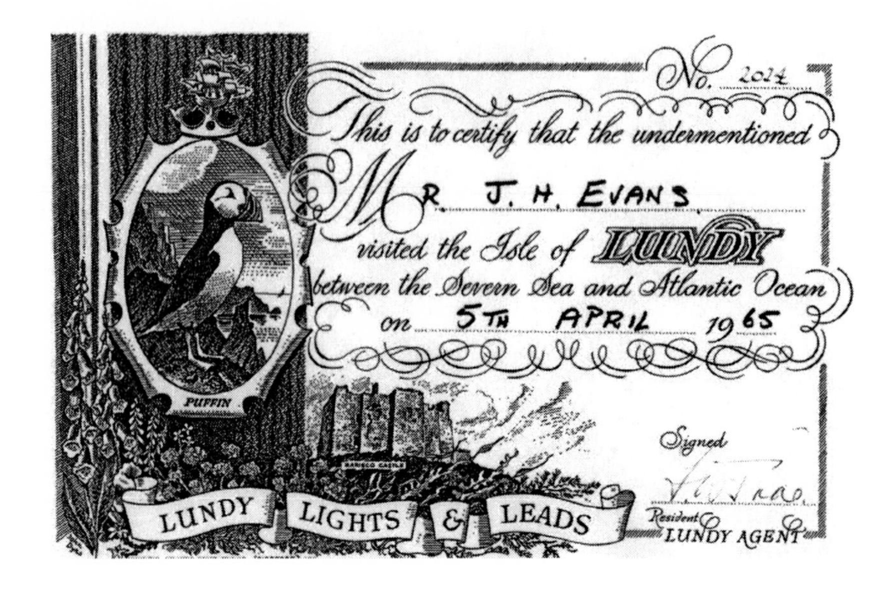

No. 2014

This is to certify that the undermentioned

Mr. J. H. Evans

visited the Isle of LUNDY

between the Severn Sea and Atlantic Ocean

on 5th April 1965

Signed

Resident LUNDY AGENT

PUFFIN

LUNDY LIGHTS & LEADS

Albion was our passenger when I taxied to take-off, and I was concerned at the effect of his extra two hundred pounds weight would have on the take-off run. A small crowd of waving islanders stood to watch our departure as I ran up the engine against the brakes. We seemed to move too slowly over this conveyer bed of rocks, and as the field began its slope downwards towards a stone wall and the cliff edge I pulled back gently on the control column despite the fact that the stall warning was blasting out a continuous noise. The aircraft cleared the wall by a matter of feet and I dived towards the sea below, a drop of about 500 feet. In this way the speed built up, the stall warning stopped its noise and I was able to climb the aircraft away towards the airfield at Chivenor in North Devon where we were to drop-off our passenger. In retrospect the take-off had been reminiscent of war time films, when heavily laden aircraft taking-off from aircraft carriers flight decks would disappear below the level of the deck only to re-appear moments later. I certainly had no wish to repeat this type of take-off, and the prospect of further visits to Lundy suddenly became anything but enticing. The then Ministry of Aviation saw to it however that we would never have to put ourselves at risk in the cause of carrying people to and from Lundy. For once I was totally in sympathy with the current rules and regulations. Sadly Albion Pennington Harman died prematurely in 1968, his brother John had predeceased him during World War II when he was killed at the Battle of Kohima in Burma winning the Victoria Cross in the process. Today I am so pleased that we visited Lundy when we did, and met the splendid people there. Following Albion's death John Hayward, the offshore millionaire, gave the National Trust £150,000 to purchase Lundy and a further group, led by the Liberal MP Mr Jeremy Thorpe, contributed another £100,000. At that time the Land Mark Trust was formed to take care of the buildings on the island. When I visited Lundy by Campbell's steamer in 1979 the island seemed unchanged. I walked along the rocky outcrop on which we had landed in 1965 and examined the wall which I had barely missed. I looked over the edge of the cliff and marvelled. But it is surely a fact 'that if a pilot fears to test his skill against adversity then certainly he has chosen the wrong profession'.

By the summer of 1965 our fleet comprised a Cessna 150, a Cessna 172 and the Aero 145. We now sought a third pilot who preferably held an Instructor's Rating to take over the duties as chief instructor, to whom I could assist as circumstances demanded. Paul had by this time been checked out on the Aero and so we were able to share the charters and the continuing flights for West Point Airlines to the Scillies at weekends. It was Dick who solved our problem, when he found a retired RAF pilot living in Llanelli who was delighted to join us for a rather meagre monthly sum. Thus it was that Oscar became our Chief Flying Instructor and a very popular one to. In fact so popular did he become with one of our female pupils, that he ended up marrying her.

Shortly after we had started the company, and money started flowing in, it became necessary to establish the normal banking arrangements. Purely by accident we found a sympathetic bank manager, who appeared supportive if not excited by our somewhat grandiose schemes for the future, and much to our astonishment granted us an overdraft facility of five hundred pounds. At the end of the meeting Paul was so excited that he opened the wrong door on leaving and walked directly into the broom cupboard, whereupon all the pots, pans and brooms fell on his head. It was a hilarious ending to a very successful meeting. Opportunities did indeed come our way, and in particular we could well have established Cormorant as a top ranking company in the UK. West Point Airlines operated out of their main base at Exeter Airport and was owned and operated by the Mann brothers. Frank Mann was the chairman of the company and his two brothers occupied the positions of Chief Pilot and Chief Engineer. During one of my periodic visits to Exeter Andy, the Commercial Manager of the airline indicated that Frank wished to meet me to discuss a business venture. This aroused my curiosity no end, and I soon found myself visiting Frank's beautiful home in a majestic position overlooking the harbour of Torquay. My reception was friendliness itself, and the proposition we discussed left me somewhat shaken and excited. In essence West Point wished to divest themselves of all the scheduled services to the Isles of Scilly. These routes from Bristol, Exeter, Plymouth and Newquay were currently operated by Rapide aircraft purchased from British European Airways Helicopters when that company moved from fixed wing to a helicopter operation. Frank's offer would include the complete route structure plus the three Rapide aircraft to operate them. We as Cormorant were already helping them on this operation with the Aero 145 aircraft. Frank then explained that he was a director of a company called Crop Culture Isle of Wight, and it was this company that carried out the crop spraying of all the banana crops of Jamaica. In conjunction with this company his two partners had designed a light twin engine aircraft largely as a Rapide replacement, which they considered would ultimately revolutionise this section of the market.

He gave me the first promotional brochure of the Britten Norman Islander, which to my eternal shame I subsequently lost. He asked me for my first thoughts on this aircraft having been given just a few minutes to read it. I pointed out that the 150hp engines planned for the aircraft were, in my humble opinion, insufficiently powerful. In this, my opinion proved correct and the standard aircraft when developed had 260hp Lycoming engines. Frank had clearly heard of Goddard and believed that Cormorant was well endowed with cash, so in light of that, his offer was quite staggering. He offered Cormorant the sales distributorship for the UK and Europe to sell and handle the new Britten Norman Aircraft (BN2).

When I next met Goddard, having already briefed Paul, his reaction was quite astonishing. He immediately telephoned the Isles of Wight and spoke to John Britten. In short he said, "We'll take the franchise and to cement the agreement we will buy the first twenty five aircraft off the production line and take an option on a further twenty five." Britten was clearly amazed at such forthrightness and Paul and I simply staggered by it. We knew that we had none of the facilities to hand to manage such a venture. Goddard clearly thought that he could deal in aircraft much as he did with fridges and washing machines. He had yet to learn that aircraft were a totally different type of commodity, and success in one type of business did not necessarily confer an automatic success in another. Britten Norman however failed to assure us of their ability to handle the order and Goddard quickly lost interest. For us this was a tragedy as Britten Norman had designed a formidable aircraft, which over the years, although mishandled by successive owners, still went on to produce and sell over a thousand aircraft. Indeed it is still in production forty years later, from its base in the Isle of Wight. Despite a number of meetings with West Point we were also unable to conclude a deal which would have seen us take over the West Country scheduled air routes, and purchase the three Rapide aircraft. Seven years were to pass before I returned to the West Country and breath fresh life into the same air routes, but this time under the auspices of a new company Brymon Airways.

Andy of West Point was again the catalyst for yet another business opportunity which came our way. Two honeymoon couples had been delayed by a traffic accident en-route to Exeter Airport, so I was called out to fly them to their destination in Alderney in the Channel Islands. I arrived in Alderney rather late in the day and found bed and breakfast at the Sea View Hotel near the harbour. While at dinner that evening alone, the proprietress of the hotel approached my table and asked me whether I would be prepared to speak to the local, in fact the only, travel agent on the island. Always prepared to further business we sat down together and discussed his immediate and future requirements. What was missing in the islands, he said, was a frequent air service linking Alderney, Jersey and Guernsey. This seemed perfectly obvious to me, and I promised to discuss the project with fellow directors. The next morning I flew a number of people for him to Jersey before returning to Swansea. Once more Goddard showed that his aspirations did not match ours, and once more we lost a heaven sent opportunity. Glossair at Staverton was subsequently approached, and it was they who set up a new operation at Alderney and named the company Aurigny (French for Alderney) Airways, which has continued to the present day. The airline constantly carries over two hundred and fifty thousand people a year plus tons of associated freight. It has now become an integral part of the life of the Channel Islands, and its profitable future guaranteed. It is not difficult to understand therefore the chagrin that Paul and I felt over Goddard's intransigence. To add insult to injury, the Aero 145, which had been promised free, was now being paid for by the company on an instalment basis, which clearly we could not afford. Now we realised that our decision to allow Goddard into the company had been a tragic mistake and one symbolic at the time of our lack of business experience and acumen. Still the damage had been done, and there was nothing for it but to soldier on. I was never to forget that aviation held great power, but how fragile I thought was its wings.

I returned to Exeter late that Friday and had a room booked for me at the Gypsy Hill Hotel at Pinhoe near the Airport. I was sitting at a table drinking coffee, when a tall young good looking chap approached me, sat at my table and asked. "Is that your aircraft parked outside?" I answered in the affirmative. "Well I could have a well paid charter for you," he said, and persuaded me to stay the night at his home in Cockington Village near Torquay where his father apparently leased or owned the complete village. That evening he took me out to a night club in Torquay despite my protests. Here I met Ivor and Patricia Emmanuel, two fine Welsh singers, whom I had seen many times on television. I was hustled away to a quiet corner and introduced to a businessman who preferred not to use his own name. I sat quietly very interested in his cloak and dagger approach. "I want you to carry out a charter for me in a few weeks," he said. "This will involve flying a single passenger very early in the morning from Exeter, and landing him in a field at the southern end of the Cherbourg Peninsula." "Nearer the time," he continued, "I will supply you with all the details, and you will receive £2,500 prior to departure, and a further £2,500 when you complete the charter." He left the club almost as suddenly as he had arrived, and when I returned to Swansea I related the story to Paul. His reaction to the proposal was typical Paul. "Well," he said, "you will certainly receive the first £2,500, but when you get there you will probably get a bullet in your head or a knife in your back. Do it if you want to, but I wouldn't if I were you!" As usual I agreed with my colleague and soon forgot about the whole episode. The following Monday morning after the return from Exeter the previous day, I took a charter to Gatwick, where I remained for most of the day. Whilst I waited for my passengers to return from London, I sat in the Terminal Building and saw a pile of daily newspapers left by departing passengers. I idly opened the pages of one of the tabloid papers, and was shocked to see a face I knew well filling almost three-quarters of a page. Staring at me was Eldon Harris from Eastbourne, the brother of Jack a great friend of mine, with whom I had taught at a school at Seaford in Sussex. Eldon was an ex merchant seaman who had travelled extensively around the world and was one huge character. Apparently he had got a young lady, called Janette, in the family way when she was at an Eastbourne finishing school. The baby had been born, and Janette had been made a ward of court by her father. Strictly forbidden to contact Janette, Eldon had late one evening, after a skinful of drinks, rang her at home. He was consequently reported to the court, arrested and imprisoned for two weeks at Brixton prison for contempt. I immediately contacted the prison and obtained permission to visit Eldon later that morning. There was a large mass of people in the waiting room who clearly represented the pitiable end of the human experience. As ever Eldon was his cheerful self and boasted the he had ordered a new suit for his short stay inside. Then he confided in me that he had seen them. "Seen who?" I asked. "Why, the Great Train Robbers, of course!" he replied, "the word is out that they are offering £5,000 to anybody who can help them escape the country." That news really shook me, as that was the amount offered me only a few days earlier in the Torquay nightclub. A few weeks later Briggs jumped prison and escaped to the continent en-route to Brazil. I was not contacted again on that subject and was thus never tempted. Many years later I was in Barbados in the West Indies when Briggs appeared there having been extracted, or rather kidnapped, by the UK police authorities. Subsequently this action had been deemed unlawful and Briggs was returned to his legal wife and child in Brazil.

For many months Stan and I had planned a holiday on the good ship Sancta Maria. We had decided to sail her from her moorings at Kemps Ship Yard in Southampton to Cherbourg in Normandy. We would be accompanied by our two girl friends from Oxford who shared the same name of Jennifer. Our first port of call was up the Solent to Yarmouth on the Isle of Wight. The old harbour master was fond of telling all and sundry the story, that when a yacht entered the harbour it hung out its fenders, but when the Sancta Maria arrived all the other yachts hung out theirs.

That first night was a wonderful and boozy evening at the George Hotel near the harbour where we had spent many evenings previously. This was the furthest that we had ever sailed the Sancta Maria, so the Channel crossing would be our first venture into the unknown. We left the Needles early the next morning in what Stan and I estimated as Force Six conditions. After many brandies the previous night it took about two hours of sailing to settle my poor stomach. The girls were similarly affected, but not Stan who stood nonchalantly at the wheel surrounded by a dozen empty larger tins and about the same number of full ones. Stan's topographical map, which just happened to be a pre World War II version, indicated a tall chimney standing on the south side of the town of Cherbourg. Unknown to us this had been destroyed in the war and had not been rebuilt. As we approached the French coast however, I could clearly see a tall chimney, but Cherbourg certainly had gone into hiding. What was visible was the chimney belonging to the Atomic Power Station on Cap de la Hague. Totally confused we drew near to a coastal buoy, with its clanging bell, identified it from a copy of the Naval Almanac, and sailed eastwards along the coast until we saw the welcoming forts of Cherbourg harbour. We stood on deck as we swept passed the outer mole and sang our version of the Marseilles to a lone fisherman on the harbour wall who appeared singularly unimpressed by our efforts. We moored in the centre of the inner harbour, where we remained for the week thankful that we had completed our first Channel crossing successfully.

With my great love of history I dragged poor Jenny from Cherbourg to Le Harve visiting the many gun emplacements, cemeteries and museums of the D-Day landings. Stan and his Jenny however spent their time examining the walls and ceiling of their cabin when they weren't knocking back the vino at the nearby bar. We spent the last night in a bacchanalian orgy at the Yalta bar, during which time I slipped outside to see that our tender was securely fastened and that I had allowed sufficient play in the rope as the rise and fall of the tide in Cherbourg is very large. I remember on a previous occasion in Yarmouth when our tender had been left hanging halfway up the harbour wall much to the amusement of the passers by. As I bent down to check the rope I tripped on a second unseen rope and plunged headfirst down the thirty or so feet into the harbour. I had fallen, as fate would have it, between a group of tenders thus saving me from serious injury or worse. Being pretty well soused had clearly helped, as I was probably relaxed when I hit the water. The only damage was to my ego, and Stan insisted on hosing me down in cold water before allowing me below deck. Everybody, but me, seemed to find it hilarious and I almost froze to death in the cold October air.

It had been Stan's responsibility to check the weather for the return trip as I was away that day visiting the museum at St. Mere Eglise. When I asked him about it, he simply answered. "C'est si bon." I took him at his word, on this occasion a serious mistake. At 0530 the next morning we slipped our mooring and passed the outer forts on a northerly track towards the Needles and the Isle of Wight. The morning was quiet and the sea calm, but as Normandy began disappearing over the horizon our world suddenly turned crazy. My estimates of the wind speed now was something in excess of forty knots, and the girls held the wheel temporarily while Stan and I attempted to raise the 'Steady Sail'. No sooner had this been accomplished than it blew away cover and all. My hat soon followed and my polite request to turn the boat around and fish it out of the water was impolitely refused. The sea condition now deteriorated further and we estimated the wave height at around fifty feet, which from our low height on the surface, looked absolutely immense and extremely frightening. Both girls were clearly terrified and nestled under the blankets in the wheelhouse. The navigation of the boat rested in my hands, and our continued existence depended on making a safe landfall somewhere. We had no radio, of course, and navigation would largely depend on the mark I eyeball.

We were now six hours into our journey and the cloud base had lowed to about four hundred feet. Forward visibility in the spray was further hampered by our intolerable climb and descent into massive waves. Stan now showed the he was indeed 'Stan the man', and apart from a ten minute escape to the toilet, stood manfully at the wheel and fought for survival. At the time when we needed assistance most, it came in the shape of a low flying Bristol freighter aircraft en-route from Cherbourg to Southampton. This confirmed at least that we were approximately on track. Three hours later Stan asked me were we where. I reasoned that any error west of track had to be avoided, while any error to the east of track was acceptable. After all the coasts of England and France converged the further east we went, and there were on offer a number of ports we could safely approach. I now told Stan to alter course by five degrees east of our present track. This decision made on the flimsiest of logic saved all our lives that day, as our previously held track would have taken us as planned directly to the Needles, and any sailor worth his salt (which didn't include us) knew that under the prevailing sea conditions the Needles was impassable to any boat or ship that day.

Darkness was now falling, and we had never been out in the Channel after dark, so a new ordeal and challenge faced us. In the distance we could now make out a black mass of land which I presumed was the Isle of Wight, but could not be absolutely sure. I now made out what appeared to be a coast guard hut and from my flying experience in this area took to be St Catherine's Point. Such were the conditions prevailing that Stan and I now decided to fire off a rocket or two to indicate our predicament. The rockets were sealed in a tin and the lid was firmly rusted in place, and despite my frantic efforts remained in place. For hours the deck had been moving on all axis and even standing was an almost impossible manoeuvre. We now turned towards the east, paralleling the coastline, and was just one of a number of ships rushing in the same general direction, which as least gave us some degree of hope. Stan had now been at the wheel about thirteen hours with just one short break, and only once had he shouted out in mid channel when the Sancta had almost broached falling side ways down the side of a gigantic wave. Now I too really began to earn my bread that day. When I had taken my commercial pilot's licence it had been necessary to learn morse code and identify flashing and occulting lights. Now the knowledge for the only time in my life came to my aid and proved our salvation. In the lowering cloud base I was able to identify the occulting red light that was the NAB light guarding Portsmouth harbour. I was dazzled by a myriad of flashing lights, and I could make little sense of those, but we were now fully confident of our position as we slowly passed up to the lee side of the Isle of Wight with the sea diminishing in fury and the wind dropping. I was now standing on deck alongside the open wheelhouse when suddenly I saw a back mass directly to the front. I screamed instructions to Stan who took immediate evasive action. The obstacle proved to be a large concrete buoy used by the Royal Navy to tie up warships and other sundry vessels. We then passed through a host of private yachts luckily without collision, and in the early hours of the morning eventually came to rest up alongside a coal barge up the River Ichen near Cowes. The trip had taken us almost seventeen hours of unbroken hell, and we had not eaten or drunk anything since 0530 the previous day. I had certainly used up all my supply of adrenaline and I'm sure Stan had to. With the girls thankfully in their bunks, Stan took up some floorboards in the cabin and fished out two bottles of good French brandy which we drank as if our lives depended on it. I awoke the next morning to a gentle kiss and smiled thinking Jenny had entered my cabin. I opened my eyes to see Stan laughing down at me. His only words were, "We made it." My response was shorter, "Bastard." We sailed up the Solent the next morning in what were Force 6 conditions. Compared to the previous day it was like a mill pond, as we stood on the deck drinking champagne marvelling at our good fortune, while Stan stood as usual behind the wheel glass in hand with his hat askew on his head, a picture I would never forget. For all of us thought, it was an adventure that would remain in our memories for the rest of our lives.

The girls left after lunch to return to Oxford. Stan and I went into Southampton Town Centre and entered the meteorological office in the main street. Behind the counter stood a serious looking chap. "What can I do for you gentlemen?" he asked solemnly. "Could you show us the meteorological chart for the conditions in the Channel yesterday afternoon?" I asked. He disappeared into a rear room, and soon reappeared carrying a rolled-up chart. "Let me see," he said as he stretched the chart out on the counter. "Portland Bill was averaging fifty five knot Gale Force 10 occasionally Storm Force 11 with winds up to 65 knots. "Were you out there in it?" he asked. "Yes," I answered, "for far too long." "What size ship were you on?" "Thirty nine tons," I answered. "My God, you were lucky!" How lucky we didn't discover for a few days when we heard the news that five ships sank that weekend, and one off St Catherine's Point. I grasped Stan's arm and we sought solace in one another's company and the warmth of a very pleasant pub. We didn't know then, but at 1700 hours the previous afternoon the sea conditions were as bad as they could get, with the tide in direct opposition to the southwesterly wind. Clearly it is smarter at times not to know the truth. Later in the week, the previous owner of the Sancta Maria, knowing that we had left for Cherbourg, telephoned Stan and offered his services to fetch the boat. When Stan informed him that the boat was already in Southampton, he said. "I don't think now that I can teach you anything about the sea." He was wrong of course, and the following year in fact, Stan went back to school, to the University of Cardiff, where he diligently studied and gained his Master's Ticket for Coastal Waters. I merely told him to get a radio fitted and preferably a radar as well!

Earlier that year I had flown GASWS, the Aero, to Oxford Kidlinton for one of its periodic maintenance checks. I was relaxing in the cafeteria when I was asked to join Charlie, the chief engineer, in his office. He looked at me rather strangely, and in his dour Scottish brogue asked me, "Who has worked on the aircraft's engines since its previous check?" "You know Charlie that nobody is so authorised," I answered. "In that case John, somebody has tampered with your engines, and that person certainly knew his business. In fact," he continued, "you could have had a double engine failure at any time, which indicates to me that somebody is trying to put you and Cormorant out of business permanently." I was of course aware that our apparent success at Swansea did not please everyone, but to sabotage an aircraft and kill the occupants was beyond belief. If confirmation was needed, a little later, Paul lost an engine on the Aero whilst approaching the Scillies. Subsequent examination of the fuel tank showed a large quantity of sand present, which can only have been poured in purposely to cause an accident. There was a complete lack of security at Swansea Airport at that time, and although we reported all these findings to the police and airport authorities little changed.

It appeared now that the company was attracting problems like a dog attracts fleas. Oscar now handed in his resignation apologetically, having found a much better paid job, but the final nail in our coffin was the financial collapse of West Point Airlines, the company who had sustained the Aero 145 operation almost from the outset, and with winter approaching we had no fallback plan. Worse was to follow when their last outstanding payment due to us saw the cheque bounce never to be redeemed. At that stage they owed us well over three thousand pounds and non-payment of this sum sealed our fate. We had been disillusioned with Goddard for some time and he was not forthcoming with any solution now. Once he had sold all his fridges and washing machines he had clearly lost all interest in Swansea and us, and his many promises of investment in the company never materialised. For three years Paul and I had worked continuously with little time off and with little money. We had carried thousands of passengers on pleasure flights and charter, taught many students the art of flying, and all this without accident. In terms of business and flying experience we had however benefited enormously and learned many lessons, which were to prove invaluable in the years ahead. Having reneged on all his promises Goddard now made himself a creditor of the company leaving Paul and I to 'pick-up the pieces'. A 'Winding-up Order' was submitted on the 13th June 1966 at the High Court of Justice Chancery Division. The estimated company financial deficiency was £6,288, and its failure was attributed to the mismanagement of Paul and myself. It was the end of a wonderful era and our dear Cormorant had dived for the last time!

CHAPTER 6

THE BEGINNING

It was Friday January 19th 1940. The colour of the sky had suddenly turned into a black threatening mass, and the classroom had been plunged into gloom. Blanchard Evans, our teacher, operated the gas-light hanging in the centre of the classroom and a bright yellow light restored normality to proceedings. The last lesson of the week was given over to 'stick-prints' a simple pleasure created by dipping various wooden shapes into paints of different colours and pressing them on sheets of paper. This was the only art lesson I ever really enjoyed, as it allowed me, when the teacher's back was turned, to create wonderful designs on Dai's head, who was unfortunate enough to be sitting next to me. War had been declared in Germany the previous September, but for us kids there had been a complete lack of any real action. This began to change in late November when mighty Russia, for reasons unknown to me at the time, attacked little Finland. Many years later this would be called the 'Winter War', and all the news reports and daily newspapers began covering it in detail. There seemed a huge amount of world-wide support for the Finns, and we all saw it as a David v Goliath conflict. But if this analogy is accepted, it appeared that the former was better prepared and the latter much less fearsome than we were led to believe at the time. The big-shots in the Kremlin decided, in their wisdom, that ten to twelve days would be sufficient to see the Finns off. In his memoirs Nikita Krushchev had stated that 'all we have to do was to raise our voice a little bit and the Finns would obey. If that didn't work we could fire one shot and the Finns would put up their hands and surrender'. This bravado was completely misplaced, and despite being overwhelmingly outnumbered and outgunned the Finns continued the fight for 105 days, during which time the Russians lost over half a million men. Dai kicked me under the desk, "Look outside", he said. The world had turned suddenly white and large flakes of snow were falling thick and fast. The roofs of the houses opposite in Pontrhondda road were now completely covered. Blanchard Evans gazed out of the window a number of times clearly appraising the situation and soon left the room to discuss tactics with Miss Roderick the headmistress. I looked at Dai alongside, now in a serious frame of mind. "Dai we have to help the Finns tonight, the Russians will be advancing," my imagination now running riot, "see you in the shed at 4.30". Dai nodded sagely and whispered, "Just the two of us?" "Yes," I answered, "we won't be needing reinforcements."

With the conditions fast deteriorating we were let out of school early to avoid the worst of the weather and at 4.30 Dai and I began our preparations. My father's shed at the bottom of the garden was at that time our Army Headquarters, but later it would be pressed into service as our Royal Air Force Operations Room. Dai donned our winter uniforms, which consisted of brown potato sacks with holes cut in them to accommodate our heads and arms. A leather strap or a short piece of rope around our waist completed our attire. Rifles were strong lengths of wood cut down from the nearby woods. We passed up the back lane hugging the walls, the snow was now deep and had started drifting in a strong north wind. We halted at every corner to check the way was clear of any Russian troops. Over the railway bridge and into the all familiar woods racing towards our many and varied hiding-places. "We'll gain the up-slope just out of the woods and take our positions there. We can hold on there until we decide to advance." Dai nodded in agreement, he was not known as a tactical or strategic thinker. We crawled in the soft snow in complete silence and almost invisible to the enemy and took our positions on the up-slope resolved to hold our ground. We knew the Finns were brave and would fight to the end. Later that evening, when I returned home, my mother scolded me for getting wet, but there what else could I expect, women never seemed to understand the important things in life.

It was the coldest winter experienced in Northern Europe since 1832, and if it was cold in Finland it was certainly cold in our small valley. The houses were generally cold and central heating a thing of the future. In our houses we kept one fire in the kitchen during the week and this was augmented by another coal fire in the front room on Sundays, to accommodate visitors should any appear. It needed a great mental effort on my part to leave my warm bed when my mother called me for breakfast in the mornings as the bedroom would be ice cold. I would flee downstairs to stand trembling in front of the solitary kitchen fire. A clothes-horse had been placed around the fireplace and my school clothes were generally aired and warm as I dressed. Breakfast was taken in a chair near the fire and usually consisted of lumpy porridge, not my favourite dish but at least hot, dried eggs as real eggs were rarely available and tea and toast. Sometimes, if I could get away with it, I gave the porridge a miss. There was no early morning bath or shower then, and it took a huge amount of bravery to venture into the bathroom until fully clothed. I suppose us kids must have smelt to high heaven in school, as some of us never seemed to bath at all. Friday night was our family bath night and it was quite commonplace to share the bath water with another member of the family. If I was first in I was given strict instructions not to pee in the water. In this way we saved both water and the fuel needed to heat it. After all there was 'a war on' and everybody constantly reminded us. The solitary toilet was down the end of the garden, but Dad soon built an indoor bathroom and toilet so that I would boast to my pals that at least we had two lavatories (we didn't call them toilets in those days).

Before the Second World War Britain was a hugely class conscious country and even where I lived in the valley of the Rhondda, a hierarchical class system of sorts developed. This tended to be based on the job your father had, where you lived and perhaps your family connections. Working class snobbery often centred around the children and their ability to pass eleven plus examinations, usually exhibited by people who had never themselves sat an examination in their lives. The people of the valley were all too familiar with hardship and danger, and many in the thirties had suffered soul-destroying poverty. So perhaps it was inevitable that they saw success in the eleven plus examination, and entry to the grammar school system as a way of escape for their children. To achieve the desired outcome many children were put under a certain amount of pressure to perform well at school. Many of us also were pushed into learning a musical instrument, and in my case the piano was chosen as the mode of torture. My mother as always decided on the course of action with my dear father acting as enforcer. How wise they proved to be, and I have enjoyed playing the instrument ever since. At our elementary school I inevitably came third in examinations, behind Tich and Mal. Tich, I believe, ended up as an accountant, but Mal spent his working life in the local colliery, his parents refusing him permission even to sit the eleven plus examination. Dai was clearly dyslexic, but the exact nature of the problem at the time simply eluded adults, and teachers who suspected that Dai's real problem was laziness or obstinacy, and his parents inability to recognise that he just wasn't very smart. He eventually became a very successful carpenter and builder. Another great friend was Archie, or to give him his full name Arthur Gwillym Cyril Owen Molyneux. As a child he suffered from a slight stutter and was consequently judged, by the powers to be, to have a diminished mental ability. He was yet another to be denied the opportunity of sitting the eleven-plus and was conveniently despatched to the local senior elementary school (later secondary modern school), where the majority of children ended up. On leaving that doomed institution the headmaster, a chronic misfit, informed Arthur that he was suitable only for mining. Arthur never took this advice, and by the process of hard work and study moved through the South Wales Police to the Metropolitan Police in London where he eventually served as a detective on the Drugs Squad.

One morning on the way to school I met up with Mal in Pontrhondda road. He was eating his breakfast at the time consisting only of a piece of bread and dripping. Suddenly in a heavy downpour of rain, as I looked across at him, I saw a stream of dirt running from his hair down the side of his face. In 1935 a special health survey had been conducted on the valley children, and it was found that fifteen percent of them were severely undernourished. I didn't need a survey to tell me that, as it was commonplace in my class to see kids faint or fall asleep during lessons, so it became a normal function for me to take some of these class mates home with me after school and join me for tea. I am sure that my mother understood the reason. I also collected other strays, and any unsuspecting cat or sheep were corralled in my father's shed, where they were kept warm and fed. The habit seemed to be catching as Dad now brought home two dogs from the mountainside. Zip the first was soon adopted by one of my dog loving aunts, but the second, Mack another mongrel, remained with the family for the next fourteen years and became the most wonderful companion to me. My mother however 'put her foot down' firmly against keeping sheep as pets, much to my disgust!

The British Expeditionary Force had already left to take up their positions alongside the French army. Nothing seemed to be happening however, and all the newspapers seemed to show were pictures of the French eating sleeping or using their railway system inside the magnificent tunnels of the Maginot Line. This non-eventful period became known as the 'Phoney War', and lasted from September 1939 until the Germans attacked the west in May 1940. Some months earlier in December 1939 when I had been breakfasting with my grandmother the headlines in the morning paper read 'The inglorious ending of the German Pocket Battleship Graf Spee'. My dear grandmother had a difficult task of explaining the meaning of the word 'inglorious' to me when I asked. So at least some fighting was taking place at sea and also in the air, but the British and French armies had done nothing, when the German army had pulverised the poor Poles in less than a month, this new type of war now described in our newspapers as Blitzkrieg (Lightning War). The Great War 1914-18 had taken a great toll of French manhood and even when that war ended the Germans were still on French soil. Perhaps it was understandable therefore that the French became defence minded in the inter-war years, and spent a huge amount of money constructing a defence line that stretched from the Swiss border to the Ardennes close to the Luxembourg border. Unfortunately the line hadn't been continued to cover the Belgium border for reasons of cost, and the fact that it had to pass through considerable industrialised heartlands. This defence line had been called the Maginot Line after the French Minister for War André Maginot, and work on it had been started in 1929 and ended in 1938. The Germans has also built a defence line and called theirs the Siegfried Line. In the meantime the Germans had landed in Norway and our forces were pushed into a quick retreat.

In France the Germans Army now faced west. At home we sat anxiously waiting for something to happen not knowing that the German attack had already been postponed eleven times before January 1940. So we blithely sang the song of the moment, 'We're going to hang out our washing on the Siegfried line', and it ended 'if the Siegfried line still there'. But even while we were poking fun at the Germans, that great genius, Adolf Hitler was finalising his plans for his attack in the west. The German General Staff could come up with nothing more profound than the re-enactment of the Schlieffen Plan of 1914, which would of necessity violate the neutrality of Holland, Belgium and Luxembourg. Fortunately for the Germans they had a real strategic genius in Erich von Manstein, who quickly realised that such an attack as planned could never be decisive, and would result in a stalemate reminiscent of the First World War. At best it would conquer some Channel ports, and free up a few airfields, which could be used for air attacks against Britain. The Manstein Plan envisaged the main effort through the Ardennes with a mass attack of German armour, crossing the Meuse at Sedan and in effect outflanking the Maginot Line. This would effectively split Anglo-French forces, and drive direct to the Channel coast at Abbeville and beyond. Manstein had consulted with Guderian, the acknowledged tank expert and founder of the Panzer armies, who considered the plan entirely feasible. After some delay Hitler adopted this plan as his own, and the attack began on May 10th 1940. As Manstein anticipated, the plan was decisive and resulted in the fall of France and the evacuation of the British Army from Dunkirk. In fact, it had proved the most brilliant and successful military campaign in modern history. Back at home, we now faced the foe alone, and the churches and chapels were full as never before, as people prayed ardently for divine intervention. At least for us kids the 'Phoney War' was over, and now we expected to see some real action.

Mass air raids were 'on the cards' and we were not to be disappointed. We soon got used to the wailing sirens, which I believe had been devised ostensibly to chill the stoutest hearts of the civil population. Evacuees now arrived and our quota came from St. Pancras in London. I remember the day well, when in threes they marched with their helpers along the road from our railway station in complete silence. Suddenly as if it were pre-ordained, there was a sustained roar of cheering and clapping to welcome those poor kids into our midst, and accordingly my family grew by one, with the addition of a Miss Helen Pretty. My chums and I now helped the adults to prepare against any German attack. We delivered gas masks to the older adults distributing them from the Air Raid Warden's Post next to the Blind Institute. We marched and drilled alongside the Local Defence Volunteers (LDVs), who in July were renamed the Home Guard, and when the first rifles arrived from America, learned to fire them on the range. These were exciting days for us but we would have felt a great deal less sanguine had we known that Luftflotte II was now stationed in north eastern France and the Low Countries, Luftflotte III in north western France, and the smaller Luftflotte V in Norway, all waiting to attack us with a force of almost two thousand bombers. In late August reality commenced when twenty-one towns and cities in the country were bombed.

The Battle of Britain, as it was called now started, and in August and September we kept the score of all the shot down German aircraft. It was more like a cricket match for us as we counted up the daily figures. Today we know that these figures were grossly exaggerated and sanitised, but at the time they did wonders for the people's morale. We hastily convened a meeting in August and our gang sat in the shed and decided we should do our bit in the air war. I proposed Archie as Squadron Leader, Dai would lead Red Squadron as a Flying Officer, and I would lead the Blue Squadron as a Flight Lieutenant. I think there was little we didn't know about RAF ranks, aircraft types and their performances. I had purchased a book with all this information and we all studied it avidly. Sometime that year Archie had given me a whole pile of comics including the 'Hotspur', the 'Rover', the 'Wizard' and the 'Champion'. My favourite story in all these was undoubtedly 'Rockfist Rogan RAF', and every week he would take on the dreaded Hun almost single-handed in his Spitfire. The outcome was never in doubt and having shot-down his opponent he would then land alongside and engage in a boxing match with the German pilot with inevitable consequences. Rockfist of course was the RAF heavyweight boxing champion as well as being an ace pilot. Not being able to emulate him, I could at least take the same rank with Blue Squadron. We substituted Spitfires with our bicycles, and to help the transformation we fixed thick pieces of cardboard to our back wheels so as they went round the rotating spokes struck the cardboard and made a huge din. In this way we terrorised the neighbourhood, and any delivery boy on his bicycle automatically became a German bomber and we would attack by striking his back wheels with our front wheel usually with catastrophic results for both of us.

I met up with the real Luftwaffe for the first time in December. I had gone to bed by nine o'clock and was soon fast asleep in my little bedroom at the back of the house. I didn't hear the siren go off that night, but as in a dream I felt my body rise from the bed and fly across the little bedroom to make a landing underneath the back window which had been kept open to avert damage by bomb blast. When I heard my mother scream I realised that this was no dream, having found myself flat on my back completely unhurt. A 500 pound bomb had been jettisoned by a German aircraft probably to assist his getaway, and had fallen just below Glyncornel House on the mountainside not more than a hundred yards in a direct line from my rear window. My mother had put on the bedroom light looked across at my father and screamed when she saw his face covered in blood. The glass table next to the bed had splintered in the blast and my father had cut his hand when reaching for his glasses. The act of transferring his glasses to his face conveyed sufficient blood to convince my mother that he had been severely wounded. A few nights later we all thought that our end was nigh. My mother opened my bedroom door and in a remarkably calm voice simply said. "You had better dress and come downstairs quickly." The Germans had developed quite a habit of dropping mines by parachutes, and from the front of the house we could see such a mine dangling beneath a chute slowly but surely coming directly at us. Mr Davies next door was fully dressed and ready to run, and was clearly prepared to allow his wife and daughter to remain behind and make their own arrangements. It took us fully an hour watching this horrible apparition, before we realised that it was nothing more than an optical illusion merely a strange conjunction of moon and cloud. The fear that was invoked however was very real, and we all returned to bed that night thanking our God. The fact that Mr Davies was about to run and leave his family was a much discussed topic in the days to come, and I knew instinctively that my father would never behave like that, if any of our family were threatened. A few weeks later he was to show what sort of man he was when he believed that my sister was in danger. The family had gathered in my paternal grandmother's bedroom on a Saturday afternoon. My sister had remained downstairs with one of the maids. As we were quietly talking a terrible scream from the shop below rent the air. My mother shouted "Gillian", but my father was already out of the room, across the landing and racing down the stairs with me in close pursuit. He was on the tenth stair (I counted them later) when Nancy, one of the shop assistants, passed below in a mass of flames her arms in the air. My father without hesitation flew through the air flattening Nancy in the progress and rolled her in a long mat along the corridor. Nancy had been wearing a cotton dress, and when the door of the shop had suddenly opened a draught of air had caused the small oil burner behind the counter to emit a flame setting Nancy's dress alight. The dear girl was in dreadful pain and I have never forgotten the look in her eyes as she gazed at me. My father's hands were both badly burned and he travelled to the hospital along with Nancy in the ambulance. My father's injuries healed in a matter of weeks, but poor Nancy died of hers just five days later. From that day my father stood even above Rockfist Rogan in my pantheon of heroes.

When the siren went during school hours we had been drilled to leave in an orderly fashion and then run as fast as we could to our homes, accompanied by children who lived further afield. It was almost a year later when the council built an air-raid shelter in the school yard, by which time daylight raids had almost ceased. We performed but one air-raid shelter drill, when we all filed in and sat mutely facing one another on the long wooden benches almost in complete darkness. The shelter remains there today and was never used in anger.

My day meeting with the Luftwaffe began with the wailing of the air-raid warning and the habitual run home with my chums. I was in the lead to the top of the hill leading to Sherwood street where I could see the front of my house. It was then I heard an unfamiliar engine noise, which caused me to stop and look-up. My pals had run on and disappeared through my front door as my mother shouted at me to follow, but I was transfixed. Above was a Messerschmitt 109 fighter roaring down the length of the valley being pursued by a Spitfire a few hundred yards behind. The Spitfire was firing madly and the spent cartridge shells fell about me like confetti, filling the gutters and pavements. Miraculously I was not struck by one, and as I bent to pick some up an Air Raid Warden warned me away, telling me they were dangerous. My mother now angrily grabbed me and hauled me indoors to safety. I have always wondered whether that German aircraft made it back to France safely, and somehow I secretly hoped he had! With my knowledge of aircraft I wondered how a single engined Messerschmitt 109 had the range to fly over South Wales and dawdle and fight. That German pilot was certainly brave I thought, and perhaps it wasn't too unfanciful to believe that the pilot got himself lost. In fact in June 1942 Oberleutnant Arnim Faber Adjutant of III Group Fighter Wing based near Caen in Normandy, landed his single engine Focke-Wulf 190 at RAF Pembrey airfield just west of Llanelli Camarthenshire in west Wales. He had been in a dogfight with a Polish Spitfire Group, and with his compass probably unserviceable and the sun obscured, mistook the Bristol Channel for the English Channel. It later became known that his grandmother was of English descent, which provided another reason for his forced landing, but one which fostered little credence.

The night war continued unabated and it was quite usual to hear German aircraft overhead as they proceeded to bomb targets further afield. The noise of their engines were quite distinct as they seemed to fly with their propellers de-synchronised, may be to frighten the populace. We huddled under the stairs, which had been somewhat fortified by a few sand bags, as soon as the siren was heard, and generally stayed there until the all-clear sounded. Dad was out every night on fire watching duties at the local hospital, and we saw little of him. The blight of our lives were the Air Raid Wardens who seemed to be full of self importance, and harried us at every turn, shouting "put out that light", a term which became a catch-phrase of the Second World War. Death and destruction came to the valley on the night of the 29/30 April 1941. But the main attack that night was made by Luftflotten 2 and 3 on Plymouth and Devonport where 162 bombers dropped over 200 tons of high explosive bombs and nearly 2000 incendiaries. It was the second of three consecutive nights that the Luftwaffe had bombed the city killing over 600 people and making 40,000 homeless. A small number of aircraft bombed Cardiff as a secondary target, killing 34 people and causing four large fires. The little village of Cwmparc near Treorchy at the head of the Rhondda Valley was but a few minutes flying time from Cardiff and some aircraft unsure of their position thought this to be the target. The attack started on Plymouth at 2150 and a little later at Cardiff.

Doctor Fergus Armstrong of that little village had a late patient with him that night, and as he accompanied him to the door he noticed many coloured lights on the hillside looking down towards Maendy. These were the flares from the early visitors, and soon the hills above the village were ringed with hundreds of incendiary bombs blazing brightly and setting fire to the hillside grass. High explosive bombs then fell plus a compliment of land mines, landing with a loud thud as the parachutes folded. The little valley hemmed in on all three sides by mountains, now heard sounds the like of which they had never heard before. In a matter of minutes twenty-seven of the villagers had lost their lives (some of them children), and more than half of its thousand houses had been damaged. But Cwmparc, if remote was not unprepared and as soon as the incendiaries fell in the words of an eye-witness "There came into action the fire bomb fighters—troops of them, a whole army of them, advancing along the main road, emerging from side streets and whooping some indistinguishable form of war cry as they swooped upon incendiaries with a kind of suppressed fury and extinguished them with a precision and certainty born of months of preparation for just such an emergency". The wardens and the rescue services got to work soon afterwards among the tumbled heaps of slate and grey stone where their friends and relatives lay. The task was not long, for the miners and their sons had little to learn about digging and tunnelling at speed. The family intimacy of village life in which I had grown up was nowhere closer than here, where every death was regarded as a personal bereavement. By lunch time the next day the homeless were all billeted in all probability, a national record. Among the youngest killed that night were two brothers and their eight-year-old sister, who had been evacuated from London earlier that year. Their parents doubtlessly thought that in the narrow valley and mountains of the Rhondda their children would find safety during the troubled years of the war. Sadly they found only death. Our street to was not exempt, and George Davis in the Police War Reserve, who lived nearby, was killed that night. His two daughters attended the same school as I did, and I was astonished at their composure and the bravery they showed. I had great doubts that I would have behaved as well had I been in their position.

Today there is a memorial garden in Cwmparc on the area known locally as the 'Bomb Site', and in the local cemetery there is a separate monument for the three young evacuees with their names suitably inscribed. The official radio announcement the following day declared that there had been 'light enemy activity over Wales but no casualties'. Such is the fog of war! That night all the German aircraft returned to their bases in Brittany and Normandy unassailed by our guns or fighters. In fact their only loss that night was a Focke-Wulf 200 Condor aircraft which crashed into the sea off the Shetland Isles North of Scotland.

My urge to fly stemmed from the early days of the war when most of us young kids at the time wanted to fly a Spitfire. I had been brought up in an age of heroes. The Battle of Britain pilots were heroes and I like many of my fellows wanted to be a hero as well. I had been born however with a defective gene, which had ensured from birth I would be burdened with the dreaded asthma, and this at a time unlike today when there were few asthma sufferers. There were no special drugs or inhalers available then, so I was forced into a personal war of attrition against the complaint. My dear mother had on one occasion been so deprived of sleep tending to my needs as a baby, that once as I turned black in her arms she had thrown me on to the bed in desperation. That action it appeared restarted the breathing process, but by all accounts it was a near thing. But it was my inherent love and ability at sport that began changing things. Probably because of asthma I had an intense desire to be as good and preferably better than the next boy, which meant I had to run faster and perform better. I would sprint after a ball, shoot or dribble and then collapse to the ground with a huge oxygen debt panting madly until I recovered. Sometimes the effort would be make me sick, but I would persevere until relief came. In this way I grew up determined to do anything on which I had set my sights, and having largely beaten asthma never met another foe remotely comparable. A family elder asked me one day 'what I wanted to be when I grew up'. When I answered "a pilot", she burst into spontaneous laughter. What further encouragement did I need!

The magic of youth is surely the sudden unfolding of vistas, and the seminal points that occur on the way, everything you think and dream about has a piercing reality that never happens quite that way again. Most of my world since birth had been in a geographic area of no more than four square miles, but my imagination, innate sense of direction and ideas had no limits. I became known locally as a madcap, and if Mr Mathew's shop window fell-in or somebody blew-up the chapel, it was to me they came to fix the blame. I was twelve when I met up with Protheroe a young evacuee from London, who was known to the local boys as the 'Mad Professor. It was to him I turned when I decided to build my own aircraft. I used the frame of an old bicycle, built some wings and attached them to the frame in a nondescript fashion. The contraption, as the boys called it, was pushed up the mountain and surrounded by an admiring thong, I began pedalling madly down the slope. When I thought I had reached a safe take-off speed I pulled back the handlebars. The next few minutes remain a blur of action where I seemed to go one way and the contraption another, undoubtedly flying but not quite in the way I had envisaged. Nursing a bent and broken nose plus a very sore shoulder, I decided then that the next time I flew, it would be in a real aeroplane. The psychologists tell us that if you are a risk taker as a child, then you become a risk taker as an adult, and so it proved!

My earliest interest in flying was stimulated through some of the films showing at the time. Tonypandy was the nearest town of any size, and was blessed with three cinemas all within a short walking distance of each other. It was my mother who hated the very thought of flying who inadvertently took me to see a film at the Plaza cinema called 'Dawn Patrol'. This film starred Errol Flynn, David Niven and Basil Rathbone. It was a story of a British Squadron on the Western Front during World War I. Today it is a well established fact that film makers have been in thrall to the aeroplane since movies began and man took flight in 1903, and has provided the focal point of scores of films. 'Dawn Patrol' by all accounts was the finest film ever made about flying in the First World War. I was spell-bound by the flying action, and unashamedly cried when Errol Flynn, the flight commander, was shot-down and killed, his helmet being dropped back over his own airfield by a German pilot. When we left the cinema and walked to the bus stop I was stopped dead in my tracks by the sound of an aircraft almost directly overhead. I stared at it much like Balboa must have done with his eagle eye when he first spied the Pacific Ocean in 1513. The aircraft was a Miles Master or a Harvard trainer, and it was in full aerobatic mode, rolling looping and spinning in sequence. It was the only aeroplane I ever saw over the valley perform like this and I was totally captivated by the event. My conversion had begun.

My maternal grandmother lived almost at the top of the mountain where houses seemed to cling onto the slopes in desperation, and goat like qualities were required to live there. She had fourteen children, thirteen of whom managed to survive, and understandably the house was always noisy and bursting with activity. One of my earliest memories was of descending the stairs to the kitchen and seeing a naked black man bathing in a tin tub in front of the fire. That man was my grandfather who worked at the local colliery and was being scrubbed clean by my little grandmother. Little of statute she might have been, but a giant in courage and spirit. One on rare night stop at the house she took me to the local fleapit of a cinema called 'Dwts' to see a film on flying called 'Only Angels have Wings'. This featured Cary Grant and Jean Arthur and was considered by the critics to be a trite and dated story of pre-war flying in Central America. It told of passenger and mail flights over the jungle sometimes in terrible weather. I was totally absorbed in the flying sequences and never noticed or cared whether model aircraft were used, or that they were able to perform square turns. Thirty five years later I delivered an aircraft from San Jose dos Campos in Brazil to Grenada in the West Indies. Whilst flying over the dense South American jungle for hour after hour my thoughts drifted back to that film and my little grandmother, mam John. Was it an accident she took me to see that film or was she somewhat prescient about my future? I was unfortunately never to find out.

Apart from films it was Roy Milton who became much the greatest influence in the future direction of my life. Roy who lived along our street had joined the RAF on July 14th 1941. He had trained in the United States and had then became a pilot in a bomber squadron based in he North of England. I was in the middle of an English lesson in the grammar school, when the girls in the form started making cooing sounds like animals at the start of the mating season. I looked up and saw Roy standing tall and proud alongside our English Teacher, the redoubtable Miss Caldicott. He was dressed in his RAF uniform with two rings on his sleeve, clearly identifiable to me as a Flight Lieutenant. When he saw me he grinned and I kicked Len Meredith at the adjacent desk and said "Hey, Len, that's Roy Milton and he lives in our street". I felt so proud and even as Miss Caldicott reproached me for my chatter I noticed that Roy grinned even more. That occasion proved to be the last time I saw Roy close-up. It was February 1944, a Saturday, and I was dressed in my football gear parading around the house waiting for the rain to stop. I had walked to the front room a number of times to check the weather, which seemed completely unrelenting. The mountain top was covered in mist and low cloud and I watched glumly as the rain bounced on the pavement outside. The street in those days was completely uncluttered with no cars, and as I idly gazed down, I saw Roy walking up the opposite pavement clad in a white macintosh, head bent against the strong wind and rain. As I watched him approach and enter his house at number 15 I was filled with a terrible fear and apprehension. The morning had suddenly turned black, all football forgotten. I rushed into the kitchen and blurted out to my mother, "Mam I've just seen Roy and I'll never see him again." My mother smiled reassuringly, "Don't be silly of course you will," she said. I never did of course, and a few weeks later number 15 received a telegram stating that Roy was missing in action believed killed—he was twenty-one years of age.

Some months had passed and one night I had stayed-up late to complete some revision for my examinations. When my mother entered the room she could see that my mind was far away. "A penny for them," she said. I came to with a start. "I was thinking of Roy Milton, mam, and one day I will find out what happened to him and write about it." Amazingly, it took almost forty years for me to begin the quest. I had returned from Miami for Christmas leaving a temperature of +28°C to the UK and a temperature of—5°C. I sat at home on the floor with my back against the radiator with a hot drink in hand, when Roy appeared in my mind just as clearly as he had been in my classroom that day in 1944. "My God," I exclaimed, "I haven't done anything about Roy." From that moment my quest begun and eventually it soon became clear that the fates had conspired against him and that he had travelled under 'no friendly star'.

CHAPTER 7

THE MAFIA, EMERALD AND A LORD'S AIRLINE

It was Christmas 1965, Cormorant had been put into liquidation, I was out of a job and my erstwhile secretary Valerie had fled to Gibraltar. My girlfriend Jenny decided also that this was a good time to give me the cold shoulder, leaving me somewhat dispirited as the holiday commenced. In a spirit of goodwill I telephoned Valerie at the Queens' Hotel, Gibraltar, where she worked, to convey my Christmas greetings only to be greeted by ominous sounds of sobbing. This immediately ceased when I promised to catch the next flight out and spend Christmas with her. The night flight in a British European Airways Vanguard aircraft passed peacefully and my stay on the Rock was made more enjoyable when Valerie informed me that I could stay in the hotel free of charge. For the next few days I saw little of the Rock and rather more of Valerie's room, not for the usual reasons, but simply because she had caught some dreadful bug.

After my enforced lethargy I was keen to explore the potential for adventure and work, which soon saw me studying Gibraltar Airline's operation from Gibraltar to Tangier with their solitary DC3 (Dakota) aircraft. There did not appear to be a small charter operator in existence, and it was Valerie who made the contact for me with the Government minister who controlled aviation matters and probably a great deal besides. The reception was cold and forbidding. I was not invited to take a seat, and following my proposal he looked at me and said, "If you start a charter company here, I will see to it that you and your company are driven from the Rock," and these were the people who espoused to be British. I retired from his office having thanked him for his kindness and courtesy, and secretly hoped he would drop dead. Clearly other options would have to be explored, and once again it was Valerie who led the way. It is quite incredible how susceptible men are to a pretty face, myself included, and particularly when it is matched to an engaging personality.

Just off the main street a turning led to a restaurant and bar belonging to one Jimmy Ragretto. It was getting dark when Valerie and I entered the premises and found Jimmy sitting at a table alone with a glass of wine in his hand. I explained to him that it was my intention to bring a twin engined aircraft down to Gibraltar from Coventry, and use it on ad-hoc charters emphasising the number of well-off yacht owners on the Rock whom could well avail themselves of such a service. Jimmy seemed disinterested in my proposition, but suddenly to my surprise a negro appeared from the dark recesses of the restaurant and introduced himself as Jim Rice. "I am interested in your proposition John," he said, "and would like to discuss it with you further. Perhaps you would like to come over to Tangier with me tonight and we can talk on the boat." I enthusiastically accepted, but left Valerie behind as she was needed for work at the hotel.

It was about 2200 hours that night as the flat bottomed sixty foot motor cruiser slipped out of her moorings and set course across the Straits to Tangier. Almost immediately I heard a thump of boots on deck and saw the blinding light of a powerful searchlight sweep the boat. Customs and Excise always concerned with smuggling had simply mistaken us for another vessel, but the sight of a gun pointing at me from close range was an experience I could have well have done without. The wardroom was comfortable, but once outside the harbour proper the flat-bottomed yacht soon began bouncing and sliding in a Force 7 sea, the ride became very uncomfortable. Fortunately the cabin was well stocked with a large variety of drinks, and we found that our stomachs began to return to some degree of normality after several brandies and sodas. Jim had already mapped out the itinerary for me when I arrived in Tangier. "Tonight John," he said, "I have made arrangements for you to stay at the Atlas Hotel in town. In the morning I would like you to grab a cab and visit the airport and check out the facilities. Unfortunately," he continued, "I won't be able to accompany you as I have to attend a funeral." Thinking it was a family bereavement I said, "Oh, I'm sorry about that Jim." "Its OK," he said, "the guy ain't dead yet." I sat there stunned, did he really just say 'the guy ain't dead yet'? I looked at Jim as he was pouring a drink and saw that he was totally unmoved by his remark. I tend generally to be somewhat loquacious after a few drinks, but on this night I felt it better to relapse into a lengthy silence.

I was suitably deposited in a comfortable room in the Atlas Hotel, breakfasted alone and took a cab to the airport. Following a light lunch I journeyed back to town and found 28 La Rue Saint Grotius. I pressed the bell having no idea of what reception lay in store. The door was opened by a very tall, not unattractive, young lady. "Hello," she said, "you must be John Evans. I'm Blodwyn Hughes." I burst into laughter at this, thinking she was having me on. "No," she said, "my name is truly Blodwyn, and I'm Welsh." "What the hell is a Welsh girl doing here in Tangier?" I asked. "Oh, I'm a script writer with Columbia Pictures, and we're making a new film called 'Avec Avec'." (A film incidentally I have never been able to locate in the records). "Come on," she said, "the boys are waiting to meet you," and she heralded me into a large lounge where five men sat on comfortable settees, all smoking fat cigars and holding well filled glasses. What was very noticeable was their beautiful dark suits, with carnations in the buttonholes, the blue chins and the swarthy dark looks. Jim stood up and introduced me to all and sundry then said. "John has this executive aircraft in England, he can fly it down here for our use only. He'll be staying with Nancy and me in Torreleminos, and the aircraft will be based at Mallorca Airport." This was all news to me of course, but I had long developed the ability to roll with the changing tide of events in my life be they good or bad. With no job back at home, Torreleminos sounded quite a splendid place to rest my head, particularly if Valerie were to join me.

The flat was on the ground floor in what must have been one of the first high rise buildings in the town. The lounge opened directly on to the beach and Valerie and I spent most of our days there sunbathing, swimming and reading the rather second rate soft back books in the apartment. 'My Wicked Wicked Ways' was my favourite, as it portrayed the life of Errol Flynn, one of my celluloid heroes since I first saw him in the film 'Dawn Patrol'. Occasionally Jim, Valerie and myself would enjoy the plush surroundings of a local nightspot, where after a few drinks and a few requests we would take the floor. Jim on the electric guitar, Valerie on the mandolin and myself accompanying on the piano. These were the most pleasurable moments in a completely indolent life style. Never once did Jim mention the aircraft again or ask me to return to the UK and fly it down. Mysteriously once a week on return to the apartment we would find the fridge and freezer full to capacity and a bundle of bank notes of various currencies sitting on the kitchen table. It took me some weeks to finally wake up to reality, that I was in the pay of the Mafia for future work not yet defined. The funeral in Tangier seemed proof enough of this. Jim disappeared mysteriously on regular occasions telling me that he had pre-arranged appointments to play the electric guitar at clubs around Europe and I of course, had no method of ascertaining the truth of this. Valerie and I were now of the same mind, having discussed our predicament at length, so together we hatched a plan and the following week at a bar in Torreleminos I put the plan to work.

"Jim," I said, "I want you to be first to know that Valerie and I are engaged to be married, and she wants the wedding service to be held at her old church on the Gower in Wales." "Congratulations, John I wondered when you would get round to it. As for going back to Wales I'll have to ask the boys." If I needed any confirmation of my position, that was it. It was indeed fortunate that I had not yet got to be closely involved with the brotherhood, and had not seen anybody other than Jim since our group meeting in Tangier. A few days later Jim provided us with air tickets for an Iberia flight from Malaga to London Gatwick. Valerie and I then made a decision to go our separate ways even if only temporarily. I flew almost immediately to Belfast to join the new Emerald Airways, where once more I was to link up with Paul Weeks, who had preceded me there. Valerie in the meantime joined British Overseas Airways Corporation as a stewardess, and with her knowledge of the Spanish language was soon employed on VC10 aircraft flying to South America destinations.

Emerald Airways was formed as the Protestant airline of the North of Ireland as a token balance to the Catholic Aer Lingus of the south. It now became quite apparent that it was almost impossible to separate yourself from politics and the north south divide. Worst of all I was forced to wear the Airline's dreaded green uniform and felt more like a pixie than a pilot. It took but a short time to ascertain that Northern Ireland was perhaps not my favourite part of the world. The killings had not started then, but the atmosphere was redolent of suspicion, bigotry and belligerence. I was living opposite the airport in an old cottage with an elderly Protestant lady, a Miss Adams, where I remained during my stay in the Province. On one of my inactive days I sat in her kitchen reading the 'Belfast Telegraph', and with time on my hands scanned through most of the paper including the jobs section. Looking down the list of vacancies I saw the letters NCNA appended to most of the advertisements. I turned to Miss Adams and asked her what was the meaning of these letters. Without hesitation, and with a great deal of emphasis, she answered, "No Catholics need apply." With this yardstick, was it any wonder that events turned out as they did?

Pilots were arriving in the company and then disappearing with monotonous regularity. Often at times it would be the wives who refused to come to the province, and with the history of the place, perhaps this was understandable. Captain Mike Lewis for example was our third choice Chief Pilot, the previous two having stayed less than a week. Mike was a first class chap who had flown world routes as a First Officer on the Boeing 707 with the British Overseas Airways Corporation. He had a very low number of hours total flying time, a fact which startled both Paul and I. His theoretical knowledge and grasp of navigation was far superior to my own, but his decision making ability as a pilot was then extremely limited. His log book indicated that he had but two hundred hours of command time, and some of that was denoted as being under supervision. To his credit however he never tried to hide this lack of experience, and admired both Paul and I, who had by this time acquired more than 1,000 hours of command in our log books. We had flown, months before, from Swansea to Belfast in the most appalling weather conditions and Mike had been so impressed at our performance that he offered us jobs on the spot. Some years later after Paul and I had departed the scene Mike became a Flight Inspector with the Civil Aviation Authority and as such was appointed as Flight Inspector to Brymon Airways when I was then the Chief Pilot of the company. During that period he undertook a ferry flight back from the States with a fellow Flight Inspector. The Beech aircraft they were flying apparently became iced up near Greenland and during landing flew into a hill killing both pilots. I know that I was one of many in the industry who mourned his passing.

During to 1960s there were few pilot vacancies worldwide. Every week the jobs column of Flight International was read avidly by aviators and would be aviators. Such behaviour did not extend however to the pilots of large companies like British European Airways or British Overseas Airways Corporation, later to become British Airways, who were firmly established on the company's seniority list with an excellent salary, pension and an eventual command position. It would be a brave man indeed who would shed such protection and fight for a job on the open market, particularly if he were married and had children. It was this failure to find jobs that had made Paul and I create our own jobs in Cormorant. Like it or lump it, we had now obtained pilot jobs albeit in Northern Ireland, and the best that could be said about it that it was better than no jobs at all. However with my highly developed sense of liberalism, I began to watch my words and thoughts while in conversation with the locals.

At luncheon one day in the 'Greasy'—the staff canteen, one of our engineers called me to say that I had a visitor waiting for me in our flight operators department. He was a shortish thick-set serious looking chap accompanied by a young pilot in uniform who had flown over from the East Midlands Airport, Castle Donington. The serious looking fellow proved to be Lord Trefgarne, and over a cup of coffee in the Terminal he offered me a job with him in the Midlands where he was establishing a new airline. As the position seriously increased my monthly salary, and offered me an escape from the stifling confines of Northern Ireland and the dreaded green uniform, I accepted with some alacrity. A week later I caught the scheduled British Midland Airways flight to the East Midlands Airport where I was met by my new boss and driven to Derby where I spent the night.

Lord Trefgarne's fleet of aircraft comprised a DH Rapide (DH89A) and two Anson aircraft, all showing signs of age. My first job was to swot up the manuals on these aircraft prior to taking the Air Registration Board's written examinations. With this successfully accomplished I then flew both aircraft by day and night in a series of exercises to prove my competency in handling all the emergency procedures. With all the relevant forms suitably endorsed, with the Civil Aviation's stamp of approval in my licence, I was now ready to fly the aircraft on public transport operations.

I quickly found that the young Chief Pilot wasn't too fussed about flying the Anson, and showed an even greater reluctance to train anybody on it. This was perhaps understandable as the aircraft, even when empty, with one engine shut down showed a marked disinclination to climb. As a result the engine was never shut down, and we simulated this emergency by setting the engine power at a zero thrust setting. To maintain flight in a straight line countless turns on the rudder trim had to be made to reduce the strain on the leg when the live engine was at full bore. On our first landing we both failed to re-trim the rudder so after touch-down the aircraft left the runway and tore across the grass in the direction of the Terminal Building. This remarkable piece of artistry destroyed any further ambition of the Chief Pilot might have had to complete my training. As we taxied back to the hanger his only words to me were, "You really have to watch the beast when she's on one." My courage and skill however was never put to the test, as the old Anson soon disappeared from the scene shortly after I completed my training on her.

Trefgarne now took me on a tour of the offices and explained how he intended to start an UK and European 'Next Day' parcel service using a fleet of Beagle 206 twin engined aircraft. These would be based at strategic airports around the country by day and then loaded with high value small parcels to be flown by night to the East Midlands Airport. Here the large number of parcel sorters would re-assemble the parcels for their new destinations and the aircraft would return to their original airports with their new loads ready for next day delivery. I merely wondered where all these thousand of small parcels were coming from, but later I must say I warmed to the project. The original idea for this operation, I believe, stemmed from a former Harvard student who had compiled a thesis on 'The transportation of small parcels around the United States' for which he was marked with a 'D' and fail for his efforts. Firmly believing in the practicality of his idea he obtained finance for his proposed operation and based it in Memphis, Tennessee. Today his company Federal Express is producing almost sixteen billion dollars in revenue, is highly profitable, and has recently ordered ten of the new Airbus 380-800 Freighters with a further ten options, the largest aircraft ever built to operate in numbers in the civil field. On a much smaller scale Trefgarne planned to operate around twenty Beagle 206 aircraft which were British designed and built. Unfortunately the Beagle Company died a rather quick death and thus ended the last significant attempt at building a British light aircraft industry. With it of course went Trefgarne's ambition for a British air parcel service. A de Havilland Rapide (known as the cloth bomber) was on the company's strength, and I was the one pilot selected to fly it, a dubious honour I suspected. Its registration was GAHKU (Golf Alpha Hotel Kilo Uniform). This aircraft carried the famous name of Sir Richard Hawkins, and had previously been owned by British European Airways and based at Land's End Airport. For years it had carried many happy holiday folk and ploughed the skies to the Isles of Scilly. I was now employed flying the aircraft on pleasure flights from the airport on an extended circuit which allowed me to regularly beat up the George Hotel in the village of Belton to the south of the field. These antics, carried out periodically during the summer, were merely to impress the attractive daughters of the household where I was staying as a guest.

Strange requests often came my way during my career in flying. The most highly rewarding in cash terms were almost always illegal, and I turned them down mainly to protect my licence and hence my livelihood. One night at the airport I was quietly approached by a football fan of Derby County Football Club who wished me to fly him the following night with his girl friend one mile above the floodlit football stadium where a match would be taking place. I readily accepted, and even removed some of the seats to create more room for them. I climbed Kilo Uniform into the night sky locating the brightly lit football stadium and levelled off the aircraft at the required altitude. I then shouted down the back that we at the prescribed level and left them to get on with it. A small door on my right separated the cockpit from the cabin and this had a small peephole through which the pilot could look and keep a weather eye on the passengers. Unfortunately the cabin lighting was so poor my eyes would have been overstrained had I chosen to watch the action, and I was fully occupied anyway in changing the aircraft trim in response to the frenzied movements of the bodies in the back. Two happy, but exhausted, people landed an hour later and I received a hefty tip for my co-operation and what they considered was my discrete behaviour.

Trefgarne seemed to change his mind at will regarding the future plans for the company. In quick succession I went down to the Air Registration offices in Redhill Surrey to sit examinations on the Bristol Freighter and the DC3 Dakota, but neither aircraft ever appeared at East Midlands. In the meanwhile another pilot had joined the company the famous, perhaps infamous, Joe Viatkin, a veteran of more than 15,000 flying hours having flown over 200 types of aircraft. Joe had been born in Helsinki of noble blood as his parents had been driven out of Russia during the revolution. Joe was an immense character with a distinct liking for booze seemingly of any kind. When he had been at Silver City Airways at Lydd Airport in Kent, his wife Olive had threatened to leave him if he didn't kick the habit. She was thus overjoyed when Joe constructed a shed at the bottom of his garden and took-up woodwork. He cunningly built a trap door and dug a tunnel to the lane below, from which point he only had to cross the road to the pub, this action apparently remained undetected. Now I was faced with checking him out on the Rapide, which had but one pilot's seat. The training pilot could only stand behind in the door, advise and hope for the best. Joe of course flew the aircraft like the ace he undoubtedly was, so I retired to the cabin, took out a magazine and relaxed in a passenger seat while Joe toddled around the Midlands. Suddenly he climbed out of the cockpit and said, "I need a piss bad". I stood up to take his place in the cabin, but he shoved me back in my seat and said, "I'm the only bloke who can leave his seat, piss out of the door, and return to the cockpit without any problem." I sat and watched as he proceeded down the aisle, opened the door, which was at the rear, did his thing and return. All this time the aircraft remained flying peacefully straight and level. "Now you have a go," he said. I sat in the cockpit levelled the wings carefully and trimmed the aircraft slightly nose down to balance my weight as I moved aft. Joe sat in the front passenger seat, quite contentedly. I had only moved roughly half way towards the door when the aircraft developed a serious case of the wobbles, with nose rising and wing dropping. Joe was convulsing with laughter as I pulled my way back to the cockpit using the passenger seats for leverage. In successive flights I attempted this trick, but always without success, I suspected that Joe had a very special relationship with this aircraft, but without doubt he was also a highly skilled pilot.

Trefgarne sent me to find Joe on one occasion as he was needed to fly a special charter. I went to his flat knocked several times without response, as I began walking away Joe appeared clad in a Victorian nightgown, looking distinctly worse for wear. I imparted the message, but he insisted on my waiting for him, so I entered his flat. Olive was half-awake on a bed which had no mattress, but merely a blanket placed over the bedsprings. She began mumbling an apology about the state of the room, where upon Joe picked up an empty bottle off the floor and tapped her sharply on the head. Olive went back to sleep quickly, and I left the flat equally quickly. A few days later Joe and I met up in Flight Operations where he described the charter. Apparently he had picked up an Anson and flown it to Bilbao in Spain full of little piglets, all suitably enclosed in a rigged net. He was without the normal animal handler and had no co-pilot. Somewhere over the Bay of

Biscay the weather became increasingly bad with a long continuous line of Cumulus Nimbus clouds (thunder storms). The little pigs, not surprisingly, went berserk with the turbulence and noise. Joe had his work cut out in flying the aircraft and became severely alarmed to find that a pig had eaten through the net and had his nose resting in the cockpit. Believing that where one pig went others would follow, Joe kicked the offending pig back to its rightful place. He was now rightly concerned that his passengers might eat through the net and continue their meal on the control wires running down through the fuselage. Fortunately for him and the pigs the weather improved and peace was eventually restored to the aircraft. I commiserated with him on his experience and said, "I expect the smell was terrible Joe." "Yes," he answered, "but the pigs soon got used to it!"

In my career to date I had flown without an instrument rating and Trefgarne had agreed to pay for this qualification with repayments being made from my monthly salary cheque. Various flying establishments around the country had by now been approved to carry out these tests, unlike in the dark old days of the early sixties. The chosen school was Air London based at the Beehive Gatwick Airport. Here I learned to fly the Twin Commanche, a small Twin Piper aircraft, under the auspices of Tony Mack, the owner of the company. Tony was a loveable, jovial man, and he and I soon became very good friends. What should have been a two or three week course stretched almost to two months until I was never certain who I was working for. Tony used me for all his charters around the country, and also as an instrument instructor largely with ex-Royal Naval pilots who like me were there to obtain their civil instrument ratings. I am sure Tony had told them I was a highly experienced pilot as they listened with rapt attention to all my instructions. I arrived one Friday morning in Tony's office, and he looked up and told me that I would be flying with Captain Belson. "How come a Captain?" I asked. "I can't renew his instrument rating," I said. Tony laughed, "he's a CAA examiner of course, and you are going to take your test around the standard circuit." I did as I was bid, and on the final approach Captain Belson turned to me and said, "That's fine, I have no problem with that." So I passed my rating, a fact that merely confirmed my belief that you couldn't separate the ability to fly accurately on instruments without an equal knowledge and familiarity with the aircraft you were flying.

I was to visit Stan Edwards that evening on the Sancta Maria in Kemp's Boatyard in Southampton, so I rang the good news through to him before I left Gatwick. As I walked along the jetty towards the boat Stan, with his seaman's cap jauntily on his head, blew the ship's siren three times to welcome and congratulate me. It was a fitting end to a very successful day and one that I had waited for some time. When Christmas arrived that year my most treasured Christmas card was from Tony. It read 'To a bloody good pilot and friend' signed Tony. The card remains in my possession today, Tony has long time departed this earth, but I am pleased that his son maintains the company Air London and still operates from the Beehive Gatwick.

Now safely back in harness at East Midlands, Trefgarne asked me to accompany him, and we flew together down to Sywell aerodrome in Northamptonshire, where he had agreed to buy a second Rapide aircraft. He merely dropped me off, so I assumed he had seen the aircraft and agreed a price. The hanger at Sywell housed a number of aircraft belonging to Dismore's the well-advertised London broker. Black Mac was the resident salesman and he directed me to the rear of the hanger, where stood an exceedingly sad looking Rapide aircraft. The cockpit was covered in spider webs and I noted that the P1 compass on the floor was well and truly rusted and could not be moved, some controls fell readily to hand, others just fell to the floor. A number of other instruments were either missing or not useable. I pointed out these discrepancies to Black Mac, whose only response was to grin and say, "Well the engines are in good shape." True to his word they ran sweetly enough, but with no radio and no compass I felt that there was a slight element of risk in flying the beast back to East Midlands Airport. Fortunately the cloud base held to about 2,000 feet and I was able to fly west until I hit the M1 and then turn onto a northerly course following the motorway until I reached my destination. I received no thanks for my endeavours despite flying the aircraft without documents, which clearly invalidated any insurance on the aircraft and on the pilot as well.

I arrived at the airport one morning to find all the staff at the windows waving madly at me. Unable to comprehend the meaning of such a welcome I parked the car and entered flight operations. There to greet me was a police sergeant who presented me with an East Sussex Police Notice seen on the next two pages. I read the document and looked at him expecting a heart-to-heart chat on morality and the public good. Instead he smiled benignly and spoke to me in a less than severe manner. "Now sir, you move about a great deal don't you?" I nodded in agreement. "Well then, may I make a suggestion?" Again I nodded my agreement. "I suggest you keep on bloody moving!" After such a severe ticking off, he stayed for a coffee and I gave him a tour of our Flight Operations department. In defence, I have to say that the so—called offences were committed on the evening of the day that England won the World Cup Final at Wembley for the first, and probably, the last time. That evening had progressed with a certain swing and followed a visit to the local fish and chip shop. I had merely demonstrated, to an admiring audience, my ability to drop kick the rolled-up fish and chip package over a nearby lamp-post. Furthermore since I had left the town some years earlier, the council had created a one-way road system, which had completely, fooled me. As to a test certificate; well—the car had only cost me a total of five pounds and I couldn't really have been expected to have a test certificate included in that sum. Thankfully however these events were acted out before the dreaded breathalyser was introduced.

Form 18

EAST SUSSEX POLICE

SUPERINTENDENT'S OFFICE.
POLICE STATION.
Lewes

Ref. B/3000/66 13th December 1966

Dear Sir/~~Madam~~,

I am directed by the Chief Constable to say that it has been reported to him that on 4th November, 1966, you committed the offences, as per the attached, in the Seaford area.

No further action will be taken in this case but I am to inform you that, if you are reported again, it may be necessary to take proceedings against you in respect of the later case.

Yours faithfully,

[signature] C/I.

for Chief Superintendent

Mr. J. H. Evans,
13 Clive Place,
PENARTH,
Glamorgan.

John Howard EVANS

1. You deposited litter in a public place.
   Contrary to the Litter Act, 1958, Section 1.

2. You drove a motor vehicle in a 'One-Way' street other than in the direction specified.
   Contrary to County of East Sussex (Various Roads, Seaford) (One-Way Traffic) Order, 1965.

3. You failed to produce a Certificate of Insurance,
   Contrary to Road Traffic Act, 1960, Section 226 (1).

4. You failed to produce a Test Certificate,
   Contrary to Road Traffic Act, 1966. S. 226(2).

for Chief Superintendent

Trefgarne's business now took yet another change in direction, when he decided to enter the Inclusive Tour Business, establishing a link with Hourmont Travel of Cardiff as a supplier of passengers. With this in mind he acquired a couple of Viscount 812 aircraft on lease from Channel Airways at Southend Airport. A ground school course was soon organised and lodgings obtained for me in Victoria Avenue Southend. Joe however, in keeping with his noble upbringing, was ensconced in a suite of rooms at the Pier Hotel to which I was soon invited. It was a cold January day and I found Joe huddled by a small two bar electric fire pretty far gone on vodka. As it was mid-morning I paid my respects, but refused to join in a round of pointless drinking, so as soon as I could I hastily fled down the stairs and out of the building. Joe in chasing after me in his befuddled state kicked over the electric fire and set the carpet alight. The last thing I remember as I ran down the street was smoke bellowing from the windows, the noise of fire engines and people shouting. Joe had boasted that the owners of the hotel were old friends of his, but I fear that friendship took a severe knock that day.

The instructors at the ground school had been hastily recruited from maintenance engineers at the airline and despite their best efforts were not among the brightest and best I had known. Furthermore they were using information from documents woefully out of date. The aircraft in fact had been operating in the United States with Continental Airways for some time, and were much changed from the original specifications, as the aircraft had received many modifications whilst in the USA. At the end of the two-week course we trooped into the Air Registration Board's examination room at Redhill, where I felt I could have by this time taken up full time residence, and en-masse promptly failed the examination. This caused Trefgarne to find a full time instructor and set up his own ground school course back at East Midlands. However it was patently evident that Trefgarne had little ability to choose good and experienced managers. His operations manager was ex-Royal Navy and his chief pilot ex-Royal Air Force, both in their own right very nice people, but ignorant of the civil aviation scene. His new ground instructor was totalled unschooled in training and teaching, facts that soon became readily evident to all. Had he admitted his lack of knowledge of the aircraft and of teaching, I am sure that we would have all sympathised, and helped him. Instead he stood before us, master of all, and told us that he had developed a whole new system of teaching with the Ws and Hs method, i.e. Why, When, What and How. We suppressed our laughter as best we could and sat and watched while he attempted to explain the intricacies of the Viscount, and

I thought Chaucer had been difficult. To add insult to injury, he told us that we needed to put up our hand and request permission if we wanted to leave the room. I looked across the room at my fellow students for their reaction. Captain Honeyman had a quizzical look on his face. 'Who is this impostor?' it said. Lindsay had one eye open pretending to be awake, and Joe was busy extracting a piece of foreign matter from his nose and clearly not paying the slightest attention. Mike, our Polish pilot, merely looked sad, but then he almost always looked sad. I waited a few minutes, stood up and told him I was about to pay a visit to the toilet. When I returned the instructor had also left the room and my fellow students, now fully awake to the drama, assured me that I had now got the sack and all this accompanied by loud hoots of laughter. On his return the instructor put on his best school master style and informed me that Trefgarne wished to see me immediately in his office. Remembering how Gary Cooper would have behaved in such circumstances, I smiled benevolently at the assembly and sauntered out of the classroom hoisting my trousers up in the process. Trefgarne as always was mellow in his remarks and just asked me to settle down and get on with it. Trefgarne and I in fact always got on pretty well, and it was always to me he turned when he wanted any of the directors or managers flown around the country. So I promised I would be a good boy in future, then promptly went sick at home, where I spent the next week learning all about the Viscount aircraft and all its systems. In the meantime I booked-up an Air Registration Board examination on the aircraft, and this time drove up north to Doncaster to sit the examination. A few days later I was notified of my success, went to Trefgarne's office and threw the paper onto his desk, and left it to him to sort out the frailties of the instructor.

It had now been arranged for us, the initial group of pilots, to train on the Viscount Simulator with Aer Lingus at Dublin Airport. It was just my luck to be partnered with Joe, who confided in me that I was the only decent pilot in the company apart from himself of course. In the past I had always enjoyed my visits to Ireland, after all they were only Welshmen who could swim, and I could recollect many riotous parties and thrilling nights. Joe's riotous nights unfortunately tended to start at breakfast time, with at least three to four Gaelic Coffees. By the time we arrived at the Simulator Building he was inevitably very much the worse for wear and in no condition to fly or act as my supportive co-pilot when I was flying. Had it been a real aircraft then I would have refused to fly with him, but this was a simulator and above all I had a sincere warm spot for the man. The next fifty hours in the simulator proved to be very exciting, perhaps it would be fairer to call it mayhem, but at the end of the course Joe received an above average grade and for me merely an average one. The simulator instructor had flown on the Berlin Airlift with Joe, and I wondered whether that had something to do with it. Sadly, Joe never made it to command the Viscount, a combination of booze did it, coupled with the fact that he had grown-up as a pilot in a more gentle age, when aircraft moved across the sky as a much slower speed.

I had now qualified on the Viscount and renewed my instrument rating on the aircraft at Liverpool Airport, but my first charter service I operated proved also to be my last. My confrontation with the ground instructor had really proved my undoing, and it appeared that I had been cast as the bad boy of the company, which had now grown to over a hundred employees. I turned up at Bristol Airport early one morning to fly the aircraft to Gatwick and onwards to Venice. I would have two captains on board, one of them being a training captain. When they hadn't appeared at the scheduled time I walked out to the aircraft and carried out all the external checks. The captains on arrival were both drunk, but not in the conventional sense. These guys were well and truly stinking, and the alcohol emanated from their every pore. Fortunately we had no cabin staff or passengers out of Bristol; these would be boarded at Gatwick later that morning. The two clambered aboard with difficulty slumped in the passenger's seats in the back and went to sleep, clearly not having gone to bed the previous night. Consequently I flew the four engined monster to Gatwick alone in the cockpit praying that no emergency would arise. We eventually sat in the Airport restaurant having breakfast, the captains drinking copious amounts of black coffee. I mentioned to them that there had been a conspicuous absence of flight navigational charts on board the aircraft at Bristol and I had been forced to use my own. They suggested that I go downstairs and photocopy the European navigational and airport let down charts belonging to British United Airways. Having no pilots' navigational logs either, I was forced on my return to the restaurant to write down all the relevant data for the flight using the table paper napkins.

Suddenly over the airport tannoy system we heard the announcement of the departure of Treffield International Airways flight to Edinburgh. This did not concern me, as on the taxi-in I had seen the second Treffield Viscount sitting at one of the departure gates. Minutes later our effeminate Cabin Services Manager rushed in and pranced up to our table, and asked us why we weren't on the aircraft ready to go. We explained carefully that we had only just arrived and had been scheduled for Venice. "No, No!" he shouted, "you are taking the Edinburgh flight." I was now rapidly running out of paper napkins, as I hastily prepared the new flight logs. I am convinced that the sixty plus American golfers on board that day would have suffered premature heart failure had they known of the state and readiness of the crew. However the flight passed peacefully enough, and I shared the cockpit with the two captains both of whom now showed some signs of normality. Back at Cardiff Airport later that evening the training captain resumed his drinking habits, and verbally abused the caretaker of the local club who consequently suffered a heart attack and died. Fortunately I had left the airport directly after landing and only learned of this sorry affair later. The events of the day had been completely disgraceful, and on my return to East Midlands Airport I tendered my resignation. In my view there was little hope for a company so badly organised, and so badly and managed. My instincts clearly told me that the company had but a short time to live, and as usual my instincts proved sound. I was only surprised, if not amazed, that the other company employees couldn't read the signs as well as I did.

Some months earlier Trefor Trefgarne, the younger brother, had been induced to put his money into the company. He then took it upon himself to hire the cabin services manager and all the stewardesses in the Gatwick area. He made a cardinal error in selecting a chief stewardess who was anything but a raving beauty. As night follows day it therefore followed, that she would not choose girls who were prettier than her, in fact the reverse was the case. To compound this folly the cabin staff uniform was devoid of sex appeal and capped with a very tall hat reminiscent of the female Welsh top hats of the nineteenth century. Both brothers now appeared to fight for control of the company with the Flight Operations at East Midlands and the Commercial Department and the cabin staff based at Gatwick. This state of affairs lasted for several weeks during which time no collective training could take place. When the great day arrived of the coming together of the clan, all the pilots were posted at all the windows of flight operations to witness the arrival of these sensual gorgeous creatures, as by this time a number of us were exhibiting serious signs of sexual deprivation. Minutes later after the disembarkation had been completed the flight operations department had completely emptied. I knew that I was fleet of foot, but even so I was left behind in the rush for the back door.

Trefgarne addressed the staff a few weeks later and assured them of the continued health and long life of the company, but I left the same day not believing a word of it. One month later on June 28th with creditors pressing, the company presented its own petition for Winding-up. According to the 'Leicester Mercury' newspaper on Saturday 19th August 1967, Treffield left debts of £203,000 and assets of only £4,800. The employees remaining after my departure were not paid, and Paul, who had eventually followed me from Emerald Airways, was one of those. Asked by a creditor why Lord Trefgarne had not attended the first meeting of creditors, Mr A. D. Williams the Official Assistant Receiver said that 'it was not compulsory for him to do so'. Sometime later Lord Trefgarne formed a new company at Coventry Airport called Midland Air Cargo, which also went bust in quite a short time. His last effort was to join a charter operator at Heathrow with Stephen Quinto, an American, this too bit the dust in record time. Eventually Trefgarne took his family's hereditary seat in the House of Lords. That institution, in its old form, also had to be reinvented. Perhaps Trefgarne had the last laugh however, when during his stint in the Lords he became a Minister in the Thatcher Government, which perhaps said rather less about him and rather more about her.

CHAPTER 8

FREELANCING, THE MED. AND WESTWARD AGAIN

By May 22nd I was back gainfully employed by E S and A Robinsons, the paper packaging people of Bristol. George Thornton was their Chief Pilot who had at one time been a development and sales pilot for the De Havilland company. Having sold a Heron aircraft to Robinsons he had been persuaded to take the Chief Pilot's job as well. I have no recollection of the circumstances which found me being interviewed at Bristol Filton Airport, no doubt one of my chums had told me of the vacancy and a telephone call had done the rest. George was on his annual leave when I arrived and I was interviewed for the job by Godfrey Auty, the British Aircraft's Corporation (BAC), later British Aerospace PLC, Chief Pilot at Filton. Auty had achieved fame by test flying the Type 188 supersonic research aircraft, a crucial part of the Concord development programme. Later at Filton I was to meet Brian Trubshaw who flew the British Concorde 002 on its maiden flight. Brian was a fellow Welshman having been born in North Wales and moved to Pembrey in West Wales in 1927. The Trubshaw name remains prominent in the Ashburnham Golf Club House in Bury Port and Brian did in fact win the Welsh Junior Golf Championship one year. The fact that I was very well acquainted with the Heron aircraft clearly did the trick, and George and I were soon flying all over the country bringing potential customers to Bristol to sample the company's wares. As we were based in the same building as the BAC flight operations many of our flights were conducted on behalf of that company, so we became constant visitors to Hatfield, Woodvale, Rochester and Belfast as well as countless RAF airfields.

I had been taken on as a temporary co-pilot as George's permanent was on extended leave until the following August. George was somewhat pernickety in his flying habits, but after my experiences with Treffield this was indeed a welcome change. He was a most accomplished pilot and I learned much from watching him perform. There was nothing of the hell-raiser in George and more often than not he was quite content to sit in the aircraft for hours between charter flights waiting for his passengers to return. He did see to it however that the aircraft was well stocked with sandwiches and soft drinks, alcohol was never a part of his menu. We were quite disparate characters, and while George seemed to be surrounded by a peaceful aura, and I constantly surprised myself by happily melting into his self-created environment. This peaceful existence was soon shattered however, when in June of that year George disappeared on a course for a number of weeks. His temporary replacement, Jock Haldane, was a former World War II Bomber Command pilot who had a temperament quite similar to my own. Maybe it was the Celtic blood that did it, but certainly we proved to be a good team. With George I was happy to be the co-pilot, but with Jock it became more a case of equals, although I was fully aware that in terms of flying experience he was many streets ahead. He seemed quite confident in my ability, and showed this by sleeping on the back seat of the aircraft while I flew it home from Belfast or Glasgow. The highlight for me however was on the flight back from Haverfordwest airfield on the 14th June when I dived down into the Rhondda Valley and buzzed my parent's home before disappearing over the mountain and back to Bristol.

The following day we flew to Bremen via Rotterdam and here we to meet trouble of an unsuspected kind. Not having to leave for a day or so we decided to seek some entertainment down town. In our book that clearly meant booze and girls. It was Jock who found Les Ambassadeurs night club, and after a fine dinner we had arrived there about ten p.m. We had already consumed a bottle of wine and a number of brandies, so the club girls appeared highly glamorous. Champagne seemed to be the order of the night, but we quickly changed this to Moselle wine, which was certainly more palatable to me and less profitable for the club. The girls were anxious to please and time passed pleasantly enough. Jock now decided to leave and pick-up more travellers cheques from the hotel, while I sought to deal with the lithe bodies surrounding me on all sides. Jock's return was marked by a vigorous naked performance by dancers in the floor show, in which it appears I played a leading part, although my memory of it, perhaps fortunately, remains scant.

The trouble really started when Jock saw the bill and started exuding steam like an active volcano. He called for the manager and demanded that the bill be immediately reduced. I was aware that Scotsman liked eating porridge oats and blowing bagpipes, but it now appeared that stories concerning Scotsmen and their money were equally well founded. The manager clearly in a pugnacious mood absolutely refused to consider a reduction at which Jock shouted loudly, "You bloody German bastard". The manager now with equal vigour called Jock "a filthy Englischer". Jock now positively roared "I'm not bloody English, I'm a Scotsman", and whacked the manager right on the nose. Next thing one of the club bouncers hit Jock from behind on the head with a baton of some kind, which only seemed to make Jock madder. Not to be left out of the action I picked up the first weapon to hand, an empty wine bottle, and cracked the bouncer hard on his head who slipped, gurgled and slumped to the floor. Mayhem followed and the lights became dimmer, I felt my body describe an upward spiral followed by a succession of thuds, whistles and flashing lights. I came to my senses being frog marched by two heavies out of the club into a waiting police car. I was amazed to find it daylight and wondered where the time had gone. In the police station we were interviewed by a police detective who spoke good English and was friendly enough. Things seemed to progress well until he said proudly "I too am a pilot and I bombed London in 1941". At this Jock said "I was in RAF Bomber Command and I bombed Bremen—twice!" The next moment we were assailed from all sides and found ourselves flung into a cell, where we were allowed to cool off for a good few hours. We were finally cautioned as to our future behaviour and taken back to our hotel under explicit instructions to remain there until called. It was now past midday and our passengers had all arrived back ready for their journey home. Under Jock's instructions we gathered them all up in a few taxis and sped to the airport. Never had formalities for a flight taken so little time, and at 1415 hours we were airborne for Bristol. As soon as we were well across the Zuider Zee Jock and I exchanged glances and spontaneously burst into laughter. I somehow thought that the Bremen police force would not be too displeased at our disappearance, and I retained a lingering suspicion that Jock had a natural aversion to Germans. Years later on a charter to Bremen with Brymon Airways I once more sought out the Les Ambassadeurs Night Club, but this time without success, so my co-pilot and I sought alternative amusement in the city. I am sure it was a pretty eventful evening, but my memories of it, are perhaps best forgotten.

Normal services were resumed when George returned to duty and my period with Robinsons ran its course. The highlight of this period was the pleasure I felt flying Dr Russell, later Sir Archibald Russell, from Wisley back to Filton. It was his genius that undoubtedly helped to guide the design of the Concorde airliner. George whispered to me that he was on board and as it was my leg suggested that I make it a smooth flight and landing. Thirty minutes later I had obliged when the tyres gently kissed the Filton runway. Dr Russell, like many others in the British civil aircraft industry, were constantly bedevilled by politicians, and the need ostensibly to build aircraft the right shape and size for the nationalised airlines of British Overseas Airways Corporation (BOAC) and British European Airways (BEA). In doing so they jeopardised the opportunity to build aircraft in numbers for the rest of the world. At the end of August I flew Heron GARTI from Cambridge to Filton without passengers. On this flight George displayed his knowledge and his ability on the aircraft. He first shut down one engine, then two, then three and allowed me to practise stalling the aircraft in all three configurations. It was my last flight with Robinsons and it had been a classic example of gentlemanly flying. We flew dressed in suits or blazers, ate well, night stopped in the best hotels and perhaps above all flew a lovely aircraft beautifully maintained. It had been a wonderful experience and one never to be repeated in my flying career.

News of my availability was soon posted to a company called Tacair, who themselves frequently flew into Filton, operating charter flights on behalf of the British Aircraft Corporation. Soon I was busy flying their Dove and Piper Aztec in a single pilot operation based at Halfpenny Green Airfield in Shropshire. Unlike Robinsons, Tacair was a rag, tag and bobtail operation, and their greatest asset being their Chief Pilot, Captain Ian Ryall DFC, another former Bomber Command wartime pilot. The company benefactor was a city gent who had been conned into buying Tacair and used it largely as a plaything. Sadly however he was rarely out of an alcoholic trance and he seemed to breakfast, lunch and dine on a diet of champagne and a succession of pink gins. During the war he had piloted a Horsa glider at the Arnhem bridgehead and had retained an interest in flying thereafter. I flew him and his girl friends on a number of occasions, and once at his request arranged a boat trip to Cherbourg where I showed them around the Normandy D-Day landing sites, and even then I had to hold up the boat owing to his drunkenness. In his sober moments, which were few, I grew to like the man, but found it completely impossible to wean him away from his daily drinking habits which were surely killing him.

When possible Stan Edwards and I spent every free weekend on the Sancta Maria at Southampton, a welcome change from the frantic world of flying. Apart from entertaining various barmaids from Southampton pubs, clubs and hotels, there seemed to be a lack of the higher bred females with perhaps lower moral restraints. The two Jennies, from our fearful journey back from Cherbourg, had somehow slipped from our lives. My Jenny, whom I had began to believe might become a permanent attachment, had decided that a more resolute, dependable and home loving man would be a better bet. This had saddened me considerably, but I had bowed my knee to the vagaries of fortune and ploughed on. Stan decided unaided to advertise for female shipmates in an appropriate yachting magazine. The response was quite outstanding, both in quality and numbers, and I was easily convinced that the two charmers we were about to meet in Southampton were both highly intelligent well bred and physically attractive. As a consequence we stopped off at a chemist shop in Warminster to purchase the necessary equipment for the weekend. It seemed that every time I walked into a chemist shop in those days to ask for contraceptives I was inevitably confronted by a female assistant. In the 1960s it was considered by many a rather daring act in sharp contrast to today. True to form I found a female assistant facing me across the counter who turned a bright red when I gave my order. She fled through a back door and a few minutes later a white-coated male appeared. I repeated my order of a dozen contraceptives and a box of seasick pills. He looked at me and then at my uniform and said "I don't wish to appear impertinent sir, but why do you chaps do it if it makes you sick?" and this in a dead pan voice. When I managed to reach the car and tell Stan, we laughed all the way to Southampton. In fact it became a standing joke that weekend. The girls turned out every bit as

Stan had described. Margaret was an intelligent, attractive and a rich young lady, while Lorraine was blond, very good looking with a wonderful sense of humour. Lorraine, Lolly for short, and I hit it off together as did Stan and Margaret. We sailed down the Solent and across to Weymouth, and despite the amounts of drink consumed, stayed in our own bunks, and the packet of contraceptives and seasick pills remained unopened. A few days later I received the following letter from Lolly, which apart from improving my ego, convinced me that here I had something rather special. How could I resist such a woman?

My dear John,

~~My dear John.~~

As your humble sailing servant/cook cum companion cum .... I would like to thank the 1st Officer very much indeed for all that instant fun packed into the weekend - its difficult to imagine it possible now. You are, and this is no attempt at flattery (I'm no good at that anyway), a remarkably amusing person and not only that, but an outstanding personality which shines above all. You should go far.. I don't usually pay men compliments like that (not many are worthy of it!) but you deserve to be told.

Seriously, though, I did have a wonderful time and I think its so much nicer to know that my enjoyment was shared by one and all. Many thanks too for sending the flowers, which will act as a reminder of our great weekend with those reckless pilots on board the Sancta Maria. It was very thoughtful of you both.

I am pleased to say I was only five minutes late for the office, but not before spending a frustrating time sitting in traffic jams on the M4. It turned out to be a busy day in the office, contrary to my predictions, which was probably a good thing, because it took my mind of my mental and physical fatigue, but, oh boy, the next day !!! I'm so sorry I was out when you rang. I went out for a drink with a friend and then on to a girl friend's flat where some birthday celebrations were in progress and I was rather swallowed up in these. I could not face the journey back to Marble Arch as I was so tired, so I stayed at her flat for the night.

[illegible]

I hope you were able to sleep it off on Monday and that your Ship mates didn't leave too much mess for you to clear up. A less exhausting weekend on the agenda this coming one, as I'm going home to Guildford, but I can see I shall be caught up in domestic activities, plus some tennis, so I shan't get a rest. I shall miss the hilarity of last weekend and I think anything after that will be everso dull.

Over,

Yours, with Love!

Lorraine

PS Thanks a million

It appeared that I had developed the ability to move seamlessly between jobs and this during a period of high pilot unemployment. A certain amount of luck clearly played its part, but I was also fortunate in having the right aircraft types stamped on my licence. Within a few weeks of leaving Tacair I was back flying the Heron with English Electric based at Stoughton Leicester East Airfield. This was without any shadow of doubt the most boring flying job I ever had. Every week day morning at 0800 hours we flew the Heron to RAF Valley in Anglesey, North Wales and returned to Leicester East later the same day. The aircraft was owned by the Whetstone based company Nuclear Design and Construction Ltd, who were building a nuclear power station at Wylfa, a tiny inlet on the northern tip of Anglesey. There rising above the cold Irish Sea like some medieval fortress were the beginnings of Britain's most ambitious incursion into the world of nuclear power. When completed and in full operation it would generate enough electricity to meet the needs of a city six times the size of Leicester. It cost the government £106 million (at 1960 values), and up to that time was the most valuable single contract ever awarded in the UK. As a part of the crew I spent the middle of each day at the Valley Hotel Anglesey, and either played golf at the nearby Trearddur Bay golf club, or more often settled for a sedate game of snooker at the hotel. The aircraft was fitted with a Decca moving map display which did all the navigation for us and allowed us to land back at Leicester East at night, an airfield devoid of any landing aids. The lonely Air Traffic Controller merely had to pass us the surface wind and the QFE (pressure at airfield level in millibars) and we did the rest.

The relationship with Lorraine now deepened and we met as often as our job responsibilities allowed. She then hit me with a bombshell, as women tend to do. It appears that she had met a Libyan gentleman on a flight back from New York months before we had met. He had fed her with a heartfelt story of how he was unable to find a suitable private secretary to work with him in Tripoli, and offered her the job with a car, flat and expenses attached. She had agreed to take this position and was leaving the UK within two months. I worked hard on her to break the contract as I had heard some terrible stories of white girls, particularly blondes, who had mysteriously disappeared in Arab countries. My argument fell on stony ground as she felt an agreement was an agreement, and unable to go back on her word. By this time I had taken Lorraine home to meet my parents, not an unknown event as she was the fifth or sixth in a line. My mother used to say that I could go all round the orchard and end up with a crab (apple). However I felt enough about Lorraine to suddenly say, "Well if you are going to Libya then so am I". From time to time my bank manager had shown concern as to the state of my bank balance even hinting that perhaps I should return to the more stable school teaching role, where at least my income would be regular. I had enthused him with visions of my next new venture and again promised huge returns from my new airline in the Mediterranean. In this way I managed to leave the bank with £500 in my pocket without even a blush. As I left his office he sighed deeply and said, "Captain Evans, I used to think that you were banking with us, but I now believe that we are banking with you".

I flew to Malta in a BEA Vanguard aircraft before boarding a Viscount, some six hours later, for Tripoli in North Africa. I spent the time in Malta sight seeing in Valetta, the island's capital, and soon learned why the island had been described as 'Hells, Bells and Smells'. I landed in Tripoli some two hours ahead of Lorraine who had routed via Naples, where she had stayed with friends. I studied the waiting crowd and soon spotted the messenger sent to meet her, who was holding up a board with her name painted in large letters. When she emerged I clasped her close in welcome and could see that the messenger looked distinctly peeved to witness my presence. When in the car I told him quite forcibly that Lorraine was not now taking the job as we had recently met, fallen in love and decided on marriage. The emerging words even surprised me. He promised to pick us up early next morning and take us to the office to meet his boss. I knew for certain that the meeting the next day would be an ordeal, and so it proved!

That night I made it clear that I would leave Tripoli just as soon as I could, and if she decided to stay then she would have to stay without me. I was quite sure in my own mind that no good would come to her if she were to stay in Tripoli, and seeing how sincere I was, she eventually agreed. The boss man proved to be a fat genial Arab who tried every trick he knew to persuade Lorraine to undertake some work, but I remained totally adamant and Lorraine remained completely silent. He was clever in his way, in that anybody who worked as a foreigner would clearly receive remuneration, which would of course be subject to local tax. Consequently, to leave the country she would have required clearances from the Minister of Work, the Tax Ministry and goodness knows who else besides, and all this to receive an exit visa. Such rigmarole could have taken many weeks and would have clearly exhausted our limited funds. Finally he realised he was beaten, but informed me that I would have to obtain clearance from the Chief of Police for us to leave the country. Walking down the main street all my fears for Lorraine were realised as we passed an open air café fully occupied by men, their looks of unbridled lust as they looked at Lorraine unnerved me somewhat. Libyan women, of course, walked the streets completely covered up with one eye alone visible.

Within hours my interview with Colonel Shalabi Chief of Police took place. He was an imposing man sitting at a desk below a large picture of King Idris the then King of Libya. He kept me standing which did not augur well for the meeting, and his first words were somewhat discouraging. "I don't like you," he said, "you are a trouble maker, and I want you and your fiancé out of this country as soon as possible." He continued in a similar vein, "If you ever appear here again believe me you will be arrested, charged and imprisoned." With those kind thoughts he casually dismissed me. It felt like the old days when I left the headmaster's study having received a beating, feeling rather sore but profoundly relieved. All the flights to Malta were full, but we were lucky to obtain a cabin on a ship of the Tirrenia Line leaving Tripoli that evening. We breathed collective sighs of relief when we boarded that ship and entered our cabin. The voyage proved to be a most memorable journey across the Mediterranean in the most sublime of conditions. The date was the 15th November 1968.

The next morning we arrived in Valetta harbour, happy but fairly broke and with no place to live, and it says something for our ingenuity that we remained in Malta for well over a year. That night we rented a shabby room adjoining a brothel where the walls were paper thin and the vibrations making it all to obvious of the activity taking place on the other side, so Lorraine and I decided that the best way to deal with this disturbance was to join them at their own game. The next day I saw an advertisement in the 'Malta Times' for a flat in Depiro Street, Sliema and took it on a twelve month lease as the only means by which I was able to avoid paying a security deposit, but the flat did have a piano which really proved the clincher.

My investigations soon showed that there were two airlines in formation on the island at that time. Air Melita an international airline was recruiting staff from their offices in the Hilton Hotel and Malta Gozo Airlines a domestic operation was being set up by lieutenant Commander Arbuthnot, a retired naval officer, based in the offices of the Development Corporation of Malta in Sliema. The fact that the passenger market seemly fairly well organised turned my attention to the potential for airfreight. Much of Malta's freight at that time was flown to the UK by British European Airways at a commodity rate of five shillings and four pence per kilo. My intensive study over several months following a walking tour (not being able to afford a car) around the island's manufacturers showed clearly that there was a great deal of unhappiness with the freight rate, but that with BEA occupying a monopolistic position little could be done. I flew to London and visited British Caledonian Airways at Gatwick where I discussed the leasing of a Boeing 320C and the costs involved. The Business Plan I prepared showed clearly that I could reduce the freight commodity rate to one shilling and six pence per kilo and still make a substantial profit. When I paraded this information around the island my potential customers were clearly delighted and supportive. The biggest exporters then were Dowty seals, BMC cars, vegetable produce for Covent Garden and clothing manufactures. I travelled to Cheltenham to meet Lord Dowty and enjoyed a tour around the company's facility, he being enthusiastic about the idea.

The Mitzi Brothers held the BMC car franchise for Malta and I became friendly with the youngest brother Maurice, whom I taught to fly in my spare time and thereby earned some money. His family's company bought car parts from the UK in containers by road and assembled them at Marsa on the island. This ensured that the flight operation would have loads in both directions hence lowering costs. The 1960s, of course, was a period well before the 'Open Skies' system which operates today, and in order to break the BEA monopoly I had to evolve a method by which I could beat the existing system. I eventually settled for a private company in which all the participating companies would hold shares and therefore the company couldn't be classed as a public transport undertaking. When I met the Maltese Director of Civil Aviation he threw up his hands and said that 'I was driving a coach and horses through the regulations', meaning of course the Air Navigation Order. Clearly he took advice on this from the Maltese Government and at a subsequent meeting, some time later, he informed me that if I persisted with my plan then the Government would pass a law outlawing any private or public company ostensibly competing with BEA. This inevitably was the end of the story, and my six months of hard work fell into ruin. At least it taught me a great deal about the deviousness of politicians if nothing else.

In the meantime Lorraine had obtained a job with Air Melita and had flown off to the States to train as an Air Stewardess with Trans World Airlines in Kansas City, Missouri. During her absence I took solace by spending some time on the beach in Exiles Bay a short walk from Depiro Street. Here weeks earlier I had spied a most beautiful girl the spitting image of Sophia Loren. She strode the beach like an Amazon with her long legs, narrow waist, large but firm breasts and a beautiful sculptured face crowned with a mass of raven black hair. From the first moment I saw her my hormones has began clattering in a most unusual manner, and I knew that somehow I had to make contact. Now alone on the beach I plucked up courage and walked across where she sat on the rocks with her Maltese entourage. She looked quizzically at me after I introduced myself and said, "You're not English are you?" Surprised I asked her how she knew. "Well if you were you'd be sitting over there with them", pointing to group of expatriates. As soon as she opened her mouth however, my sexual hormones fled for cover. Her voice was like broken glass or perhaps like a camel with laryngitis. I thought of buying a set of air plugs, but that I thought could severely damage the relationship, so although we remained friendly that's all it ever became.

I now became known around Luqa Airport and earned a crust or two by flying passengers in a single engined Cessna aircraft over to Catania in Sicily on shopping excursions. On climb out from Luqa Airport I could invariably spot Mount Etna standing out in the distance which at least took the sweat off navigation. I also made flights to the islands of Pantelleria and Lampedusa in addition to pleasure flights around the island of Gozo. Patrick Starling was an Englishman resident in Malta and was involved in the film industry, Malta having a large film studio. At the same time he was training in the UK for his British Private Pilot's Licence and flew with me a number of times to maintain his level of competence. I took him on his first night flight and we climbed the aircraft to 8000 feet above the island of Gozo. Suddenly after a few minutes at this level the engine refused to make power above idle. It was if the throttle had been locked in the closed position. I tried everything I knew to return power to normal without success and started to glide down the well illuminated coastline towards the airport. I contemplated a landing in St. Paul's Bay, but as one of the world's heavy sinkers I quickly removed those thoughts from my mind. I stretched the glide as much as I dared juggling height and speed as best I could. By this time Luqa had held any conflicting traffic, and as my descent continued the engine still stubbornly refused to co-operate. I cleared the runway threshold with less than twenty feet to spare and rolled to a stop. As I debated the best way to get us to the terminal building I pushed the throttle forward in disgust, only for the engine to burst into a vigorous roar. It was an incident never satisfactorily explained and the engine showed no further ill effects after successive ground runs. I shuddered to think of the consequences had I been at a lower level over Gozo as Patrick too wasn't the best of swimmers.

The news now arrived of a coup d'état in Libya where King Idris had been toppled by Colonel Muammar al-Quaddafi, who established an Islamic State, reducing foreign interference and proclaiming a 'People's Republic'. As it had been a military coup I wondered what had happened to Colonel Shalabi my old antagonist. During the following week the world press covered the news, repudiated the change and governments openly declared their lack of support for the new regime. At the same time private emissaries of the same governments were in secret talks with Quaddafi offering him support of all kinds, particularly in military arms. Dick and Jimmy represented a large US credit card company, who were the front men for the sales of US military aircraft to Libya, and they and many such like representatives soon flooded into Malta. I had met Dick and Jimmy many times in the offices of the Development Corporation so was not surprised when I was asked to join them one day for a lunch appointment. At this they asked me to represent them in Tripoli as their expert on military aircraft. I protested that I knew little of the latest military offerings, but they insisted that it would be sufficient for me to mug up on the various technical documents. This offer coupled with a very large fee was sufficient inducement, particularly as my finances were by now in a somewhat parlous state. On the evening prior to our flight to Tripoli Dick went down with a serious infection and our departure was delayed a week. In the meantime two of our party, Claus and Falzon went ahead to prepare the groundwork for a succession of meetings. Within days we received messages that both these men had been arrested and imprisoned for money laundering activities. Strenuous efforts were now made to obtain their release through the Maltese authorities and the British Embassy in London without success. Dick and I consequently never visited Tripoli and months later when in London I met up with Claus and heard his story. Both he and Falzon the Maltese had been arrested on false charges, imprisoned and tortured. Both men had been semi-starved and for periods each day were hung by their finger tips with thin wire and severely beaten on the soles of their feet, a torture known as bastinado. Claus had found his cell door unlocked on two consecutive nights and had ignored the obvious bait, but the third night he broke loose and walked south into the desert and not directly westwards where he knew the guards were waiting to shoot him. Almost a week elapsed before he luckily fell into a frontier post on the Tunisian border and was rescued. Claus was or rather had been a big tough German, and any lesser man would never have made it. I examined his hands where the evidence of the wire marks were still clearly visible, and although previously a man of almost seventeen stone, he had been reduced to a shadow of his former self although his spirit remained undimmed. As for Falzon he was never seen or heard from again, at least to my knowledge, and had Dick not suffered his stomach bug, he and I would in all probability have suffered the same fate.

Air Melita in the meantime had gone bust, and the Managing Director and his secretary had been arrested attempting to leave Malta by boat to Sicily. I had left for Geneva and with John Doyle, the President of Piper Aircraft Corporation in Europe, delivered a single engined aircraft back to Malta. This was quite exciting as it was the first time, and last, that I would cross the Alps in a single engined aircraft. We managed to reach 13,500 feet skirting between Mont Blanc and the Eiger. I breathed a sigh of relief when at last we were able to descend over the plain of Lombarday and into Geneva Airport. That night we slept in the comfort of the Christopher Columbus hotel and in the morning flew directly to Palermo on the north coast of Sicily paralleling the Italian mainland down its length. After refuelling we completed the short hop to Luqa Airport in Malta. The flight had lasted just over six hours and was a fitting climax to my stay in Malta. A month later Lorraine and I were back in the UK both jobless again, soon however we were both gainfully employed once more, but flying with different airlines.

Lorraine having been trained by TWA in Kansas City had no trouble obtaining a stewardess position with British Caledonian Airways, looking a real picture in her Scottish Tartan. I was interested in a relatively new carrier Westward Airways who were operating the Gatwick Heathrow Shuttle and flights down to the West Country and the Isles of Scilly. I walked in on Captains Fry and Prowse in the coffee shop at Gatwick Airport and within an hour had been taken on board, and commenced my training the next day with Captain Wrefford. Fry and Prouse were both ex-BOAC Captains with a wealth of experience on world-wide routes flying the Boeing 707. To fly the BN2 Islander as a single pilot however required a completely different kind of training and skill, and to their credit they had undergone a complete course of retraining at Thurston's Aviation flight school at Stapleford Tawney in Essex. Howard Fry was the managing director of the airline and was at that time the prospective

Liberal parliamentary candidate for St. Ives in Cornwall where he lived. However he never succeeded in winning that parliamentary seat. Captain Prowse was known as 'Pants Prowse'. It was alleged that he had turned up one day at Heathrow for duty, with BOAC having forgotten to put on his trousers. He was the operations manager of Air Westward and a very tall thin person who habitually wore a monocle. Who said that there were no characters left in aviation? I was now able to reacquaint myself with the Isles of Scillies and the West Country in general, an experience I enjoyed immensely. The Gatwick Heathrow shuttles were less enjoyable and you certainly needed to keep your 'finger out', particularly when in the early morning you came off the Epsom beacon and cut on to final approach joining the long line of jets arriving from the States and elsewhere. In fact once established on finals for landing, safety dictated that I flew the Instrument Landing System (ILS) slightly offset to keep the Islander outside the severe wake turbulence caused by the big jets. This was not too difficult under visual conditions when you could see the aircraft ahead, but generally this was not the case and I just had to take 'pot luck'. On one such occasion at less than 200 feet above the ground, the Islander was thrown into a ninety-degree bank and became almost inverted before I regained control. This, I have to say, said less about my flying ability and rather more about the innate stability of the aircraft. Again it was necessary when established on the glideslope to maintain an approach speed of 150 knots, which was higher than the cruising speed of the aircraft. This was necessary to maintain separation between the aircraft on the approach. Again it was impossible to lower the flaps as the approach speed was usually in excess of the flap lowering speed. On touch down you left the runway at the first possible turn off to see the next aircraft, inevitably a jet, flashing by almost instantaneously. Officially the time lapse between approaching aircraft was two minutes, and you really had to keep your wits about you. The Air Traffic Controllers at London airport in my view were first rate, their voices calm and unhurried, which must have been in sharp contrast to the stress endured, and I joined the long list of pilots who admired their professionalism. Many times I flew the shuttles with no paying passengers so on those occasions with the collusion of our passenger desk at Gatwick, usually manned by David Smith, we filled the aircraft with friends and the prettiest girls available from the other airline desks. The management of the company forbade us to cancel any flight even when no fare paying passengers were booked, a policy which I considered an advanced form of madness. Indeed most of the company staff were confounded by this edict which contributed greatly to the subsequent demise of the company. Lorraine was now flying long haul with Caledonian and opportunities to be with one another became extremely rare. As a consequence we mutually agreed to call it a day, and went our separate ways. It had been a great relationship and we had enjoyed much fun together, but life as they say goes on!

Returning from Plymouth one Saturday afternoon with a full load of passengers I encountered severe and continuous icing problems. I was constantly operating the hot air system to destroy the ice forming in the engine carburettors. By the time I reached the Epsom beacon I found myself number four in a holding stack for landing with my fuel level quantity gauges looking distinctly shaky. I informed Air Traffic Control of my fuel state and confirmed my intention to divert to Gatwick if I were to be held for length of time. I was assured that I was next to be released out bound for landing and soon this happened, and as I awaited instructions to turn on to final approach an Air France aircraft called up with an emergency and I was forced to continue the outbound leg until I was over east London. The fuel gauges were now reading an all time low, and eventually I landed with less than ten US gallons on board. After landing I now found myself wondering how to obtain fuel for my onward flight to Gatwick, as Westward in its wisdom had selected a Canadian company at Heathrow to handle all our aircraft and passengers. Unfortunately, this company had been blackballed by the unions, thereby making it impossible to lift any fuel at the airport.

Once the passengers had departed I discussed the situation with my ground handlers. Apparently a union meeting was in progress at the airport and he suggested that I walk in and make a request for fuel. I was not at my best that evening having already flown seven sectors that day in anything but good weather, but I decided to 'have a go'. I pushed open the swing doors reminiscent of a cowboy saloon, and put on my best imitation of a Gary Cooper smile and entered the hall. Two or three comrades were on the stage addressing an audience of around fifty airport workers. As I advanced down the aisle the comrades lapsed into silence and stared at me, and as if by command fifty pairs of eyes followed their example. "Excuse me," I found myself saying, "I fly for Westward Airways and I require some fuel". There was a prolonged uncomfortable silence then the meeting's chairman stated the obvious, "Your handling company is banned at this airport and my members won't supply you". They then continued their meeting as if I had never existed, and so I backed down the aisle and through the door bowed but certainly not beaten.

When I returned to the aircraft I asked my agent to find a clean fifty-gallon drum. Fortunately he was a person with a certain presence and a keen entrepreneurial spirit. With our acquired drum we drove down to the Esso garage on the airport and filled up with four star petrol. My solitary passenger was a great guy, and the three of us lifted the drum onto the wing of the aircraft and poured in the fuel. My passenger excited by this turn of events now asked me whether the aircraft engines would operate on car petrol, "I bloody well hope so," I said, "but don't worry I'll give them a good run-up on the ground first". The flight went without mishap and after landing at Gatwick I thought the matter would be quickly put to rest. I was wrong however, and my action was reported to Captain Prowse. I was soon summoned to meet him at his pleasant and palatial home near

Epsom. He looked at me as if I had brought a bad smell into his home, and told me in distinct and clear terms that I had fallen short of the high standards required of an airline pilot and all this with his monocle firmly in place, it was really hilarious. He further suggested demotion from the line and a move to Land's End Airport in Cornwall to carry out the rather mundane activity of flying passengers on pleasure flights around the local lighthouse. In turn I suggested that I should be promoted in view of my initiative at Heathrow and completing my schedule to Gatwick safely. At this somewhat bold suggestion his monocle fell from his eye, and his face turned a slight but distinct red colour. I finally put him out of his misery by agreeing to leave the company subject only to his accepting certain financial terms, which he did gladly.

I was now free again and within the month was once more in the air with GKN Guest Keen and Nettlefolds a huge company, flying their executives around the country in some style. This continued until October when my life was to change in quite a remarkable manner. One thing I felt sure about though, that I must be the only airline pilot ever to refuel a public transport aircraft at London Heathrow with four star petrol from the forecourt of the local Esso garage.

The Author and his flying partner Paul Weeks
arrive at Swansea Airport August 1963.

Lifting a willing passenger over the boundary fence to Paul.

The End of our Pleasure Flying Dreams
the two partners look on disconsolately at the mess left by the council after they had dug-up the passenger car park, and they called this an area of outstanding natural beauty?

The ladder was used by the two pilots to get passengers from the common, over the fence, and into the aircraft. Here, Michael Bagshaw, Son of the Airport Manager, demonstrates his skill.

Paul with arms folded, Valerie (Miss Carmarthenshire), and Author pose in front of the Aerol 145. (Swansea 1965).

Janet seems more interested in the camera than the lesson.

A rather better picture of Valerie.

The Airfield on St Mary's Isles of Scilly

This picture looking North shows the tarmac part of the East/ West runway just 280 metres long sloping down to the rocks. The longer runway was only constructed in 1991. (Dally Collection).

Plymouth Airport (circa 1931). Apart from the construction of a small passenger lounge and offices, little had changed when Brymon started scheduled services 40 years later.

The Author standing nest to Mrs Cruse (of 90 years) after her first flight. Mr Mackrill our greatest supporter, stands next to his stepdaughter.

The Cormorant fleet circa 1965.

Cormorant Aviation Services Limited

Pleasure Flights

Daily from

Ramsgate Airport

(March 25—October 3)

See Ramsgate, Margate, Broadstairs and Cliftonville from the Air.

Free Transportation to and from the Airport from our Kiosk on the Front.

ADULTS 15/- CHILDREN 10/-

(Parties of four or more only 10/- per Person)

Denny Bros., Printers, Bury St. Edmunds.

These were the days of Radio Caroline and the Mods and Rockers.

Stand Edwards and the author spent fifteen hours in a Storm Force 10/11, crossing from Cherbourg to Shouthampton in the 'Santa Maria' above (October 1965).

A Skyvan of emerald Airways, Belfast.

Ground School Training at Shorts Belfast, 1966. Paul Weeks is at extreme left back row. The author is extreme right front row. Mike Lewis Chief Pilot became a Civil Aviation Flight Inspector, (extreme left from row), and was killed in the 70's, ferrying an aircraft back from the United States.

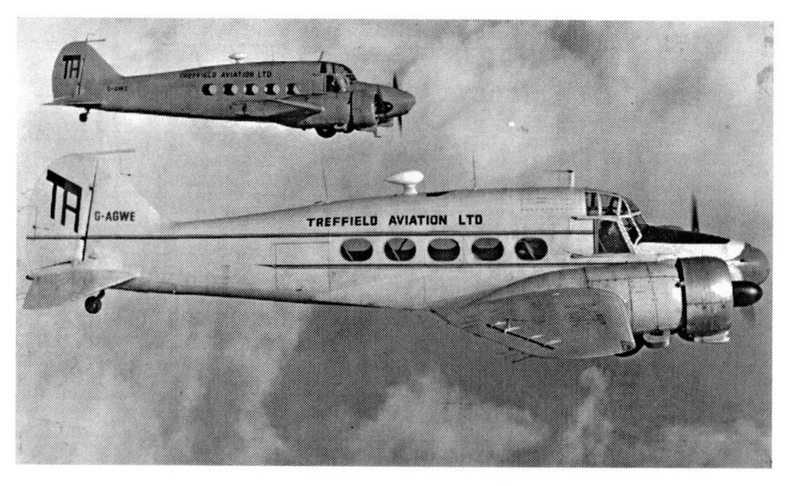

Two Treffield Aviation Ansons in formation over the Midlands (circa 1966). An event never likely to be repeated.

Treffield also flew Viscount Aircraft similar to the above.

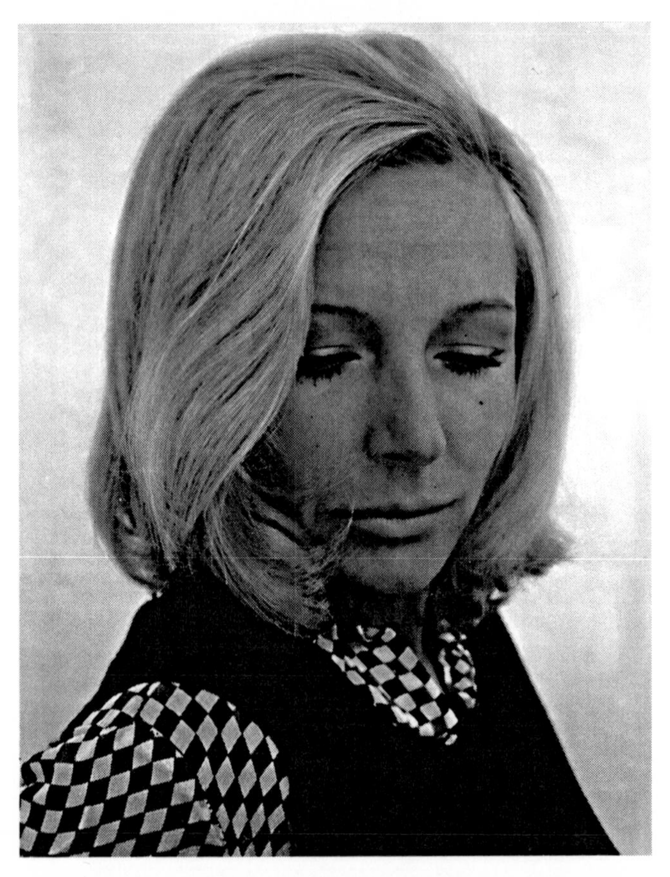

No wonder they wanted to keep her in Tripoli,

Sweet Lorraine (Lolly).

The Author with

Mum

Dad

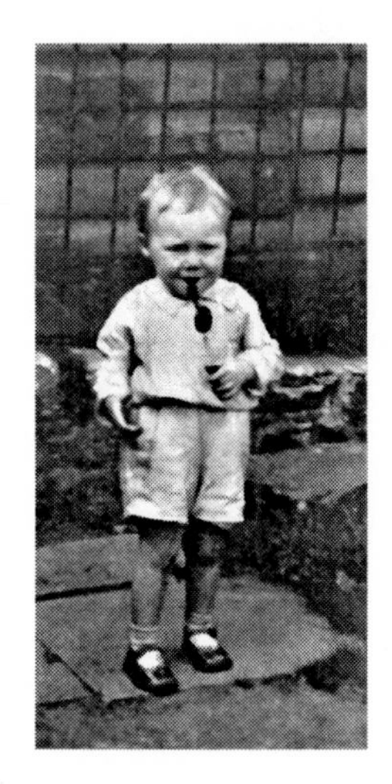

Pipe (clearly an Airline Executive in the making)

Bat

Rest of the Family, sister Gillian and Aunt Glenys, with Snowy and Mac.

The gang, photographed by author after Sunday School. How well dressed we were then.

First girlfriend.

Flying the D.H. 89A RAPIDE at East Midlands Airport 1966. This particular aircraft (GAHKU) named ;Sir Richard Hawkins', had been one of the three BEA aircraft based at the Lands End Airport until 1959, when helicopters took over the service to the Scillies from Penzance, heliport, (Author is seen here, holding the propeller in place).

One of our passengers flanked by the author and our illustrious agent Len Dalton. Scillies (circa 1972).

Len resting on the steps of a Brymon Twin Otter at the Scillies.

A grateful passenger ahngs on to the author in Jersey. (see BIA hanger in background).

Len once more, having borrowed a captain's uniform.

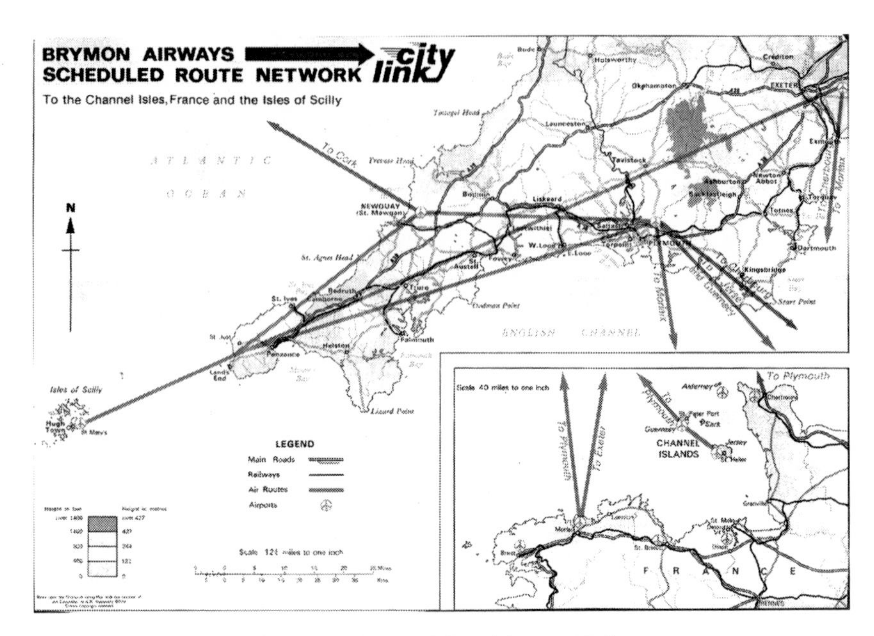

Brymon Route Map (circa 1975).

The First Brymon Airways Twin Otter (DHC6).

Lyn, one of our attractive stewardesses posing beneath the tail of a Brymon Islander.

An Air Wales Bandeirante in flight over Brazil, prior to delivery (circa 1979).

A typical group of valley boys, Roy Milton is on extreme right of picture, with belt holding up his trousers (circa 1930).

Roy in Americus, Georgia (circa early 1942).

To obtain his wings Roy flew the above aircraft whilst in the U.S.A.

1. Stearman PT 17A—Americus Georgia
2. Vultee Valiant BT 13A—Macon Georgia
3. Harvard AT 6A—Dothan Alabama

Roy on extreme right with some of his crew on their Halifax bomber (circa 1943).

Roy's favourite aircraft Sierra-Sue. This aircraft was list over Berlin in January 1944 with another crew, (all killed).

The Halifaxes of 427 Squadron trundling out for take-off. Yet another raid on Germany (circa 1943, Leeming, Yorkshire).

When his Halifax exploded, Roy's body was thrown forwards out of the aircraft to the position indicated in the picture.

Some of the villagers in Beuren. Mathilde Becker (now Hemmes) in front, on right with black hat, discovered Roy's body on the snow. The crew were buried by the grave digger, standing alongside (with stick).

Ludger Schattel who acted as the author's interpreter in Beuren (February 1984).

The penultimate resting place of Roy and his crew. At the end of the war, they were re-intereed in the Cologne military Cemetery.

The Honours Board at Tonypandy grammar School (now a Community College). Roy's name, JRG Milton, is second from top (the G has been omitted).

The Author's Great Uncle H.H. Evans, wears the Edward Medal for his heroism in rescuing miners in a pit explosion in 1910. (This picture courtesy of the National Library of Wales, Aberstwayth).

John Victor Evans, son of H.H. Evans above, left Oxford University in his first year and took a commission in the Royal Welch fusiliers at the outbreak of World War I. He served for 3½ years in Mesopotamia and France, before suffering gas poisoning on the Western front. In 1922 he became the President of the Oxford Union.

My beautiful valley home (the absence of cars indicate that this picture was taken in the early 1930's). Pontrhondda primary school is on the right of the picture.
(see shelter in playground, backing on to the allotments.)
(marked with an X)

'Springwood' Hyde Park, New York
The birthplace and home of Franklin Delano Roosevelt (America's 32nd President). The author (far right) is in conversation with an American friend, waiting for the guided tour to begin.

CHAPTER 9

BEATLE FLYING, RACING CARS, FLYING FISH AND SUNKEN TREASURE

As soon as my head touched the pillow it seemed that the telephone at the side of my bed started ringing. It was Jim, a flying instructor at Fairoaks airfield, "John we have a very important charter booked for tonight, a VIP," he said. I glanced at my watch, it was just passed eleven o'clock, "Goodnight Jim", I said, "I'm very tired and anyway I'm outside my flying duty hours." I put down the telephone pulled the blanket over me when the telephone rang again. This time it was Brett, my co-pilot, "John we have a VIP for this charter tonight". I interrupted him and shouted, "Brett I'm in bed, I'm tired its past eleven o'clock, goodnight!" I slammed down the telephone. A third time it rang, again it was Brett, "John please listen, our VIPs are John Lennon and Yoko Ono." "For Christ sake Brett the only VIP on my aircraft is me", I shouted. "Please John, we can't really afford to turn this charter down, and the people are waiting at Gatwick Airport!" "Christ can't a guy get any sleep", I muttered. "OK", I said finally giving in, "I'll meet you at the airport at 1145."

It was April 1971 and I was living as one of the inmates in a rather grand old house in Woking Surrey. I had recently left Westward Airways and joined Brymon Aviation Ltd at Fairoaks Airport. I had spent the first three to four months glued to a desk preparing the manuals for submission to the Civil Aviation Authority for the company's Air Operators Certificate. Two days before the VIP charter with Lennon and Co, Brett and I had flown an empty aircraft to Liverpool Airport to load a ship's generator and fly it to Bremen, where a large ship was stranded waiting for this essential part. Brett and I landed at Liverpool at 0950 hours expecting to be airborne again for Bremen within the hour, however, I had not taken the British workman into account. When the generator eventually arrived at the airport it was encased in a large wooden frame. Four workmen struggled to lift it into the aircraft through the large cargo door without success. Just one look at it and it was clear to me that the crate was too large for the door, but the workmen had a combined IQ about fifty points lower than that of a not too agile minded orang-utan, and failed to see the obvious. Ever practical I suggested that they use the ever-present hammer and knock out a couple of planks of the crate. This they refused to do on the grounds of demarcation. Apparently it needed a carpenter to be brought on scene for such a delicate operation. As I was aware that the weather was deteriorating over the North Sea, I was eager to be off, so I was brazen enough to suggest that I use the hammer myself. This appalling suggestion was viewed with horror, and all work stopped forthwith. "There'd be a strike if we allowed you to do that", said the leader of the group, echoed simultaneously by his mates. Eventually a carpenter was found and the crate placed in the fuselage and tied down to my satisfaction. The last thing I wanted was a ton weight of generator moving about in the back of the aircraft in a thunderstorm, which looked from the weather forecast to be a distinct possibility. Four hours after arrival at Liverpool airport GAXXJ departed on the first leg to Amsterdam. After a fifty minute refuelling stop we crossed the Zuider Zee and landed at Bremen at 1830, the weather proving much better than forecast. No sooner had we parked the aircraft than two burley German workers in soft boots, white overalls and helmets with attached lights were on board, and within twenty minutes the generator has been whisked away en-route to the local docks. The comparison between the British worker and his German counterpart was all too evident. 'how did they ever lose the war?' I thought. Brett and I entered the hotel dining room later that evening absolutely ravenous. We had been on duty over twelve hours without a bite of food. The room was almost empty and the waiter was obviously displeased at out appearance. He spoke no English and the menu was written in German only. I took out my English-German phrase book and opened it on the table. The first phrase that took the eye was somewhat lunatic, but what the hell I thought so in my best German I said, "Fetch me a policeman I've been struck by lightening". The result could not have been visualised, as the rather strait-laced waiter fell about consumed with laughter. In matter of seconds he clearly had a brainstorm and miraculously could now speak English without blemish, Brett and I ordered and enjoyed a superb meal. Later the next day we arrived in Gatwick and I returned to Woking later the same evening. I had just gone to bed when the telephone began its insistent ringing about the Lennon charter.

At twenty minutes after midnight on the 18th April 1971, I flew the aircraft off the concrete taxiway of Fairoaks Airfield without the help of any external lighting. The Gatwick controller querulously questioned our departure airfield, as Fairoaks had been closed over six hours. I left Brett to arrange the aircraft refuelling and to file the flight plan to Jersey as Bordeaux our destination airport was fogged out. I wandered into the Terminal Building to search for our nocturnal passengers. Today, Gatwick is a thriving airport, utilised on a twenty-four hour basis with crowds of people arriving and departing at all hours and sleeping in any available space. In 1971 however it was very different and few people were to be seen at that time of the morning. A small group were standing near the Information Desk, and as I approached, one of them wearing strange clothes and a funny hat came to meet me. I instantly recognised the well known face of John Lennon the famous Beatle. "You must be our Captain," he said pleasantly. "Perhaps," I said, "but who are you?" This caused him to roar with laughter. "You will have to excuse these clothes, I wore them in the 'Yellow Submarine'." "Good Lord," I said, "I had no idea you had been a sub-mariner." This caused another loud peal of laughter. (I honestly had never heard of the film The Yellow Submarine). From that moment on our relationship became a friendly, informal and a happy one. I have often been asked my views on John Lennon having spent almost a week in his company. Despite the fact that he had become an icon in the popular music industry and achieved world-wide fame he appeared to me to be totally natural, unspoilt and a really nice guy. I was horrified when I heard of his murder in New York in 1980.

At 0235 hours I lifted XJ into the night sky over Gatwick. There was a complete absence of cloud and the visibility excellent. Crossing Southampton Water I could see the English coastal towns stretching into the distance. The voice of London Airways controller now disturbed the tranquillity of the moment. "XJ what time is Jersey open this morning?" It had been my impression that Jersey remained open on a twenty-four hour basis, and I stared across at Brett whose job it had been to check this out. His silence on the matter had convinced me that the airport was indeed open. "I thought it was open 24 hours", was my hopeful reply. "I'll check," said the controller as once more silence reigned. A few minutes he called again, "Jersey does not open until 0530 hours local time." "Thank you sir," I replied, "we'll just continue on our way." Jersey was normally a forty minute flight and now I had the choice of slowing up and continuing, or returning to Gatwick and having my passengers wait around. I made the correct decision and reduced the power slowering the aircraft to a plodding ninety knots. When we arrived at the island, I commenced a slow and deliberate circuit around the coastline. "Brett," I said, "you have control I'm grabbing some sleep," and I pulled my coat tight around me, stretching out in my seat and closed my eyes. It seemed only minutes when Brett nudged me awake, "Lennon's manager wants to talk to you," he said. I turned in my seat to listen to what he had to say. "Captain, I seem to have seen that lighthouse down there a few times in the last hour." "Absolutely correct Sir," I replied, "The airport doesn't open until 0530, (it was now 0330 hours), and we are circling the island, but we'll be the first aircraft to land." "Thank you Captain, I thought I'd better ask." At 0530 we heard the newspaper flight calling up from 50 degrees North, but I ensured that XJ touched down first. As we left the aircraft I was amazed at the growing crowd, clearly not there to greet me, but how they could have known that Lennon was arriving at that hour completely foxed me. The Bordeaux weather remained unchanged so I suggested breakfast at the Airport Hotel and a short rest over until the fog at Bordeaux Airport lifted. The flight from Gatwick to Jersey, normally around forty-five minutes had taken just over three hours. Fortunately however, there were no complaints from the customers.

The flight to Bordeaux was uneventful and we touched down at 1100 hours. Brett and I bunked down at the Airport Hotel fully expecting to return to Gatwick the next day. When the call came however, it was to continue the flight to Palma Majorca. At Montpelier, our intermediate refuelling stop, John Lennon approached me, "Captain how much does an aircraft like this cost?" he asked. Thinking he was about to make an offer I replied, "about £17,500, give or take a bit depending on its equipment," said I. Then a minor shock to my system when Lennon said, "How would you like to fly as my personal pilot?" My answer was strictly business like, "Well it would depend on the conditions of contract," I said smiling. There the matter seemed to die a natural death and no more was said during our remaining days together. I am sure that Lennon and Yoko were preoccupied with more important matters, as soon we were to discover. We arrived in Palma at 1925 hours and stayed in a hotel down town, while Lennon and Co. travelled to somewhere on the other side of the island.

The lights went out as soon as my head touched the pillow and I blissfully spent the following day in the sun. Not having heard from our flying companions we indulged ourselves the second night. I was still tired however, and was pleased to say goodbye to my female companion of the evening, while Brett's companion was easily persuaded to retire with him to his room. I had been on the road for nearly three days, so before I went to bed, I busily scrubbed my only two drip-dry nylon shirts and hung them in the bathroom to dry. I was asleep by 2300 hours, but my rest was rudely disturbed shortly before midnight by the shrill ring of the telephone. Could I be at the airport as soon as possible as the illustrious group wished to be flown to somewhere in North Africa? Sadly I had to disturb young Brett who by this time was busy exercising his manly privileges. "Sorry Brett," I said, "but we have to be at the airport in thirty minutes, see you downstairs in ten!" A series of wild oaths was his only reply. Carefully I squeezed my two shirts as dry as possible, wrapped them in paper and put them in my flight bag. There was no possible way I could wear them in the state that they were in. I put my uniform and coat over my pyjamas and with Brett was soon en-route by cab to the airport. Just like Gatwick, Palma Airport was almost devoid of passengers in the early hours and I soon spotted my group sitting disconsolately at the far end of the terminal. They looked a sorry sight, like a bunch of refugees. Lennon insisted on an apology for our late call up. "You see, John, we came here to kidnap Yoko's child by her first marriage," I couldn't focus on the remainder of his apology. Kidnap kids in Spain I thought, to which unwittingly I would have been seen as a willing accomplice. I had heard sufficient stories about Spanish prisons, and had no desire to learn more, particularly at first hand.

Tetuan in North Africa seemed to be favoured this early morning, so Brett and I rushed to flight plan, fuel the aircraft and check the weather. With these tasks almost completed, Lennon's manager arrived on the scene and informed me that the destination had now changed to Monte

Carlo. The process of preparation was now re-started and almost at the same time we completed our tasks, up came the manager once more and changed the destination to Madrid. My temper now snapped, "Look," I said, "if you bloody change the destination once more, you can fly the bloody aircraft yourself, I'm going back to bed." My outburst seemed to do the trick and at 0205 hours on the morning of 22nd April, XJ winged across the Mediterranean crossing the coast at Valencia and arriving at Barajas Airport, Madrid at 0440 hours. Once again Lennon and his group disappeared into the hinterland, while Brett and I rested our weary limbs at the Airport Hotel. I had never flown in my pyjamas before, and I never was to again, but at least I had saved the occasion to carry a famous Beatle.

Later I was to find out what really happened in Majorca the previous day. One paper described the events as follows:—

Lennons Questioned in Spain

By our Madrid Correspondent

Spanish police in Majorca escorted Beatle John Lennon and his wife Yoko Ono to a magistrate's court yesterday for questioning over Yoko's daughter Kioco who is seven.

Court sources said the couple were taken to the Magistrate, after the girl's American father, Anthony Cox, filed a complaint to police that she had disappeared from a playground.

Police went to the Melia-Mallorca Hotel and found Kioca with her mother and Lennon. All three were taken to court.

Lennon, asked if he had been arrested, said late last night, "No not exactly. I am trying to sort out this mess. I'm contacting a lawyer to help me."

Early today, police said that Lennon was still at the court.

The Lennons arrived in Madrid two days ago by *private aircraft* (my underlining). Later Lennon sporting a normal haircut flew with his wife on a scheduled flight to Majorca.

Next morning we were asked to be at the Airport at 1000 hours to fly the Lennon group back to Majorca. Lennon's arrival seemed to have drawn out all the teenage kids from Madrid and many others beside. Now I received a nasty shock when the Airport Director refused us permission to fly our aircraft back to Majorca. His argument was that as a Public Transport Operation we could not undertake the flight as Iberia, the national airline, held the sole rights of passage. I then argued, "Well we are not a public transport flight (which we were), but a private flight." The Director simply replied that no private flights were allowed to fly to Majorca either! As a final gesture I informed the Director and his cohorts that my grandfather had fought in the Spanish Civil War for Spanish freedom, however I didn't say on which side. This remark, which was false anyway, was met with a stony silence. Beaten but unbowed I returned to the Terminal Building and informed Lennon of the situation. He graciously thanked me for my services, we shook hands and Brett and I, together with Lennon's transport manager, returned via Bordeaux to Gatwick, and the remainder of the Lennon group caught a scheduled Iberia flight back to Majorca. I never saw John Lennon again but the trip had been fun, and he had been a pleasant unassuming travel companion. I am pleased today that Liverpool Airport has been renamed Liverpool John Lennon Airport, a richly deserved honour.

The charter flights described above were among the first conducted under the newly formed Brymon Aviation Ltd, a company set up by two New Zealanders Bill Bryce and Chris Amon, at Thruxton, Hampshire, later moving to Fairoaks Airport near Woking, Surrey. It was the amalgamation of the names Bryce and Amon which gave rise to the name Brymon. Bill was an excellent salesman and Chris a Grand Prix driver with Matra-Simca at that time. They operated a flight school with new Cessna light aircraft for which they held a franchise together with an aircraft sales company. They had purchased a Britten Norman Islander (BN2) essentially to operate public transport flights, only to realise rather late in the day that to do this they needed an Air Operator's Certificate (AOC) granted by the Civil Aviation Authority. I walked into this situation having been flying out of nearby Gatwick. The AOC presented few problems and I was aided and abetted by my Civil Aviation Flight Inspector, Captain Mike Lewis, who had been my Chief Pilot in a previous post with Emerald Airways in Belfast.

On the 30th April I took a charter to Nantes in Brittany from Gatwick, carrying a so-called wine party. As they boarded the aircraft, I informed them that there was no toilet aboard and that the flight would take roughly 2½ hours to complete. Flying at 6,000 feet between Jersey and the French mainland, Brett nudged me with his elbow his eyes as large as saucers. "You won't believe this," he said, "but the woman behind you is pissing into a Champagne bottle." "Well tell her that the Captain doesn't drink the stuff, just in-case she asks," I replied. After landing, we found that a few gentlemen had urinated over the seats and on the floor, and a number of bottles full of warm urine had been left behind for us to clear up. I turned to Brett and told him that he would find me in the airport restaurant when he had finished. "What do you want me to do?" he asked naively. "Just clean out the aircraft," I said, "after all it is the co-pilot's privilege after every flight." Brett's answer was muted but also unprintable.

Under the terms of the Air Operator's Certificate, a minimum of two pilots had to be listed, and Bryce had pushed Brett in my direction and I had accepted. Unknown to me, he had put up a few 'blacks' at Fairoaks where he worked as an Assistant Flying Instructor. Once, he had submerged an aircraft undercarriage by taxiing on to a waterlogged and forbidden part of the airfield, and on another occasion, had opened up the engine on an aircraft, which had its tail in the hanger, blowing down a tall ladder. Unfortunately, an engineer happened to be sitting on the top of it working at the time! No harm came to him however, but Brett had invoked the wrath of the airport owner, who wished him banned from the airport. Much persuasion apparently had been needed to keep him in his job. Brett was a quiet likeable chap, a product of a privileged background and a public school education. Why the English persist in calling the private school system a public one defeats me, as the general public could never afford to pay the fees. Today these schools euphemistically like to call themselves Independent, but even that is debatable. As I had accepted Brett, warts and all, I received an invitation for dinner at his family home, a large attractive house in Ascot. I sat at the dinner table, beautifully prepared with Brett, his mother and father, and had just commenced the main course. The peas were somewhat small and hard, and I had just managed to place a few on my fork precariously balanced in the air and poised to enter my mouth, when his mother farted loudly and unambiguously. My peas flew high into the air, but the family continued their meal completely unabashed, as if this was the most commonplace and natural thing to do at meal times. How I controlled myself in the ensuing moments remained a mystery, but I bent over my plate, my eyes down and did my utmost to control my shaking limbs. I thought back to my Sunday afternoon's chapel in Wales as a boy, when one or more of our group would release silent farts. Mr Lewis, our Sunday School teacher, a large man with powerful hands had a well developed nose for these occasions, and he would grip your leg just above the knee and squeeze until you almost screamed an apology, then he would say, "Go outside, boy, and shake yourself!"

The next charter was the longest I ever undertook in my flying career and involved flying forty road tyres from Birmingham to Palermo in Sicily for the 44.39 mile Targa Florio road race, in the Italian 'Competizione

Automobilistica Internazionale Di Velocita'. This was the 55th Anniversary of this exciting road race, and as fate would have it, the last one. The aircraft was at maximum weight which reduced our range, so I planned refuelling stops to Bournemouth (Hurn) Airport, Jersey in the Channel Islands and Clermont Ferrand and Marseille in France, where we night-stopped. The following day, the 12th of May, we flew across the Mediterranean to Palermo in Sicily having stopped to refuel at Ajaccio on the island of Corsica. The difficult period of the flight occurred between Clermont Ferrand and Marseille, when were flying at our maximum height of 10,000 feet in thick cloud at night. Brett was flying the aircraft, when his shout of alarm disturbed my short nap. "Look at the speed," he cried, it had fallen from 135 knots very quickly to 90 knots, which at that weight was not far above the stall. All the instrument readings were fine, but one look outside at the landing wheel and wing strut told the full story. We were a flying 'Christmas tree' with a thick coating of ice. The highest ground beneath us was 8,900 feet and therefore we had no margin to descend, as we would not reach lower ground for a further 45 minutes flying time when we reached Montelimar, and it was only then that I could contemplate a descent to break clear of the ice. We both knew therefore that an engine failure in the intervening period meant 'curtains' for us, as the maximum ceiling we could maintain at that weight and temperature was about 5,200 feet on one engine. I nursed the aircraft for the next hour with Brett operating the hot air to the engine carburettors, until with a collective sigh of relief we were able to commence a descent to Marseilles and the warmer Mediterranean air. Ice was still falling off the aircraft as we taxied into our stand.

After our landing at Palermo we journeyed by car to the small town of Cefalu, also on the north coast of the island where we were to stay until the race had been completed on the 16th May. In the hotel I met Joe Bonnier, the famous Swiss racing driver, and it was only then I discovered that the tyres I had flown down were for his racing team. The next day he asked

Brett and I to join him in a circuit of the famous race track. Up to that point in my life, my concept of car racing, gleaned from my childhood, was of cars racing endlessly around a figure of eight racing circuit until one was declared the winner. I climbed into the car with Joe and we began climbing higher and higher up into the Sicilian Mountains. I expected naively to see the racing stadium entrance appearing before me at any moment. Now Joe began hurling the Fiat car around 'S' Bends and blind corners at 80 mph or more with sheer and vertical drops of 3,000 feet or more bordering the narrow road. I began to be seriously concerned, as this was certainly not any idea of an afternoon out. "When do we get to the track Joe?" I asked. "This is the track," he replied, defying death on another impossible corner. "Look Joe," I pleaded, "just let me out here and I'll walk the rest of the way." He burst into laughter at this and told me that the track went on for a further twenty-five miles or more. I gritted my teeth, hung on to a strap and sat it out bravely. To my credit, my trousers remained unstained, although I have to say the margin was very small. The thrills I ever really needed in my life came with flying, so when the great day of the race arrived, I resorted to the pleasures of the hotel swimming pool, and relaxed. When Brett and I did the pre-flight checks, prior to departure from Palermo, I noticed several tufts of grass protruding from the port engine propeller boss. Brett began pulling and continued pulling until a large pile of grass lay on the ground. He then put his hands into the interior of the boss and gently pulled out three or four bird's eggs of varying colours. Our last act of humanity before leaving was to rebuild the nest in the nearby hedge and replace the eggs. I fervently hoped the mother would soon return and find her chicks unharmed.

Many charter flights followed and we traversed the land, visiting Birmingham, Prestwick, Belfast, Paris Beauvais, London Heathrow and Jersey, and then repeated the sequence. We carried some bigwigs of the racing car fraternity from Gatwick to Le Mans for the twenty-four hour race. As I had a few spare seats, I took along Richard, who rented an adjacent room to mine in the large house in Woking. Richard in my view had two major problems. He always appeared as a picture of impeccable sartorial elegance. In fact I do believe he mowed the lawn dressed in waistcoat and cravat! Secondly, he loved his ordinary run of the mill motor car with a passion beyond human belief. I had recently purchased a Ford Consul for five pounds from a hard-up colleague at Gatwick. It was certainly in a dreadful state with a heater that only seemed to come to life in the summer and switched off completely at the first suggestion of winter. The windows would not shut and I dared anybody who might want to steal it. The engine, however, ran beautifully, just like the old Singer sewing machine, rarely missing a beat. When I arrived at my Woking lodgings with my new acquisition, Richard was so appalled he formally resisted any notion that I was a well paid pilot, in fact he didn't believe I was a pilot at all, such is the male snobbery and affection for motor cars. When I asked him whether he would like to accompany me to Le Mans, he could hardly refrain from sniggering. After much persuasion and a visit to our base at Fairoaks he finally realised that I was on the level and consented to come. On the 12th June 1971 we crossed the English Channel, hugging the valleys between towering clouds with their embedded cumulus nimbus. The static in my head set was almost par for the course, but Richard sitting next to me in the co-pilots seat seemed in some distress.

"What's the matter Richard?" I asked.

"It's the static, its really hurting my ears," he said.

"Well put some paper in it," I replied nonchalantly. After landing at Le Mans I saw the passengers away then saw Richard totter around the tail of the aircraft.

"What's the matter now Richard?" I asked.

"I've got paper in my ear," he replied.

"Well bloody well pull it out!" I retorted unsympathetically.

"I can't, can you do it?" I looked into his ear but couldn't see any sign of the offending paper.

"Why did you stuff paper in your ear Richard?" I asked.

"Well you told me," he moaned.

"Rubbish I told you to put paper in your headset, not your ear. Never mind we'll sort it out when we get to the hotel." Jackie Stewart's team had booked the hotel accommodation for us, and when we arrived, I steered Richard directly to the bar, thinking a few drinks might help to obliterate his pain. Unknown to me he had a very low tolerance for alcohol and after the first tall glass of Pernod had disappeared, his face took on a completely new look of peaceful solemnity. After a second glass he began to look as if he were heartily pleased with life. The third glass of Pernod went down at an amazing speed, his face taking on a beatific smile as he slid gently off his stool onto the floor. The French waiters paid scant attention to this development and gingerly stepped over him as they moved about their business.

The lounge door suddenly opened and a noisy bunch of Brits entered the room. "What's wrong with him?" they asked, looking at Richard. "Oh he's OK," I said, "he's just got paper stuck in his ear." The Brits burst into loud laughter, but one of the group took me seriously and identified himself as a doctor. "One moment, I'll fetch my bag from the car," he said. Despite his best efforts with a pair of forceps he failed to disturb the paper, and I was faced with putting Richard to bed in his stricken state. At the top of the stairs Richard was trying to open his bedroom door by sticking his key in an illusory keyhole about a foot from the floor. Laughing madly I bent to help him up to a standing position, took a step back and fell backwards down the stairs. Fortunately my alcohol intake had sufficiently relaxed my body and no serious injury ensued, but I ached all over for a week.

The following day after our arrival at Fairoaks Airfield I drove Richard to the out patients department of Woking Hospital and as we entered unannounced we met a large coloured nurse in the corridor. "Can I help you?" she said. "It's my friend here, he needs help," I said pointing to Richard, who was still in a half stupor and pained condition. "What's the matter with him?" she asked. "Oh he's got paper in his ear," I said, waiting for the inevitable giggle, which was not forthcoming. "Well come this way," she said, and led Richard away. Within minutes Richard returned triumphantly holding the piece of paper in his hand. As I told him later some people just have to learn the hard way!

Playing snooker with Richard and the Major, (a retired army officer living in the same lodgings), at the Woking Conservative Club did nothing to satisfy the demands of my more creative urges. I became restless and clearly needed a change of work and scenery. The fisherman of Cornwall answered my call and I was asked to base our aircraft at Land's End Airport, to fly their catches of crawfish and lobster to France. Bill was at first reluctant to see his aircraft and pilots out of his sight but after a strident argument or two, he agreed. Bill was one of those chaps who seemed to relish conflict, perhaps the term 'a bloody good row' would be nearer the mark, and I often asked him when his parents were going to marry. However although he had a solid enough business sense, trust was not a term normally associated with him. Before we left for Land's End however, I nearly came to grief in the most unsuspecting manner. A British Airways Trident Captain came along and asked to be trained on the Islander aircraft. As his retirement from BA was approaching he sought an Islander endorsement on his licence, in order that he could continue flying in general aviation when he left the company. Now the Islander is a very easy aircraft to fly and landing it is a fairly innocuous event. As a seasoned CAA approved Instrument and Type Rating Examiner myself, I assumed that the conversion would be totally trouble free. To practise circuits and landings, we flew to Bournemouth (Hurn) Airport where we virtually had the circuit to ourselves. None of his landings could be described as good, but at least they were safe. We completed eight approaches and landings on one and two engines, then taxied in to enjoy a coffee or two before returning for the night detail. We now repeated the same routine on a perfectly clear night with little wind. Once more the landings were rough but safe, and I, anticipating the completion of the detail, relaxed a little, sat back and told him to complete a final circuit and landing. The circuit and approach were perfect, but his round-out for landing was almost 30 feet too high. I was about to tell him to overshoot, when unexpectedly he closed both throttles and the aircraft just fell out of the sky! I rammed both throttles forward against the stop to arrest the free fall, but it was too late. We hit with a force that physically hurt me, snapping my wrist watch chain and hurtling the watch somewhere into the dark recesses of the aircraft. The reaction from the BA pilot amazed me. His pride had been sorely dented and he screamed a volume of invective, which I would never have believed possible from a rational man. He "didn't want to fly the fucking aircraft", and so it went on. I taxied the aircraft in very slowly, feeling almost as embarrassed as he certainly was, but lost for words and in a semi-shocked state. When I examined the external surfaces of the aircraft I was amazed to find no wrinkling of the external surfaces. In fact I could discern no external sign of damage at all. Later, when the engineers checked the aircraft in detail, they gave it a clean bill of health. For me that was a minor miracle and merely supported my long held view that the Islander was indeed a superb aircraft. Indeed after flying the type for over 4,000 hours I never had cause to change my mind. The BA captain apologised to me later for his behaviour, and following the events of that night finally decided that general aviation was not for him. A few years later he retired gracefully from the airline business after 15,000 hours of accident free flying.

It was July 3rd 1971 when I eventually flew Islander GAXXJ from Fairoaks to Land's End Airfield to renew my acquaintance with the West Country. I had always felt a remarkable attachment to the area, following my early days with Cormorant. There appeared to be a magic flying there, which defied description and logic. It was almost like entering a time warp, when the rest of the country didn't seem to exist. Pleasure flying around Land's End and the fifteen minute hops to the Isles of Scilly were now the order of the day, interspersed with fish carrying flights, first to Quimper and later to Brest in Brittany. The fish lorry would arrive from Penzance and the lads would load the corrugated cardboard boxes aboard the aircraft. The aircraft tended to cube out before it weighed out (fill-up by volume before it was overweight), but nevertheless we usually loaded about a ton and a half of fish. I flew the first fish flight on the 9th of July and climbed to 7,000 feet to avoid some nasty looking weather. On arrival at Quimper, a refrigerated lorry arrived and the fish were soon away to be introduced to the restaurants in the Bay of Audierne. I was met on my return by the chairman of the Penzance group of fishermen, who casually asked me at what height I had flown the fish to France. When I told him 7,000 feet he nearly burst a blood vessel. "Don't you know you may have killed all the fish?" he said. Totally mystified I told him that I had considered the fish dead when they had been put in their boxes. He slowly explained the process, that the fish were kept alive by surrounding them in ice whilst in transit. Clearly I had been somewhat unfair to expect fish, usually quite happy on the seabed, to be equally happy at altitude! From that moment on, I flew them at the lowest possible height commensurate with the weather. Happily it transpired I had only killed twelve fish on my first outing, but at least I had saved them from the pot. Months later when Brett and I shared a cottage in Cornwall for a short time, he brought home a lobster for dinner. When he dunked it into a pot of boiling water I heard the fish "scream", albeit faintly. From that moment on, I decided that since I couldn't replicate life then I had no right to take it. I may be called squeamish but that's the way it was and has remained!

Land's End airfield, near the town of St. Just, is subject to clammy sea fogs, and on such a morning Brett and I motored into nearby Penzance, ostensibly to visit a number of used book shops. That morning, the 24th August, I was very lucky in obtaining two first editions. The first was 'The Turn of the Tide' by Arthur Bryant, based on the War Diaries of Field Marshal Viscount Alanbrooke, and the second 'Crusade in Europe' by General Dwight D Eisenhower. Extremely pleased with myself, with my books under my arm, I climbed out of the car at the airfield and crossed the tarmac to my office near the old Terminal Building. As I passed near the aircraft I was approached by an army captain. "Are you flying to the Scillies this afternoon?" he asked. As the fog had now started lifting I replied that I would indeed be going. "Would you have seats for me and my three sergeants?" "Yes of course." I replied, adding that we would be taking-off around 1400 hours. "How much are the tickets then?" he asked. "Ten pounds for the four of you." I replied. "Will you take a cheque?" "Well," I said, "you look honest enough." We both laughed and walked to the tail of the aircraft where he wrote out the cheque, which I merely thrust into my pocket and then walked across to the office. As I put the books down on the table, the book 'The Turn of the Tide' fell open displaying the portrait of Field Marshal Viscount Alanbrooke. I quickly discerned the resemblance between the Field Marshal and the army captain outside. I took the cheque out of my pocket and saw that it was signed 'the Hon Brooke'. It was too much of a coincidence to be true, so I walked out and found him still standing near the aircraft. No sense in messing about, its not my style anyway, so I came straight to the point. "Are you related to Field Marshal Viscount Alanbrooke?" I asked. "Damn clever of you to notice the resemblance," he said. Needless to say he sat, by request, in the co-pilot's seat to the Scillies that afternoon and we became firm friends thereafter. In succeeding years he often stayed at my home in Cornwall and flew with me on all our routes. Later he became the godfather to my two children, Sian and Gavin, and how they loved him. More than a wee bit eccentric, he would drive them around in his old and battered three wheeled Morgan car, and sit with me into the early hours discussing the war, his father and other generals. At my children's Christening he wore his father's 1952 suit, and odd socks, a characteristic that I share with him to this day.

There appeared to be considerable secrecy surrounding our next charter. We were to fly as cargo, artefacts from a sunken wreck off the Isles of Scilly to London Heathrow Airport, to be sold at auction in London by Sotheby and Co. The name of the ship, the 'Hollandia', and the nature of the cargo were unknown to me at that time, and it was many years later before I discovered the full facts. The 'Hollandia' had been built in the yard of the Dutch East India Company in Amsterdam in 1742. She sailed on her maiden voyage on the 3rd July 1743 under the command of Captain Jan Kelder, and was reputed to be carrying some 129,700 guilders in silver. She left Texel for Batavia (modern Jakarta), and ten days later the ship struck the Gunnar Rock in Broad Sound off St. Agnes Island, Isles of Scilly, in the early hours of the 13th July 1743, with complete loss of life. Brett and I had stayed on the Scillies the weekend prior to the charter, and in my mind I had linked the charter cargo to the sinking of the English fleet under its naval commander, Sir Cloudesley-Shovel, on the Western Isles of Scilly in 1707. In this, of course, I was completely wrong.

It had rained on the Sunday evening, and on the following day, Monday 17th January 1972, Brett and I were ready at the airport for a 0945 hours take-off. Because the weather appeared to be indifferent in the London area, I took it upon myself to visit Air Traffic Control in the tower to check the meteorological actuals and forecasts for the various airports, and put in the flight plan. This left Brett to see to the loading of the cargo, and check its weight and distribution, in completing the 'Load and Trim sheet'. When I returned to the aircraft, I met Rex Cowan, the expedition leader of the diving team, who had discovered the 'Hollandia'. He was already sitting in the aircraft, together with two of his associates, and with the cargo loaded we were ready for departure. When I opened the throttles to taxi out, the aircraft seemed very reluctant to move, and I turned to look at Brett and queried the weight. He confirmed that the aircraft was at its maximum all up weight, so I attributed the problem to that and the fact that the grass was sodden wet. I chose runway 13, the longest runway (600 metres, all grass), for take-off, and taxied to its very end, before running up the engines and checking all the instruments. The acceleration was painfully slow, and by the time we had reached the high point of the runway (the Isles of Scilly airfield is shaped like an inverted saucer), I instinctively knew that the aircraft wouldn't make it. I therefore braked hard, cursed madly, and managed to stop in the remaining distance. Once more I taxied back to the end of the runway, and this time revved-up to full throttle against the brakes, letting the aircraft shudder in anticipation, before it began its chase for flight. As we passed the high point of the runway, we were barely at take-off speed, but this time I let her go, until near the cliff edge I coaxed her gently into the air. The speed was still barely above stalling, so I lowered the nose towards the surface of the sea, and picked up a further ten knots. It took the next twenty-five miles, to Land's End, to make 2,000 feet, and a further twenty-five minutes to reach 5,000 feet, our assigned flight level. A full thirty years was to pass before I discovered that the poor aircraft had been in excess of a ton overweight that morning, and it had been something of a miracle that we had made it. Possibly in the secrecy of the moment, and the rush to depart that morning, the weights had been confused; perhaps even that pounds weight had been inadvertently substituted for kilos. Two hours and ten minutes later, with Heathrow in fog, I diverted to Biggin Hill airport in Kent, having been able to inform Sotheby's of our change of plan. Consequently, they were already on the apron, waiting to meet us with their security guards and vans when we arrived. This whole episode had strangely slipped my mind until I was reminded of it by a former Brymon colleague late in 2003. By telephoning friends on the Scillies, I was able to re-establish contact with Rex Cowan, and speak to him for the first time since we had parted company at Biggin Hill that day in 1972. His memories of that flight, and particularly the take-off, remained vivid, and he described them to me in has own words as follows:—

> **On 18th September 1971 the wreck of the Dutch East Indian 'Hollandia' was discovered after a three year search by a team of divers directed by Rex Cowan and led by Lt. Cdr Jack Gayton. Much treasure was discovered. This, consisted mainly of Mexican pieces or coins of 8 reales, known as pillar dollars, and Dutch ducatons. These were to be shared between Rex Cowan, the divers and the Dutch Government. It was decided to nominate Sotheby's to auction the coins in London and New York.**
>
> **The coins were held in a safe deposit at Lloyds Bank in St. Mary's the Isle of Scilly. They had been smuggled into the bank during the week in shopping baskets covered with conflake boxes in the interests of security. For that same reason it was decided to charter a plane from Brymon in a nominee name to fly the treasure from Scilly to Heathrow where the Sotheby representatives would take charge of it.**
>
> **The charter plane arrived the weekend before the 17th January 1972. Parked on the airfield it rather dented our cover, causing speculation amongst the islanders. On the morning of the 17th Lloyds Bank opened its doors at crack of dawn and the bags and boxes of silver coins, around 25,000 were driven up to the airfield. It was a rainy overcast day. To conceal the nature of the cargo, the airline was told that six passengers with luggage was to embark. In fact, the original plan was for two passengers, Rex Cowan and the archaeologist**

Peter Marsden to accompany the treasure. When the coins arrived at the airport the bags, heavy and dense were loaded in to the rear of the aircraft—but at the last minute a third passenger, Noel Pearce a former Naval Petty Officer and ship's diver, decided to go along. That added weight to the plane.

The plane taxied for take off onto the grass runway. It was wet. Almost at the end of the runway at full power I noticed that it had not reached its rotation speed. I took a deep breath. The pilot of course aborted the take-off and returned to the apron. I believe he thought it was mainly due to slippage on the wet grass. He tried again. This time, my knuckles were white as the plane gained speed on the runway. I dared not look at the speedometer. It seemed to me that we were not going to take off—and indeed when we came to the end of the runway just over a cliff I thought we would crash into the sea—and the treasure and us would return to Davy Jones locker. But just as we left the runway the plane dipped, but gained lift just as it left the cliff—and off we (just about) took!!!!

During the flight, the weather closed in and the pilot decided to divert to Biggin Hill. A radio message got through to Sotheby's who raced to meet the plane as it landed.

CATALOGUE

OF

COINS
AND OTHER ARTIFACTS

INCLUDING CANNON, PEWTERWARE ETC.

RECOVERED FROM THE

WRECK OF THE DUTCH EAST-INDIAMAN

"HOLLANDIA"

(SUNK 1743)

SPECIAL EXHIBITION IN THE MAIN GALLERY FROM 5TH APRIL

WHICH WILL BE SOLD BY AUCTION BY

SOTHEBY & CO.

AFFILIATED COMPANY: PARKE-BERNET GALLERIES INC., NEW YORK

New York Representative: SOTHEBY'S OF LONDON LTD.
President: P. M. H. POLLEN

Auctioneers of Literary Property and Works illustrative of the Fine Arts

AT THEIR LARGE GALLERIES, 34-35 NEW BOND STREET, W1A 2AA
Telephone: 01-493 8080

Day of Sale:

TUESDAY, 18TH APRIL, 1972

AT 10.30 A.M. PRECISELY

On view Friday and Monday, prior to sale 10 a.m. - 4 p.m., or by previous appointment. (At the Coin Department, 3 St. George Street, 1st Floor)

1971/1972 No. 9

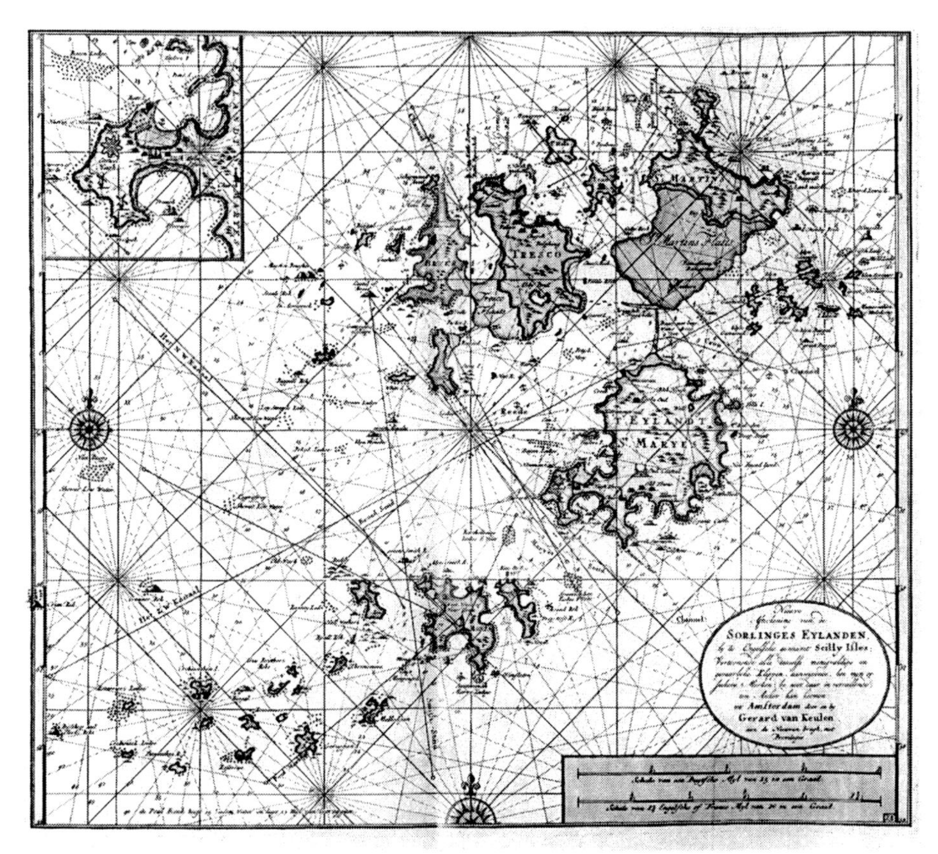

An early Dutch Sailing Map of the Isles of Scilly

I had now been informed by the CAA that, in their wisdom, they had appointed a new Flight Operational Inspector to oversee our operations. Soon Captain Jim Hengle arrived at Land's End, ostensibly to check-out our paperwork concerned with our Air Operator's Certificate and also to fly with Brett, who was in a complete funk about having a CAA official looking over his shoulder. They flew to the Isles of Scillies and returned later in the day, a total time of thirty minutes. I asked Jim what he thought of Brett's flying. "Oh, his flying is OK, but please show him how to switch on the radio!" It merely showed how human beings could be so irrational and nervous when under test.

The days of that summer were indeed glorious and on many occasions from the airfield I was able to see the Isles of Scilly just protruding above the horizon in the distance. Indeed the six months I spent at Land's End were among the happiest of my flying career, and so similar in many ways to my earlier days with Cormorant. Once more I controlled the day by day events, largely free from external pressure, breathing the wonderful Cornish air and living 'high on the hog' with Brett at Bosarven House near St. Just. Captain Jim Hengle now suggested that we move for the winter to a new base further up the coast at RAF St. Mawgan near Newquay. He felt that the winter weather at Land's End would make it almost impossible for us to continue our operation. I concurred with his reasoning, and by the beginning of December, with the permission of the Newquay Urban District Council, I had established a small office on the eastern side of the airport, from where we continued our fish flights to Quimper and Brest. Before leaving Land's End however, Brett and I had to conduct a charter flight from Shannon Airport on the west coast of Ireland. Here we were to pickup a load of crawfish and lobster and fly directly to Quimper. Although we arrived at Shannon early in the afternoon, there was no sign of the Irish fisherman and their load of fish. Hours passed and I sent Brett about the almost deserted airport in search of them. He found himself with his customary doziness inside the huge duty free store, which had been closed for hours. He extracted himself however, and eventually the fishermen arrived eight hours late without a hint of apology. We got airborne at 0415 hours in the morning and one and a half hours later crossed the tip of Land's End. It was indeed a magical moment for me, and the shallow clouds separated, as if on demand, and I saw Bosarven House and the small town of St. Just quite clearly in the early morning light. I looked across the cockpit and saw Brett's face, placid and concentrated as usual. Maybe it was my Celtic blood, but this for me, was the true 'witching hour'. This area of Land's End and the Isles of Scilly always held me in its thrall. It was indeed a kind of magic kingdom and I revelled in those moments.

I spent some six months or so at Land's End when I suddenly realised that something had been missing. Clearly it was the absence of the female of the species. Oh I had flirted with the waitresses in the restaurants in Penzance but that was all, my life fully occupied with the vagaries of the flying business. Brett on the other hand had met a young and beautiful university student, living on a farm almost directly opposite Bosarven House. Apart from her dark beauty she had a remarkably high intelligence, certainly too high for a lowly co-pilot. Brett was in her thrall however, and who could blame him for this temporary lapse into pottiness? To impress the lady he decided to buy his own private aircraft, a Champion Tri-Traveller, and went to Biggin Hill in Kent to conclude the purchase. It was eventually parked outside our offices at St. Mawgan with the full fury of the winter storms imminent. Unfortunately, his courtship with the lady soon petered out and with little appetite to fly his own aircraft, the poor thing remained outside in the wind and rain looking extremely forlorn. One Saturday I suggested that we fly to the Scillies. Brett as ever reluctant to fly it, left it to me and we spent an enjoyable day in the islands. The wind had now increased to over forty knots and we were back over St. Mawgan in forty minutes. The wind was even stronger there and its direction eighty degrees off the heading of the solitary runway. I landed the little aircraft almost across the main runway and obtained permission from Air Traffic for Brett to jump out and hang on to the in wind strut, otherwise it was almost certain that the aircraft would blow over onto its back. A sense of wickedness now overtook me and surreptitiously I slowly opened the throttle and the aircraft left the ground with Brett still hanging on the strut. The Air Traffic Controller must have had kittens when he saw Brett flying down the runway hanging on by his fingers to the aircraft for dear life! I gradually lowered him back to terra firma without harm, but the strut under Brett's weight developed a curious V shape. This was the final straw and within the space of a few weeks Brett had resold the aircraft back to its original owners.

CHAPTER 10

FLY THE BRYMON WAY

When Christmas 1972 arrived I took-off for Wales to see my parents, leaving Brett to guard the shop. He had now switched his affections to another sweet young thing living in Wadebridge, so he was happy to remain in Newquay over the holiday period. A few days later he telephoned me to say that I was to call BOAC Associated Companies at London Heathrow, who wished to interview me about a Training Captain vacancy in the Middle East. A successful interview followed and when I confronted Bill Bryce, the owner of Brymon, with the news he became somewhat emotional. "Christ John, you can't leave me now, . . . and how much money do you want to stay?" It was typical of Bill that he saw most things in terms of money. "Tell you what Bill," I said, "I'll start an airline down here in the southwest, run it and make it work." "Gee John all airlines loose money" protested Bill passionately, continuing in the same vein ad-nauseum. Bill loved to talk tough, and sometimes he would act tough, indeed at times I was sure that he shaved using a blowtorch. But I could act tough too, and endowed with a stubborn streak, I carried the argument on this occasion, he relenting, and agreeing to my proposition. We argued about the airline name for some time but eventually I conceded, and by 1973 it was called

Brymon Airways (we traded in 1972 as Brymon Aviation). Although my relationship with Bill would run, from very good to very bad, I have to say that he showed great courage in backing my idea and putting his money at risk. As most people are aware, the airline business is not without its risks, and there may be some truth in the old adage 'that to make a small fortune in the airline business you need to start with a large one!'

It had always been an ambition of mine to start an airline in my native Wales, but this opportunity in the southwest was a wonderful opportunity, and I intended taking it. Our first secretary suffered badly from body odour and I quickly discovered her inability to spell correctly, but an advertisement in the local Newquay paper brought forth a response I was looking for. I entered the empty office one morning just in time to answer the telephone before it rang-off. The well-modulated accentless voice said "Is the position of secretary still vacant?" Her name was Carin, a name I had only ever seen once before in the name in the name Carinhall*, the estate owned by Hitler's buddy Goring situated north of Berlin and named in memory of his wife. In this context I asked her was she German. "No," she said, "Karin (spelling it with a K) is a Swedish name, my mother being Swedish." I immediately pictured a beautiful blond Swedish girl so my response was immediate, "Come up and see me sometime!" I said and a few days later she did when I knew immediately that she was a serious departure from the norm, and was hired forthwith. She was an immediate, indeed a stunning success with our passengers, and better still laughed at nearly all my jokes. Within a year we were living together and without any conscious effort or planning on my part suddenly found myself the father of two bouncing babies, a girl Sian and a boy Gavin. I had been well and truly hooked, and within a short time actually began to enjoy the experience. The kids grew up good looking and intelligent and thereby, clearly following their mother.

* Carinhall was indeed spelt with a 'K' (Karinhall), after his Swedish wife.

There is a Biblical promise that the meek shall inherit the earth, however kids from my background tended generally to be far from meek, and I was certainly listed among that number. I was well prepared therefore to fight hard for any route we wished to operate. This of course was well before the 'Open Sky Policy' which operates today. In our case we found British European Airways Helicopters of Penzance objecting to our application to the Isles of Scilly, their case being presented by that formidable advocate Arnold Heard and his team. The Chairman of the Civil Aviation Board at the hearing was a Mr J.H. Lawrie a friendly but imposing figure. I had rounded up a collection of supporters from Plymouth, Newquay and the Isles of Scilly who would give evidence on our behalf, and the previous day I had flown them from the West Country to Biggin Hill in Kent, there we had been met by John Gardiner who was to represent us. We were briefed that night at our hotel in Bromley, and faced the following day's events with some confidence. The hearing took a serious and predictable route, that is until Joe took the stand. He was a larger than life character from the island of Bryher in the Scillies who had little regard for people from the mainland and even less for the pomp of the occasion. When it was suggested by a BEA representative that it was possible at low water to walk to Bryher from St. Mary's, Joe fairly blew up! "Don't be bloody silly, you'd bloody well drown," he roared in his broad Scillonian accent. The room exploded in mirth and even the Chairman of the Board rocked with laughter. When I took the stand I was asked, by the Chairman, why I thought the new routes to the Scillies could be successful. I pointed out that these routes were not in fact new, (as if he didn't already know that), and that Mayflower Air Services had operated them successfully in the early sixties. I also pointed out that it was only Squadron Leader's Cleiffe's accident on the Scillies, (the Managing Director of Mayflower), that had prevented continuation of the services. It was with some temerity that I told the Chairman, that Cleiffe had written a book about the experiences, and that he, meaning the Chairman, should read it. This caused another great wave of laughter in the room. When the Chairman smiled at me benevolently, he assured me that he would indeed read the book and I was sure that we had won the day. When Arnold Heard congratulated me after the hearing it only served to confirm our victory. Soon we were told officially that we had been cleared to operate scheduled flights from Newquay and Plymouth to the Isles of Scilly. The application to operate to the Channel Islands being unopposed. In 1972 and 1973 I flew a number of first flights for the Airline (see overleaf) and Brymon Airways was well and truly launched. My joy was also enhanced by the many letters of congratulation I received from my colleagues in the industry, but pride of place went to the telegram (overleaf) which arrived from John Britton and Desmond Norman the aircraft manufacturers of the Islander on the Isle of Wight.

BRYMON AVIATION
1st FLIGHT
PLYMOUTH - JERSEY
18th JUNE 1972

AIRCRAFT - B/N ISLANDER
REG. No. G - AXXJ
PILOT: Capt. J. H. EVANS
FLIGHT No. 0404A
FLIGHT TIME 1 hr. 00 min.

Capt. J H Evans.

BRYMON AVIATION LTD
FIRST FLIGHT COVER

O.B.P. Phillips
63 St. Mary St.
Chippenham
Wilts.

BRYMON AVIATION
1st FLIGHT
NEWQUAY - SCILLY
17th JUNE 1972

AIRCRAFT: B/N Islander
REG. No. G-AXXJ
PILOT: Capt. J. H. Evans
FLIGHT No. 0113G
FLIGHT TIME: 0hrs 35mins

Capt. J H Evans

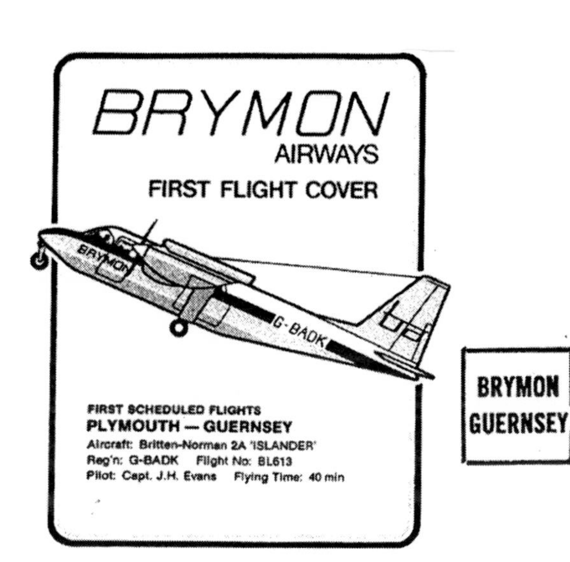

BRYMON
GUERNSEY

BRYMON

PLYMOUTH

FLINT ENTERPRISES
Flint Cottage.

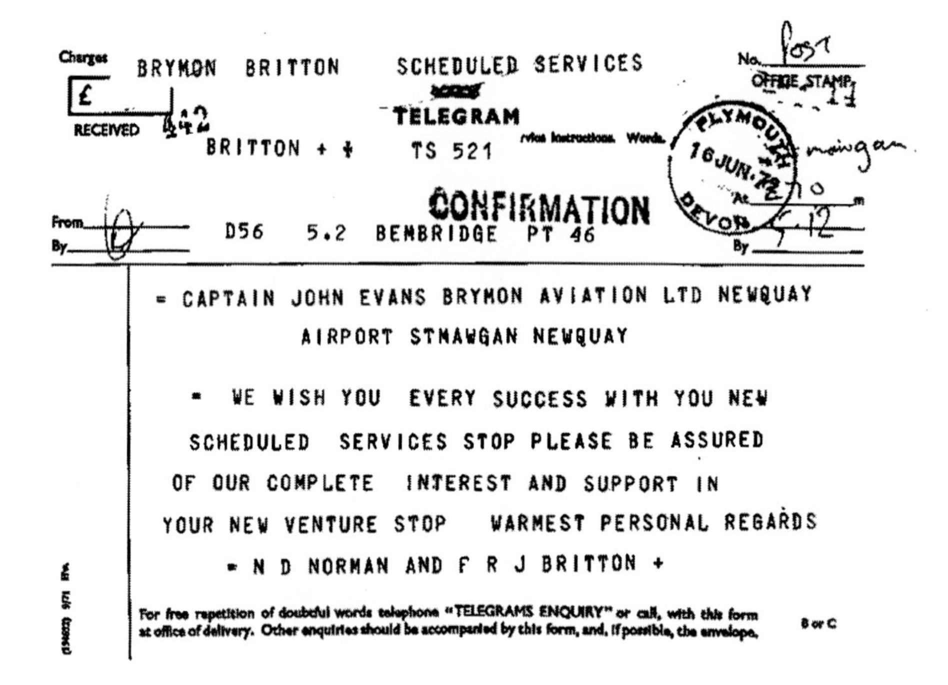

Charges £ RECEIVED 242

BRYMON BRITTON SCHEDULED SERVICES

TELEGRAM

BRITTON + + TS 521

No. Post

OFFICE STAMP

PLYMOUTH 16 JUN 72 DEVON

From / By

CONFIRMATION

D56 5.2 BEMBRIDGE PT 46

= CAPTAIN JOHN EVANS BRYMON AVIATION LTD NEWQUAY AIRPORT STMAWGAN NEWQUAY

= WE WISH YOU EVERY SUCCESS WITH YOU NEW SCHEDULED SERVICES STOP PLEASE BE ASSURED OF OUR COMPLETE INTEREST AND SUPPORT IN YOUR NEW VENTURE STOP WARMEST PERSONAL REGARDS

= N D NORMAN AND F R J BRITTON +

For free repetition of doubtful words telephone "TELEGRAMS ENQUIRY" or call, with this form at office of delivery. Other enquiries should be accompanied by this form, and, if possible, the envelope.

B or C

I had now purchased a large caravan and with our limited knowledge and ability at carpentry, Brett and I converted it to a small reception lounge for our passengers at Newquay Airport. My daughter Sian, just a few months old, would be taken along every morning to the airport where she would be fawned over by the departing passengers as her mother checked them in for their flight. Obviously the flying bug must have entered my daughter's genes, as later in life she obtained her Private Pilot's Licence to my great joy and surprise. Squadron Leader Doc Foster now entered my life. He had been in the RAF since 1942 and was currently flying Nimrod aircraft out of St. Mawgan. He would wander down to the caravan each evening after his day's work and beset me with his stories of his dashing flights around Bear Island in search of Russian submarines. Make no mistake Doc was a thoroughly pleasant man, whom we all grew to like and even love, but his repetitious stories "bore the pants" off us. I started to hide from him, or plead an excuse to leave early if he caught me unawares. Doc loved flying and wanted to continue after he left the RAF. In other words he wanted a job with us and by a constant wearing-down process evinced a promise from me to take him on subject to his obtaining a Civil Instrument Rating with the CAA and passing a Type Rating Test with me on the Islander aircraft. I was unsure that I had made the correct decision as in my experience, military pilots like Doc normally expected a flying batman to accompany them during flight to look after such worrisome chores as navigation and the tuning of radios etc. He soon departed for Stansted for his test with the Civil Aviation Flying Unit. When he returned he looked as if he had developed a very painful stomach complaint. Despite his great experience the examiner had failed him, and he had taken this rather badly. I sympathised with him and welcomed him to the 'real world' of civil aviation. To help his state of mind I told him of my experiences with CAFU many years before, and of my many heart breaking and costly visits to that 'Temple of Doom' which was CAFU and Stansted Airport. Somewhat reassured he practised assiduously for his next attempt on the Nimrod simulator suitably adjusted to replicate the Stansted Test routes. Some weeks later he walked into my office smiling triumphantly, the holder of a British Instrument Rating, and he simply walked through the Type Rating test with me, proving what an accomplished pilot he was. In a short time Doc proved himself to be a priceless asset to the company, achieving great popularity with staff and passengers alike. Like many pilots he seemed to have a perpetual stock of jokes, some of which he could even tell the passengers.

Before any of our pilots were allowed to fly to the Scillies with passengers they went along as passengers to take a good look at the place. As the Training Captain, I then took them and watched them performing approaches and landings on the different runways. Finally they were line checked flying the route with passengers, but sitting alongside and carefully watched by a company line check captain. It was only at this point, that a pilot was considered competent to fly passengers as a single pilot. How different this, to my first introduction to those beautiful islands. The weather was always an intriguing factor and I always emphasised to the pilots that they should remain on the ground unless they were absolutely sure of making a safe landing. I was in the restaurant at Plymouth Airport on the morning of Doc's first passenger flight to the Scillies. He had made a complete foul-up that morning, and had been unable to land and was consequently en-route Plymouth. To say he was embarrassed was an understatement and clearly believed his balls were going to serve as bookends. I sat in the restaurant studiously reading the daily paper when he entered and took a seat at the table. He tried gently to attract my attention, but I in turn I glued my eyes to the written page and said nothing. When I eventually lowered the paper, I looked at him and said, "Good God, Doc, what are you doing here? You should be on the Scillies!" He looked like a child having been caught with his hand in the cookie jar, but I soon put him out of his misery. "Doc," I said, "it could happen to anyone, but please ensure that it doesn't happen again, that's all." Relieved but still in a state of shock he rushed out, jumped into the aircraft without first removing the chocks from in front of the wheels and opened up the engines with a great roar. He accelerated forwards driving the chocks before him, tearing many yards of divots out of the ground as he taxied to the fuel pumps. I refrained from mentioning this to him when we next met, but a number of people did, and Doc remained in a passive and humble state for the next few days.

Aviation in the 1960s' and 1970s' seemed to have its full share of characters, unlike today, largely through a residue of World War II personnel. Percy Pierce a Plymouthian was just one of those who loved aircraft and the aura that surrounded them. He had exaggerated his age to join the wartime RAF, and had been trained as a flight engineer surviving fifty-four raids and two crashes. He was still only seventeen years old when he took part in the first 1,000-bomber raid on Cologne in 1942. Had Percy been an officer, he would have certainly been awarded a Distinguished Flying Cross (DFC), and probably more, but as a working class boy and a lowly sergeant, he received nothing. This merely showed that the class system was alive and well and permeated the military even in times of war. A Canadian pilot I knew, put it succinctly when he refused his commission saying about his crew, "I could die with them in the air, but on the ground I couldn't share the Mess or eat with them." Percy seemed to live at the airport and I gave him carte blanche to take any empty seat free of charge and pop-down to Jersey or Guernsey to pick-up a bottle of duty free. After the war ended he had returned to his hometown of Plymouth, married, had a couple of boys and took a job with the Post Office. His wife eventually ran-off with the local milkman leaving Percy to bring up his children alone. His main weakness after his marriage ended was women, and his endless pursuit of them. The word 'philanderer' might come to mind, but Percy really had little idea of how to deal with the opposite sex. His physical appearance left much to be desired, and he had a hairline that struggled to cover the back of his neck. He must also have wished at times that his name was Pilgrim, so that he could have made some progress with the girls but this was not to be. Instead he would stroll through Woolworth's or Marks and Spencer ogling the various female specimens, then come to the airport and bore me by describing them intimately. I tried to introduce him to my direct method of engagement, but Percy was not of that ilk. He usually found me in the Airport Restaurant at Plymouth and would sidle up close and conspiratorially ask me, "Are there any attractive females joining the company soon?" "Don't know," I would say, "I haven't much interest in that sort of thing." "Bollocks," he would cry roaring with laughter, "you're the syph and pox king around here!" One would gather from such conversation that Percy was a sex fiend and that I was a constant visitor to the VD clinic. The trouble with Percy was that he had a dirty mind, clearly a left over from the wartime RAF. He eventually got his commission, but this in the Air Force Cadets, so every Saturday when I heard the patter of many feet I knew it was Percy and his platoon of kids marching round the airport.

One day Gypsy John, one of our pilots, so named because he insisted on wearing one earring, arrived back at St. Mawgan with the brake fluid pouring out of the main wheel assembly. Without brakes I couldn't conduct a Base check on Brett, which was due, additionally I was about to introduce my latest recruit, Dave Thomas, to the aircraft, having taught Dave to fly at Swansea during my Cormorant days there. He had been a very experienced glider pilot, and had scrimped, saved and worked at a variety of jobs to raise the money to obtain his Commercial Pilot's Licence, so when he had rung me for a job I had no hesitation in offering him a position. Brett, Dave and I flew to Exeter that afternoon to get the brakes fixed with our maintenance base operator, West Country Aircraft Services. John Skinner, a fine engineer and a good friend to me, worked on the aircraft well into the evening fixing the brakes. It was now dark and the airport had been closed for some time. I had walked under the wing to examine the brake assembly, when my forehead had come into contact with the fuel drain. It was only a superficial cut but it bled profusely, and to help stem the flow I tied my handkerchief around my head. I now looked like a Japanese Kamikaze Pilot and one with a thunderous headache. Unable to refuel with the airport closed, I calculated there was sufficient fuel in the tanks to fly to St. Mawgan with just a few gallons to spare for the wife and kids. The weather had been perfect all day, and there had been no hint at any change. With no runway lights available John Skinner and his assistant Bill took their cars down to the runway intersection, and faced one another across the runway with their headlights full on. I had so much confidence in Dave, that I allowed him to do the take-off with me sitting alongside in the right-hand seat. Safely aloft we climbed to 6,000 feet in a cloudless sky and flew the direct track to St. Mawgan, directly over

Dartmoor prison its lights clearly visible. Dave now contacted St. Mawgan to obtain the latest weather and landing instructions. The three of us in the aircraft sat bolt upright when the controller told us that the cloud was 8/8s on the surface, with the sky obscured in fog and visibility down to fifty metres. I immediately swapped seats with Dave and told Brett to take the right-hand seat as the situation looked rather serious. When the controller called up and asked "XJ, what are your intentions?" I had no alternative but answer, "To land." At that time of night Plymouth Airport was closed, and Cardiff Airport out of reach with our remaining fuel. I accepted 'Radar onto runway 13' and commenced the approach my headache forgotten. I briefed Brett to shout as soon as he saw anything resembling a light. I was at 100 feet when the controller terminated the talk-down and now started giving me advisory height to the touchdown point. I had now slowed the rate of descent when Brett shouted, "A light at 11 o'clock." I assumed it was the runway lights on the left-hand side of the runway, but I couldn't be sure. Next moment we were rolling along seemingly in the middle of St. Mawgan's very wide runway. We all laughed in relief when the controller said, "XJ I can't see you." Well we couldn't see anything either! Very slowly we made our way back to the terminal and parked. As we walked out to the car we met a bunch of British Midland crew, who were returning from the pub in the village. "Where have you guys come from?" they cried. "Just landed," said I, "the kamikaze pilot." They all hooted with laughter and disappeared into the fog whence they came. The British Midland Viscount parked overnight just 30-40 yards from the road was totally invisible. That night my wife made up two extra beds.

Ever since I was a kid it seemed that danger had been a constant companion. When ITN Television called and wanted a pilot to fly them south of Land's End to take pictures of a ship in distress I was pleased to accept the charter. The fact that the ship was sinking and packed with nitro-glycerine explosive only seemed to add a certain spice to the proceedings. It was getting dark when I found not one but two ships in approximate position 60 nautical miles south of Land's End. One ship was low in the water clearly the freighter, and the other a Royal Navy destroyer. A lifeboat was ferrying the crew off the freighter when I arrived, and I was content to fly in circles while the TV cameraman got on with his job of filming. It was now almost dark and the destroyer flashed a steady white light at me, telling me to keep my distance, or more pointedly 'bugger off'. I climbed to 6,000 feet and widened the flying circle as I certainly didn't want to be too close when the seawater and the nitro met. I had all but lost the ship in the darkness when suddenly night turned into day. The explosion hurled debris and smoke way above my height and tossed the aircraft about like a leaf in the wind. The light illuminated the sea around for miles and the colours were quite fantastic, at least so said the cameraman, as I was too busy trying to bring back some semblance of control to the aircraft, which had almost become inverted.

The Atlantic Hotel on the Scillies was my favourite venue when I was lucky enough to spend a whole day on the island. Len Dalton was the company's inspiring agent who met every flight with a smile and a helping hand. This day I had invited him to lunch in the Atlantic Hotel restaurant, which delightfully looked out over the beautiful bay of St. Mary's. When he appeared he looked extremely worried, indeed very unlike his usual self. He simply stood in front of me and said, "John, your other aircraft has crashed and the pilot killed." The bottom simply fell out of my world. Brett had been with me from the very beginning of the company, and he was the only other pilot flying that morning. I tottered to the hotel telephone and rang Air Traffic Control at Plymouth Airport. A sense of relief flooded through me when I heard that the crash had not involved Brett, and a company aircraft. Then total despair when I was told that Paul, my station manager, had been killed, together with his wife and two young children. They had taken-off in marginal conditions to fly to London and the light aircraft had somehow crashed into a bungalow in Torbay. Paul and his children apparently died instantly, but his wife had actually survived despite quite appalling injuries. The accident report suggested carburettor icing had caused the engine to lose power, and in stretching his glide to land on some adjacent playing fields, had stalled the aircraft, causing it to dive into the roof of a house. Only the previous day I had warned him not to fly in conditions outside his abilities, particularly since he only held a private licence and flew infrequently. Later his wife, not fully recovered from her injuries appeared as a guest on the Jimmy Young television show for charity and soon became quite a celebrity in her own right! Just a week later my wife and I represented the company at the funeral in Torbay. It was absolutely gut wrenching to see the two small coffins alongside that of their dad.

It always appeared to me that warm fronts with their rain, low cloud and poor visibility timed their arrival in the West Country to coincide with our busiest days namely Saturdays and Sundays. On one such Saturday I found myself besieged at Exeter Airport by a retired British Army general. He asked me a wide range of questions regarding the flight and the amenities available on the Isles of Scilly. I easily answered his questions regarding the flight, but suggested that he waited until he arrived on the island where our agent would satisfy all his other queries. The flight went smoothly enough and a smiling Len, as cheerful as ever, was there to meet our arrival. Unfortunately, his meeting with the general got off to a bad start when the general addressed Len as 'my man'. Now Len had left the mainland many years before to get out of the "rat race", and if he was anything at all he was undeniably his 'own man'. As Len bristled, the general continued, "now what do you people do here in the summer?" "We fish and fuck," said Len without blinking. Whether or not the general heard the answer, I couldn't be sure, but he continued unabated, "and what do you do here in the winter?" "There isn't any fishing," said Len. I presume that the general had a happy time in the Scillies, certainly he hadn't carried a fishing rod so maybe he stayed on and took Len's advice.

The year 1973 had been a good one for the company. Passenger loads were good and the Brymon name was becoming very well known, particularly in the West Country. With a passenger load factor close to seventy percent, it had become evident that on certain flights we were turning passengers away through a lack of seats, and this was certainly evident in the peak season. The need for a larger aircraft for the route structure was now a must, and it would require one with an excellent short take-off and landing capability. The De Havilland Canada Twin Otter / DHC6 seemed the perfect choice, and had already operated in Africa under our Civil Authority's authorisation, so putting it on the British Register would not constitute a problem. In fact, it would be the first of its kind in the UK, thus opening the market for the Canadian company. With its nineteen seat passenger configuration and its truly amazing take-off and landing performance, it promised to take the airline into a higher league than hitherto. In February 1974 Brett and I flew to New York Kennedy Airport with British Caledonian Airways enroute for Toronto. Neither of us had seen fit to obtain a US visa, believing that as we would be in transit, one would not be required. Consequently, on arrival we were placed in the custody of a Customs Officer, who watched us very carefully until we boarded our Air Canada flight. Apart from the wonderful hospitality of the Canadians the most memorable part of our training, involved our circuits and landings at the Toronto Island Airport. On the down-wind leg we were confronted by the immensely high CNN tower building, not yet completed, but still high enough to protrude into the cloud base above our height at 800 feet. In terms of its performance the aircraft outperformed the Islander, largely through its large high wing and its reverse thrust capability. Because of delivery schedules however, it wasn't until October of 1974 that we were able to put the aircraft into service in the UK with great success.

Earlier that year I carried out a charter for BBC Television, who wished to cover the first sailing of the Plymouth—Roscoff ferry. Having filmed the departure of the ship from Plymouth they now wanted to film the arrival of the ship at Roscoff. I flew the film crew across to Morlaix airfield in Brittany, the nearest to the port of Roscoff. It was my first visit to Morlaix and I was enchanted by the warm reception, particularly when I made it known that I was a native of Pays de Galles. Musing over a delicious coffee, I thought how wonderful it would be to start the first ever direct scheduled air service between the southwest and Brittany. The more I thought of it the more sense it seemed to make and the keener I became. I reasoned that an air service to parallel the sea crossing had a guaranteed market and must make economic sense. I turned to the airport manager and in my imperfect French said, "Monsieur, je voudrais commensez une ligne regulair entre Plymouth et Morlaix!" He looked at me in some astonishment. Was it my attempt at speaking French, or the idea that surprised him most? I couldn't be sure, but within minutes I was whisked by car down to the town and the offices of the Chambre de Commerce. There for the first time I met Xavier le Clerc, who as far as I could make out was in charge of transportation affairs. He and I became quite good friends, and often times he would stay as a guest at my home in Cornwall. Some years later, after he had started his own airline Britair, my wife and I stayed at his home on the beautiful north coast of Brittany. He explained that in order to grow his airline he needed larger aircraft, and to further this aim, he like me in previous years, had visited the home of Embraer the Aircraft Manufacturer at San José dos Campos in Brazil. At that time the company was offering low cost finance to any purchaser of their aircraft guaranteed through the Bank of Brazil. When President Mitterand visited Morlaix sometime later, Xavier found him very well informed on aviation events in that region of Brittany. Mitterand asked Xavier why it was that Britair was interested in purchasing Brazilian aircraft when suitable French aircraft were available.

Xavier explained that the French banks had shown no interest in funding French or any other aircraft, so he turned to the Brazilian manufacturer for help. President Mitterand made a number of telephone calls immediately once he heard this, and Xavier was told to expect calls from a number of French banks in the immediate future. This duly happened, and Xavier soon changed his order, and switched his allegiance to the French ATR 42 an aircraft manufactured in Toulouse. In the meantime President Mitterand had also contacted the Chief Executive of Air France, and soon the aircraft of Britair were flying on Air France routes, and guaranteed financially. This ensured the economic viability of the company, guaranteeing its long-term future. Xavier turned to me and suggested that I do the same thing for Brymon Airways, and approach Margaret Thatcher for help. This remark prompted a loud wave of laughter, and more than a few ribald remarks.

The rain was hissing on the windscreen as I climbed the Islander out of the Scillies. The warm front of the previous day, a Saturday, had completely ruined our schedules and we were still in 'catching up' mode. The front had now passed, although St. Mawgan remained below limits. The Plymouth and Exeter weather however was improving as I levelled the aircraft at 5,000 feet and told the passengers that we were now crossing Land's End. We were still in cloud and approaching abeam St. Mawgan when I noticed a small fluctuation in the starboard oil pressure gauge. The Islander's gauges were not the best in the business, and often time it had become difficult to differentiate between an engine problem and a faulty gauge. Some weeks earlier on a flight to Jersey, I had just made my customary radio call at 50 degrees north, when I noticed a rise in the starboard engine oil pressure. It is a fundamental part of good pilotage that one cultivates the roving eye, constantly scanning the instrument panel either in a clockwise or anti-clockwise direction. In this way any change in the instrument readings becomes readily obvious, and alerts you to any potential problem, on this day the oil pressure was seen to be increasing slowly, but the oil temperature reading remained steady. In fact the engine sounded fine and a quick look out confirmed that it was still attached to the wing and making power. Satisfied, I decided to take no action particularly as Jersey was less than thirty minutes flying time away. On arrival, after the passengers had departed, John Skinner, an engineer now with Jersey European Airways and a friend from Cormorant days, wandered out to talk to me, "Hi John, come out here and take a look at the aircraft's tail." I followed and saw that the engine oil from the starboard engine had been thrown up completely covering the tail section. "Had you flown another ten minutes, I guess you would have had a rather nasty fire," John said. Now on this Sunday I was once again faced with a similar errant pressure gauge reading, but I now noticed also a small but definite rise in the oil temperature reading. That was enough for me, and having forewarned the passengers, I shut down the engine and feathered the propeller. A quick look around saw ten worried looking passengers gawping at the stationary propeller. The Plymouth weather had now improved and the landing made without difficulty. At touchdown I was heartened to hear the passengers burst into spontaneous applause, a clear indication of their worry. The West Country Engineers now busied themselves with the engine problem and when I conducted an air test a little later, it behaved flawlessly. My wife and baby daughter were my only passengers for the short flight back to St. Mawgan. At about sixty knots on the take-off run there was huge bang from the same engine, and above the noise I heard my young daughter scream loudly. It is a good policy to think for a few seconds before shutting down an engine. Many a good man has left this earth through the simple expedient of shutting down the wrong engine, but my daughter's scream must have increased the adrenaline flow, and the engine was shut down and the propeller feathered in a flash. I now had full power on the live engine and slowly 'milked-in' the flaps. Turning the aircraft to port against the live engine I added a few knots of speed as I dived down towards the

City of Plymouth, the airport being almost six hundred feet above sea level. I struggled down-wind barely reaching fifty feet above aerodrome level and made a safe landing. With a full passenger load I surely would never have made it, and the experience certainly provided some food for thought. The Air Traffic Controllers told me that they saw a fire in the engine and a huge ball of black smoke. They were also convinced that the aircraft would surely crash into the trees at the westward end of the runway. I'm glad I was able to disappoint them, and Percy, a witness to the events, acted fastest and by the time we were safely on the ground the taxi he had ordered was ready and drove us back to Cornwall and home in some style. It had certainly been a difficult and tiring day. I considered the fact, that in almost 4,000 hours of flying the Islander I had never shutdown or lost an engine in anger until that day. Then it had happened twice on the same day, statistically almost an impossibility. The day was June 6th 1976, the anniversary of the D-Day landings in Normandy. It had certainly been D-Day for me!

I often asked myself how slender the thread by which a man's destiny hangs, and I was shortly to ask the question of myself once more. I had completed the final flight the day from Jersey to Plymouth. Later I would fly the aircraft across to St. Mawgan to drive home. In the interim however I would generally find time to kick a ball about outside our Plymouth offices with the baggage boys and anybody else left on the premises. This weekly session was conducted with a certain joie de vivre and in a small way contributed to the company's 'Esprit de Corps'! After such an energetic display I would climb the aircraft to 2,000 feet, and 'beat-up' the airfield for the benefit of my erstwhile foot-balling chums. On this day I dived low across the airfield in a northeast to a southwest direction. From that angle, and being near the ground, it was impossible to see the Terminal Building owing to the rising ground in the middle of the airfield, and I was unaware of the north-westerly breeze which had increased in strength. Suddenly at 150 knots and a few feet above the ground, events moved swiftly and I was horror struck to find a telegraph pole looming directly above me and filling the windscreen. I heaved back on the control column and shut my eyes fully convinced I had made my final mistake. Next minute I found myself still alive and the aircraft above 2,000 feet, I was still in total shock when I landed back at St. Mawgan fifteen minutes later. As I entered my house the telephone was ringing. It was Percy who had been watching my departure from Plymouth, "Jesus John," he exclaimed, "do you know how close you came to buying it today? The bloody post passed between the side of the fuselage and the propeller!" Very subdued I asked him how high the post was. When he answered, "about twelve feet," I reached for the brandy bottle, stretched out in my chair, and considered if fate does intervene to ensure that a man's life follows a predetermined course. My thought processes were soon cut short however, when I fell deep into the arms of Morpheus.

For some unknown reason the position of Station Manager at Plymouth Airport developed into a perennial problem, caused in part I suppose by my own inadequacies. Richard (of paper in the ear fame) had taken the post at the commencement of the Airline, for no other reason other than I liked him as a person, and felt he would not let me down. He had no previous experience in the airline industry, but I had a soft-spot for him, and with his brand of innocence he did indeed bring some light relief into a sometimes difficult work schedule. I had invited him one evening for dinner at my home and he was something like a hour late when he rang and told me that he had got lost, and had just arrived at Par. My riposte was to tell him that in fact he was 'well below Par', a joke I fear that failed to register with him. A salesman selling telephone message recording machines had been bothering me for some time. Recording telephone messages was a fairly new development in the early seventies, so I eventually arranged a meeting between him and Richard. I warned the salesman that Richard had a temporary, but severe, hearing problem, and it was necessary on meeting him to speak rather loudly. I then told Richard that he was to meet this salesman, who also suffered a similar disability. A group of the lads gathered outside Richard's office on the said day, and waited for the inevitable fireworks. After a short time the noise became louder and louder and the door suddenly burst open and the salesman stalked out. Dear Richard, red faced and non-plussed, told me later that he had never met such an irate person and suggested strongly that we had no requirement for a recording machine. We had all been prostrate with laughter but Richard never suspected a thing. His inadequacies at work now began to show as the pressure of business developed, and although he remained a picture of sartorial elegance and smiled like a beaming sheep, in the interests of the company sadly he had to go. He was replaced by Paul who, as already described, killed himself and his children in a light aircraft. Bill then arrived, who had more than a fleeting resemblance to James Cagney. He however, clearly believed that he had joined a rest camp and soon departed. The next arrival was experienced enough, but decided in his wisdom to ignore the arriving and departing passengers. When I reminded him of his prime duties, he threatened to take me bodily apart. He too left the company rather rapidly and I began to think the position was cursed. Things changed however with the arrival of Mike Johnson, who had previous airline experience with British European Airways at Heathrow. A few weeks later I also interviewed an applicant as his deputy determined to put this problem to rest. When I entered my office for the interview, I met Terry Fox for the first time. He materialised with long hair, old jeans, crumpled sweater and dirty trainers. After a few strong words about his appearance, he re-appeared some days later as a well-dressed human being and was immediately engaged. I was never to regret either of these two appointments.

Brymon had now taken over the lease of Plymouth Airport and fire fighting had become one of is responsibilities. In order to save money Bill

Bryce, the owner, and Terry Fox were trained as auxiliary firemen. One afternoon two light aircraft from Germany crashed into one another at the end of the westerly runway. When Air Traffic Control sounded the alarm Bill set off like an Olympic Sprinter, jumped into the Emergency Response Vehicle, a posh name for a Land Rover equipped with two fire extinguishers attached to the front bumper. This was driven by Bill around the corner of the Terminal Building, in order to pick-up Terry, who had rushed out in anticipation. Terry had just taken hold of the rear end of the vehicle, when Bill took-off in a spurt of dust. Terry did well to hang on for the first fifty yards or so, his feet dragging behind. From the Terminal we all watched in high amusement as it appeared a re-enactment of the chariot race in the film 'Ben Hur'. Terry's muscular strength soon gave out, and he was left prostrate on the grass. Unhurt, however, and in true Brymon spirit, he ran the rest of the way. There were no casualties in the crash, the two German aircraft were towed away, repaired, and were gone within the week.

Sadly by late 1975 the atmosphere in the company had deteriorated. Even a mild request by the pilot for some form of contract of employment was ignored, despite the fact that this had now became law in the UK. Regular meetings between the staff and management and a laid-down policy on salary structure was also refused. Inevitably all the pilots joined British Airline pilots Association (BALPA) and sanity returned only when Bill agreed to all the demands, but not before harsh words had been said and irrevocable damage done to the fabric of the company. What a difference to the heady days of previous years, when we all worked so well as a team. In fact during that time there had been virtually no absenteeism, through sickness or any other cause, a good measure of the morale of any company.

Often present at Plymouth Airport in those days was Peter Cadbury, the then Chairman of Westward Television. We had met a number of times when he had flown his own aircraft into the airport and had discussed Brymon informally, and also his possible interest in setting-up his own airline. I had for some time worked on a business plan called Air Wales, which discussed the operation of profitable air routes out of Cardiff. Cadbury had been sufficiently interested to read my work, and asked whether my proposition could work if based on Exeter Airport, and I agreed that this was indeed very probable. In the latter days at Brymon my health deteriorated with all the unrest, and I felt that a change was necessary. My maxim was, and remains, that if a job isn't fun, then it wasn't worth a candle, and it had now ceased to be fun! A little later I resigned with great sadness and took-up the position as Chief Executive of the newly formed Air Westward, initially based at the Westward Television Studios in Plymouth. On the 10th November 1976 the headlines in the newspaper, 'The Western Evening Herald' read, 'My Airline Scheme', by Cadbury. In summary it said, "Peter Cadbury last night took the wraps off his multi-million pound plan for a West Country Airline. Air Westward is a wholly owned subsidiary of Westward Television. This company will be running regular flights to Paris, Edinburgh and Wales from Exeter Airport. Tomorrow Mr Cadbury and Mr Winston Brimacombe, the new Executive Vice-Chairman of Air Westward and a Director of Westward Television, will fly to America to look at the new Metroliner aircraft which will operate for Air Westward." In the last paragraph of a long article it said, "the Chief Executive of Air Westward will be Captain John Evans, a one time Chief Pilot of Brymon Airways." I was then quoted as saying, "I am extremely pleased to be associated with such a magnificent venture; in my opinion it has all the ingredients of a wonderful success story". Plans for the airline to acquire Swearingen Metros were shelved in April 1977 when the manufacturing company fell into financial difficulties, consequently the route-licence applications with the Civil Aviation Authority were withdrawn. Some days later I was invited to lunch by Ronny Perry, the Managing Director of Westward Television, while sitting in his office, he asked me what I would like as a pre-lunch drink. I asked him for a dry sherry, and as he handed it to me said, "Oh by the way John you're fired." So it was after that almost six years of continual flying, I was once again out of work, but this time with the added responsibility of a wife and two children.

CHAPTER 11

RETURN TO THE LAND OF MY FATHERS

Sometime in February 1977 I received a telephone call from Victor Alanbrooke, telling me that the powers to be had requested that he take his hereditary seat in the House of Lords. He knew full well my feelings about that institution, nevertheless I felt a certain pleasure, that he had thought my opinion worthy of consideration. Perhaps he was surprised when I suggested he take his rightful seat. The reason being that his presence could only improve the place. So it was on March 1st 1977, (St. David's Day), as I was quick to remind him, that I visited the Lords to witness the great day. It was in fact the first time that I had ever visited either of the two Houses of Parliament. It turned out to be a most pleasurable occasion, with a guided tour followed by a splendid meal. It has been described as the finest club in the land, and nothing I saw disproved that claim, and even the wine bottles were marked 'House of Lord's Wine'. The day's enjoyment was further enhanced by an accidental meeting with Manny Shinwell, (Baron Emmanuel Shinwell 1884—1986), who at that time was in his ninety-third year, an astonishing man, who almost convinced me that I was an old acquaintance of his. In 1935 he had defeated Ramsay MacDonald (who had been the first Labour Prime Minister) at Seaham Harbour Durham, in a bitterly contested election. As Minister of Fuel and Power, he had been responsible for the nationalisation the coal mines in 1946, and had held many other offices of state. He had been awarded his Life Peerage in 1970. He was a little man in stature, but great in other respects. He had served a five month prison sentence in 1921 for incitement to riot, clearly a man who held strong principles and had not been afraid to stand-up for them.

Back in the real world following the demise of Westward Airways, I had a great need to 'recharge my batteries' and so I took the family for a holiday to Eloanda in Crete. There the superb weather and the wonderful seafood improved my mental state and once more I was ready to face new challenges on my return. I soon found myself at a meeting in London with the Ministry of Overseas Development discussing the position of General Manager of a small airline in the Falkland Islands, a British Crown Colony in the South Atlantic, 320 miles off the east coast of Argentina. The chairlady at the meeting having offered me the position, then made thinly veiled attempts to dissuade me from taking it. The Falklands appeared to be a 'God awful' place, where it rained for periods every day and where the seawater was usually at, or below, freezing. She suggested that I consider my decision very carefully, and gave me up to two weeks to think about it. Back in Cornwall, my wife was in favour of going, saying that it was a wonderful opportunity for us as a family to see and experience a part of the world we would otherwise be unlikely to visit. Just five days before my deadline, I received a call from DK Aviation of Grimsby. DK was the Aircraft Broker who had held the UK franchise for the Swearingen Metro Aircraft and had been involved in the attempted sale of the aircraft to Westward Airways. Now David King, the Chairman of the company, who had read my Air Wales business plan (on which Air Westward had been based), now seemed very excited by the prospect of operating the original ideas expressed in the plan, but this time with the new Brazilian Aircraft, the 'Bandeirante', for which he intended to obtain the UK franchise. I agreed that the aircraft could indeed operate the air routes as envisaged in the plan, and consequently soon found myself having a Board in Grimsby with the Directors of Cosalt Plc (the old Grimsby Coal and Salt company), who would be largely funding the new airline. Having satisfactorily passed that obstacle, 'Air Wales' was duly registered as a company, and I became its Director of Operations. A few days later Bill Bryce offered Brymon Airways for sale to the Directors of Westward Television. The 'Plymouth Times' of Friday June 24th 1977 lead with the headline, 'Exclusive—Airline offers to sell—claim', A selling price of £1.4 million was discussed and rejected by the Board as unrealistic, but sometime later Air Westward did start an airline under that name. Several months on, when Air Wales had been operating for some time, on a very beautiful summer night, I was operating the Cardiff to Brussels service and working a London Airways radio frequency, when I heard a Brymon Airways aircraft calling. A few minutes later an Air Westward aircraft, returning from Amsterdam to Exeter, also called up on the same frequency. I felt a great sense of warm satisfaction at that moment, as I had been instrumental in forming all three companies. I handed the controls over to my co-pilot, turned down the cockpit lights and relaxed in my seat feeling rather pleased with myself at that very singular accomplishment.

It had been on the 25th April 1935 that S Kenneth Davis had founded Cambrian Airways based at Cardiff Airport, situated then at Pengam Moors on the eastern side of the city. From that day the symbol of the Welsh Dragon had been adopted as an emblem on the company aircraft. By 1967 British European Airways had begun playing a much greater, and influential, role in the airline, and by 1975 both the name Cambrian and the Dragon motif had disappeared and with them the last vestiges of a Welsh national airline. The irony was that these events had taken place at a time when a greater feeling of nationhood had begun to develop, coupled with a resurgence of the national language. I had however to some degree or other foreseen these aviation developments, and as early as 1969 had been in touch with Stan Handley, the Transportation Secretary at the Welsh Office, who had provided me with much needed assistance in developing my new 'Air Wales' business plan. Strange to say, I received much greater help from the authorities then, than I ever received after the establishment of the Wales Assembly.

I was now spending my time divided between my family in Cornwall, preparing the formalities for the airline at Cardiff and at Grimsby in the offices of DK Aviation, where I was preparing the manuals for the airline operation. DK had found a typical English guesthouse for my stay in Grimsby. The landlady was clearly a member of the 'Landlady's Malevolent Society', who in a thunderous tone introduced herself by stating, that the front door of her establishment was locked at 10 p.m., and I'd better be inside by that time. She would have been driven out of the Gestapo for cruelty, but nevertheless described herself as a kind and liberally minded person. I have to admit however that during my period of residence I saw little evidence of her liberal ways. She had stressed that there were few rules in her household, but this was disproved when I paid my first visit to the guest bathroom. Sitting on a shelf behind the toilet were printed a whole list of house rules, which included bath times and suggested levels of water used, very reminiscent of war time. At the bottom of the list one brave guest (probably on a single night stop) had printed the words, 'and you do not collect £200 when you pass Go!', a message which caused me huge merriment and one I found particularly apt.

David King was clearly his own public relations machine, and in his press release dated 27th July 1977, the heading was 'DK Aviation to start National Airline for Wales', so clearly reminiscent of Peter Cadbury's press release of Air Westward. It went on to say that—"Following meetings in Cardiff with leaders of industry, the Welsh Office and the Development Corporation for Wales, David King said, 'I was astounded to find that such a important market has remained ignored for as long'. He continued, 'The formation of Air Wales at this time is obviously tied to the degree of autonomy in Wales, which will require more direct talking between people in Cardiff and Brussels.' He concluded, 'This airline is based in Wales for Wales, what we need is the support from the business man and people of Wales, we can do the rest!'" Having introduced the ideas for the project in the first case, I became somewhat uneasy to find, that I had now been ignored, and not been named as a director of the company, although this was remedied some months later, I soon realised that should the airline succeed under my guidance, the most I would receive would be some tit-bits, from the 'rich man's table'. If it all failed however, I realised that I would be the inevitable 'fall-guy' having the responsibility to run the airline, but without any real authority, the worst of both worlds. While David was mixing with the executives of Welsh institutions, I was still grappling with the intricacies of the airline formation and dealing with the innumerable requests for information from the Civil Aviation Authority. Whilst in Grimsby, however, it would have been criminal not to partake and enjoy the fresh fish available in the fish docks. Indeed DK Aviation had their offices within the Cosalt building in the fish docks, so at lunch I merely had to cross the road to partake of the most marvellous fish and chips. I quickly learned that the fishermen did not eat cod, describing it as the 'garbage of the sea'. Their preference was haddock, to which I soon converted.

The next few months were horrendously busy not just with the preparation of airline manuals etc., but also with the social and business functions that the creation of a national airline entailed. The Development Corporation of Wales (now defunct), under the leadership of its Chief Executive Meirion Lewis, was forthright in its support for the airline, and among my early engagements under their auspices was a dinner when the principal speaker was the then Prime Minister Mr James Callaghan.

I then met the Chief Executive of the Clwyd County Council, who had a direct interest in our first proposed air service linking North and South Wales. In fact they were so keen on this service that they were prepared to provide a financial subsidy of £10,000. In October David King was the main speaker at the Development Corporation luncheon at the Hydro Hotel in Llandudno in North Wales. When he mentioned my name as the founder of the very idea of Air Wales the remark was greeted by rapturous applause. I have to mention here however that the invited audience was largely Welsh. My next stunt was to persuade Colt Cars of Cirencester to sponsor the airline, by providing four cars all beautifully painted in Air Wales colours, and all for free, through the courtesy of Michael Orr, the then Chief Executive, whom I had known from previous days when flying for Brymon.

In October 1977 Mr Paice of the Civil Aviation Authority rang me to confirm that all our Air Transport Licences had been granted, and in December we began our first scheduled service operating between Cardiff and Hawarden (Chester). However it was our service between Cardiff and Cherbourg in Normandy, that brought about the greatest economic opportunity for the company. It occurred when we brought back a number of truck drivers from Cherbourg to Bournemouth (Hurn) an intermediate stop. These drivers were employed by TNT (Thomas Nationwide Transport), UK, one of the largest trucking and transport organisations in the world. Through this contract, I soon met up with Peter Allesbrook, the Chairman of TNT UK, later knighted for his services, and arranged a meeting with him and my fellow directors at his Upper-Brook Street London office. Allesbrook was prepared to invest a seven-figure sum in Air Wales on the basis that this figure would be matched by DK and Cosalt respectfully. This in the words of the major Air Wales shareholder was "too rich for them," the offer was therefore rejected. It appeared to me however that my fellow directors preferred to have a large slice in a small company, rather than a small slice in a much larger company. However there was another reason, which I was unaware of at that time, but which came to light later. The opportunity we then missed became all too evident in 1978, when TNT entered the UK Express Parcels Market, via the purchase of an existing carrier, Intercounty Express. In their first ten years TNT revolutionised that market place, by introducing the UK's first nationwide, next day, guaranteed door to door delivery service, establishing itself as the unchallenged market leader. TNT UK was to develop into one of the most profitable and successful parts of the Worldwide TNT operation. Some 9,000 people were to become employed in the UK alone, with a transport fleet of over 4,000 vehicles. Clearly, I had provided a once in a lifetime opportunity, for Air Wales with its brand name, to achieve a long term position and status in the Air Transport Industry. This unfortunately was never to be!

A number of Brymon Airways' staff had followed me to Air Wales, among whom was Ivan Ulic, or Ivan the Terrible as my children called him. Ivan had been with Brymon two years as a Captain and had been born in Titograd in Yugoslavia. Brett also rejoined me on his return from flying in the Seychelles. Terry Fox, the ever-present deputy Station Manager from Plymouth Airport joined me as Ground Control Manager as did David Parsons, who had been my Station Manager at Newquay. I had desperately wanted Doc Foster as my Chief Pilot, but family ties in Cornwall prevented this. In February 1978 Ivan, the new Chief Pilot, and myself, flew to Brazil for pilot training on the Bandeirante aircraft (EMB-IID). We travelled with Varig Airways from London Heathrow to Paris Charles de Gaulle, and then via Recife to Rio Janeiro. The highlight of that flight for me was to view the Canary Islands from the cockpit of the Douglas DC-10 as it passed above at 31,000 feet in the early morning light.

I was to spend the next few weeks in Ground School, then on to Simulator Training and finally Flying Training on the aircraft. My flight instructor was Martins da Rosa, who proved a skilled flight instructor, and a wonderful host generally, having a huge weakness for lager. My initial intention had been to remain with the other pilots and then ferry the aircraft home with them. However as my presence was urgently needed in Cardiff I finished my training first, and flew the scheduled airline back to London. A week or so later my two pilots ferried the aircraft via Recife, across the South Atlantic to West Africa, and then on through Portugal to Cardiff. All this made possible by the addition of a large auxiliary fuel tank in the rear fuselage. The Air Transport Licences were approved by year end and included routes from Swansea and Cardiff to London Gatwick, Chester Hawarden, Brussels, Dinard, Brest and Bordeaux. In a telex from Grimsby dated 9th January 1978, I learned that in view of my services to the company, I was to be appointed to the Board of Directors. This appointment to be with immediate effect, 'Congratulations John', was added, and the message was sent by David King. This left me somewhat unexcited as it merely confirmed that without the presence of a Managing Director I would have the full responsibility for the airline without the complete authority. In other words if the company went 'pear shaped', it would be down to me, and if successful David would be up there taking the bows—'C'est la Vie'!

By May 1978 our Bandeirante, registered G-CELT, flew the first passenger service between Cardiff and Brussels. British Airways Engineering on the south side of the Airport were doing a splendid job in servicing and maintaining the aircraft, and only twice in our first year of operating were we grounded for technical reasons. By the end of the first year the company had operated over a 1,000 flights from Cardiff to Brussels, averaging a passenger load factor of 55 percent. Also when occasion demanded the aircraft was used to Brest mid-week and every Saturday in the summer period on a service to Bordeaux. The close relationship with Sabena Belgian World Airlines was certainly 'paying-off', and we were able to offer our passengers fairly comprehensive interline facilities through Brussels to the rest of the world. Today sadly, Sabena has disappeared from the ranks of the world's airlines. It started its flying in 1923, and the word Sabena was simply an acronym for Société Anonyme Belge d' Exploitation de la Navigation Aérienne. It was one of the world's oldest airlines and an important link between the motherland and Belgium's great interests in Africa. However, in the airline business there is clearly little room, for sentiment, and cash flows and statements of profit and loss 'rules the roost'! Amazingly, Sabena, it appears, never made a profit in its seventy-eight year history!

The finances for Air Wales were all controlled from Grimsby, so I was surprised to find a letter on my desk from the finance house Lombard North Central. Apart from alarmingly high quarterly payments it indicated that we were paying interest at fourteen and a half percent per annum. The decision to fund the Embraer Aircraft through Lombard had been taken prior to me being appointed to the Board, not that I could have altered that decision had I been a director anyway. However conventional wisdom had pointed to using finance from the Bank of Brazil, where at that time interest rates were set at seven and a half percent. Again the company was paying for out Piper Chieftain Aircraft placed on our books at £190,000, when the going rate for such an aircraft in excellent condition was only £150,000. It was clear that strange things were happening, for which I could not obtain any satisfactory answer. You really didn't need to be a 'conspiracy theorist' to suspect that the company was being used for ulterior motives.

David King had now established a flight operation in Saudi Arabia and some of the Air Wales pilots were sent to Riyadh to operate the service. All the training costs, however were borne by Air Wales, and all my attempts to verify the accounts were frustrated by the Board. Finally the whole exercise in creating the airline in my view was seen to be fraudulent, as the only objective in mind all along, had been to obtain the UK franchise of Embraer Aircraft for DK Aviation. For this purpose two Bandeirantes had been ordered and expectations of success in Grimsby were high. Flight International Magazine soon published the fact that CSE of Kidlington Oxford was challenging DK for this franchise. CSE had been around for many years and already held the American Piper Aircraft franchise for the UK and the Middle East. Furthermore, they had a formidable array of existing facilities at Oxford, for maintenance, avionics and spare parts and as DK had none of these, there could only have been realistically one winner. A short time later it was announced, that CSE had obtained the franchise and the whole 'raison d'être', for Air Wales had suddenly disappeared. I had anticipated this outcome for some time and quietly held meetings with Members of Parliament, the Welsh Office and the Welsh Development Agency with a view to acquiring public finance, and re-structuring the airline's finances and changing the Board of Directors. In March 1979 David King was quoted in the Daily Western Mail Newspaper as saying, "Air Wales is not in financial difficulty, and talks are aimed at strengthening the company's financial structure. But whatever decision emerges it seems certain that the airline will continue to operate as Air Wales."

During the year, I had written and had printed a twelve page booklet entitled, 'A Round Wales Air Service', depicting the advantages to the Welsh economy of air links between the various parts of Wales. The company was already operating a South Wales—Northeast Wales service, and a genuine interest had been generated through the local councils and other Welsh bodies. It had been pointed out in the booklet that such a scheme would unlikely to be profitable, and therefore would require Government subsidy, and certainly in the short to medium term. This scheme would have been of inestimable value to the Wales regions and infrastructure generally, but despite the fine words political will was absent and the opportunity missed. Twenty-five years on under a Wales Assembly, I once more presented a re-vamped version of the earlier scheme. The minister's answer to this was to commission a consultant's report at significant cost to the taxpayer. Today the internal routes can be operated under the European Public Service Obligation System (PSO), yet there remains little sign of action. What is certain is that the consultant's report having been generated at great cost will be placed in the Assembly Library, where it will merely gather dust. What Wales needs are better politicians and brighter bureaucrats, but this will never be achieved, until the people of Wales take a far greater interest in the political process and 'go out and vote'!

What had started in a 'blaze of glory' ended almost before it began, with a whimper! Any scheduled airline needs a three year operating period to 'bed-down' its routes and begin to generate reasonable operating results. Air Wales was never given that opportunity. Many working in the company had become aware for some time that the demise of the company under the existing regime was inevitable, despite the help of its many friends. Mr Dafydd Wigley, Plaid Cymru MP for Caernarvon, always a good friend to the company, tabled the following question in the House of Commons on the 19th February 1979.

PQ NO 298/78/79

HOUSE OF COMMONS

PARLIAMENTARY QUESTION FOR ANSWER ON MONDAY 19 FEBRUARY 1979

AIR WALES

MR DAFYDD WIGLEY (CAERNARVON): To ask the secretary of state for Wales, if he will take steps to ensure the necessary support for Air Wales for the company to consolidate and expand their air services in Wales.

MR BARRY JONES:

Decisions about the development of this company's services are a matter for the commercial judgement of the operator concerned. My right hon and learned Friend has already accepted for transport supplementary grant a measure of revenue support for the service between Cardiff and Hawarden.

WRITTEN ANSWER

Any faint hope I now had of keeping Air Wales 'afloat' rested with the devolution referendum, which was to be held on St. David's Day, 1st March 1979. I naively thought that should Wales vote for its own Assembly that such an event could bring about a belated rescue of the airline. Instinctively I believed in self-government for Wales, and did all I could to support the idea by appearing on television and speaking on the radio. However, I was to be severely disappointed and the final result proved disastrous. In answer to the question, 'Do you want the provisions of the Wales Act 1978 put into effect?" i.e. Do you want your own assembly?

243,048 (20.3%), voted For
956,335 (79.7%), voted Against

It had been the first time ever that the people of Wales had been given the opportunity to vote on this subject and they had overwhelmingly rejected the idea. Their result said to me that the people of Wales were totally lacking in self-confidence and political aspiration, and therefore simply didn't deserve an Assembly or a National airline, the knowledge simply adding to my existing misery.

David King entered my office unannounced and took a seat on the settee and gazed vacantly into space. Although our relationship had become somewhat strained, they remained cordial to the end. I shuffled some papers on my desk and waited for him to break the silence. Slowly he turned and looking directly at me said, "Well John what are you going to do now, have you got a job lined up?" "Oh yes, I'm going out to the West Indies," I casually responded. He looked surprised at this, as indeed I was myself, as I really hadn't had any time to consider any future job moves. Why I had mentioned the West Indies could only have been the result of some sub-conscious thoughts presaging any action. That evening on the 6th of April 1979, I took G-CELT into the air for Air Wales' last flight to Brussels. Returning to Cardiff some hours later, I flew the aircraft above a well-defined layer of cloud. It was almost as if the aircraft was suspended in space. The stars were bright this night, and it seemed almost possible to reach out and touch them. Here in the warmth and security of the cockpit, the fate of the airline seemed of little consequence, in the vast scheme of things. I was a firm believer in my own destiny, wherever the path should lead; a perspective perhaps reinforced that night by the wondrous panoply of stars. Tomorrow I felt, would certainly be another day, another airline, another aircraft, and even perhaps another country, where one again I would stare at a dimly lit instrument panel, and raise my eyes once more to the stars. I landed that night with unusual care, taxied in and completed the 'shut-down' checks slowly. My co-pilot departed, leaving me alone in the darkened cockpit. I caressed the control column gently, said a little prayer, and wished the aircraft well in all its future flights. Then I walked somewhat wearily away to the Terminal Building.

CHAPTER 12

'DON'T WORRY THE NATIVES ARE FRIENDLY'

'Into each life some rain must fall', are the words of an old song. Well fate had been pouring buckets of the stuff into mine, and in keeping with my habit of taking holidays between jobs, I decided to take one now. Phil Bannister, the Sabena Passenger Manager for the UK and Ireland, had been a good friend of mine throughout the Air Wales period, and it had been largely through his efforts that Sabena had offered such great support to the company. He now obliged me by supplying tickets for me and the family to travel from London to Mexico City. We had never visited that country before and I longed above all else for a sunny beach where I could stretch-out and relax in the company of my wife and children. Yesterday and tomorrow seemed a long way off. We flew from London Heathrow to Brussels, on a Boeing 707 via Montreal to Mexico City. After a few days visiting the sites we embarked on an Aero Mexico DC9 and flew to the coastal resort of Zihuatanejo in Polosi Bay, roughly 120 miles up the coast from Acapulco. We cavorted daily on the beautiful beach but sometimes I was dragged unwillingly to the local shopping mall near the hotel. It was in one of these local shops that my wife fell into conversation with the owner of the store, who had married a Mexican woman. He was of Swedish origin, and my wife who was fluent in that language soon began a lengthy conversation. When it came to an end he turned to me and asked me from what part of the world I hailed. When I said Wales, he told me that he had recently seen a piece on Wales in the local newspaper. My interest aroused, he continued enthusiastically 'Apparently just recently your country had an opportunity to establish your own government, and run your own affairs, yet you turned down the opportunity. What sort of people are you?" I mumbled some response and fled the shop in shame, I felt strongly that the people back home should realise that what is important is not how they see themselves, but how they are perceived by the outside world. Voting no to an Assembly, had sent out a clear message that Wales lacked the self-confidence to run their own affairs, and not worthy to be called a nation. I slept badly that night and made a vow to myself that if Wales ever had a future opportunity to vote on a referendum for self-government and voted yes, then I would once more return to Wales to set-up another national airline.

It was on the beach at Zihuatanejo that we met Jim Cavil, an American from San Francisco. He was well read and much travelled and was keen to hear of my experiences in civil aviation. It appeared that he had a great friend who happened to be the chairman of a regional airline in Belize. Having heard from me that I was now unemployed, he promised to telephone his friend, who was currently looking for a managing director for his airline. The next day after a long telephone call I was offered the position in Belize subject only to my sending a faxed Curriculum Vitae on my return to the UK and signing the letter of agreement, which would be sent to my address forthwith. Well jobs have been obtained in stranger circumstances, but I for one couldn't think of one. Back in Wales just over a week later I received the letter, together with a further letter from a colleague in Brussels, who had fixed me up with a meeting in London for a managing director's position with a French airline in West Africa. At Heathrow I had picked up a current

Flight International Magazine and my wife had alerted me to an advert in the 'jobs' column for an airline chief executive's position in the Caribbean. This advertisement (normally a box number) carried a telephone number so I, with my innate sense of curiosity made contact, and was asked to attend for an interview at Luton Airport the following week. I had it so arranged that I would attend for that interview in the morning, then motor into London to attend the Board for the French job in the afternoon. The ex-RAF wing commander who interviewed me at Luton was clearly out of his depth in the civil field, but quickly informed me at the conclusion of our talk, that he would place me on the short-list for the position. If successful I would set-up and operate this new airline based on the island of Grenada, the most southerly of the Windward Islands, just 100 miles north of Venezuela on the South American continent. In 1974 Grenada had become an independent Commonwealth state, but in 1979 the New Jewel Movement had sized power. This sounded very much like the new challenge I was seeking! The meeting in London that afternoon must have been reminiscent of a pre-Second World War RAF Commissioning Board. These three elderly gentlemen consultants eyed me indifferently from behind a large and elevated desk, ensuring that from their positions they could look down at me. I had already decided on the drive down that this job was not for me, and when they, asked me "What does your mother and father do?" I had great difficulty in maintaining my composure and not bursting into laughter. I looked directly at the Chairman and answered brightly saying "my mother and father were in the iron and steel business." They liked that answer, and glanced at one another with renewed interest and enthusiasm. "Perhaps you would like to elucidate further," said the Chairman, so I did. "My mother irons and my father steals," I said. The remainder of the interview, I seem to remember, was somewhat short, but I walked out happily smiling. So now it was to be Belize or Grenada in the Caribbean. A friend had already informed me that the mosquitoes in Belize were as big as bats, and although this was something of an exaggeration it was enough to tilt the balance towards Grenada and the beautiful beaches of the Caribbean. The next day I telephoned the wing commander and informed him that I had been offered the position as Chief Executive in Belize, and they required an answer in a couple of days. This was a mild exaggeration, and simple blackmail, but it did the trick and he confirmed my appointment in Grenada later that day. So there it was, the Caribbean, and I would be making good my remarks to David King a few weeks before, a self-fulfilling prophesy! Ever since I was a child I had thought of and planned various schemes then worked to achieve successful outcomes, forming an airline was merely one example. Perhaps, of course one's life is pre-determined from the outset, but I would like to think that such creative thinking was a function of free-will, but somehow I still had my doubts!

I flew alone with Monarch Airlines from Luton with my family to follow two weeks later. This would give me an opportunity to 'size-up' the job, and prepare the way. The flight was jammed-packed with holidaymakers and routed via Gander to St. Lucia. My new employer was one Eric Clancy, who was there to meet me, standing on the tarmac holding up a board and on it my name clearly written in large letters. As if reluctant to enter this new world and start life afresh, I waited in my seat until the aircraft had almost emptied then grabbed my bag and descended the aircraft steps and introduced myself. He was a young millionaire from England who had moved to Grenada and had seen the commercial opportunity of creating a new airline based there. He had already bribed the St. Lucia customs officials to avoid the usual formalities, so it was straight across to his Piper Aerostar aircraft for the forty minute flight down the Islands to Grenada. It was becoming dark as we landed, and in the tropics the transition from daylight to night is quite abrupt, and certainly surprised me. Clancy left the aircraft, and began speaking to some airport officials rather earnestly near the Terminal Building. He then rushed back to the aircraft and told me of a change of plan, and that we were now going to Barbados. Clancy was still in the left-hand seat as we levelled off at 3,000 feet. Suddenly he turned to me and asked whether I held a night rating, as he clearly didn't. Following eighteen hours or more of travelling, the time zones and temperature changes, I was dog-tired, but his remarks woke me up with a start. "Yes, of course I have a night rating," I said, whereupon he asked me to fly the aircraft. I had already spent a few hours on this type of aircraft, but here I was desperately tired, in a strange part of the world at night and sitting in the wrong seat. I then asked him for the area and navigational letdown charts for Barbados. "Oh I don't have any," he said, as if it was the most natural thing in the world, to waltz around the Caribbean Islands at night without charts. "But I know the radio frequencies," he continued, like a small boy trying to please. Despite my fatigued state, I flew the aircraft from the right-hand seat which wasn't too easy as it was only equipped for a single pilot operation with all the flight instruments grouped on the left hand side. Viewed from my seat and particularly at night the instruments would appear to show a difference from their actual reading, a phenomena known as 'parallax'. What a way to start a new job I thought, questioning the wisdom of the decision in coming here. It was at this stage also, that I began doubting the sanity of the guy sitting next to me. At least he knew the approach frequency of the airport, and consequently I was able to obtain the rest of the information from the air traffic controller, and so tune in the aircraft navigational instruments and land safely at Barbados Grantly Adams Airport. The next hour we spent wandering around the airport apparently looking for Clancy's wife, who had flown to Barbados earlier on a scheduled carrier to meet up with her father, who was passing through. The events that followed over the next few weeks proved that story to be entirely false however. The missing wife was eventually found breast feeding her baby behind a pillar in the Terminal Building, and collectively we proceeded to the Holiday Inn, where I spent my first night in the Caribbean. Although I had already begun having doubts about the behaviour and competence of my new employer, nothing was going to upset my sleep that first night.

The following day, the third of August 1979, I flew the Aerostar back to Pearls Airport Grenada, the Spice Island, with the Clancy family aboard. Clancy drove me in a Jeep, which was to be mine, to the South of the Island to a small cottage with a swimming pool overlooking a very pretty bay. This was to be the residence for my family and me when they arrived some two weeks later. Now I set about the business of familiarising myself with the islands of the Caribbean, visiting Barbados (this time with the appropriate charts), Trinidad, St. Lucia and Mustique in quick succession. I had no office at first, so I worked out of a small bedroom in the Clancy's household, lacking any normal facilities for preparing airline manuals. Clancy's wife, Gill, was a tall very attractive blonde, and one day with Clancy off the island on business, she walked into my office clad only in the briefest of bikinis. At first I thought she was making a play, but this clearly was not her intention. I quickly became aware of the bruises on her body, running down her back, buttocks and thighs. "How the hell did you get those?" I asked. "Fell down on some stones near the swimming pool," she replied, her eyes telling me otherwise. Casually I asked how she had met her husband. It appeared that he had advertised widely for a personal assistant to tour the world with him, and she had come out on top of a long list of applications (What a good idea I thought, must try that one day.) Subsequently they had married, honeymooned in Las Vegas and settled in Grenada, and her newly born baby joined one by a previous marriage. I now rejoiced, as my wife and children arrived in St. Lucia on the Monarch flight, and I flew up to St. Lucia in the Aerostar to fly them down to Grenada and their new home. I confided in my wife the concerns I held about Clancy, reliving the state of his wife's body, and his irrational behaviour on that first night flight to Barbados, which had set my 'alarm bells' ringing. There was something clearly amiss, and I did not want to be around and involved if and when the situation deteriorated. J had been in many tight and dangerous situations, both on and off the ground, and my instincts had served me well thus far. They were now telling me to 'look out', and perhaps indeed 'get out'.

The day I was to make my first flight to Puerto Rico en-route to San Antonio in Texas with Clancy as companion, a tropical front saw the weather at its most vicious, outside of a hurricane. The pyrotechnics of lightening over the island and the incessant noise of thunder, coupled with torrential rain, could be likened to Dante's Inferno. Certainly I had never witnessed any weather like this in Europe in all my days of flying. Being without a telephone I jumped into the jeep and drove the few miles to the Clancy household, in gale like conditions. His temper this morning, for whatever reasons matched that of the storm, and his opening salvo began with the words, "You don't want to fly do you?" spraying out the words like machine gun bullets. Taken aback by this reception I merely answered, "I came here to check with the airport the forecast meteorological conditions for the flight." What I heard didn't please me any, but I agreed to go on an hour's drive to the Airport. Conditions were so bad, that the bridge spanning the river near the Airport had been washed away, so we were forced to take a more circuitous route. The latest weather did indicate that the storm was slowly edging westwards, and although I was uneasy with the conditions, I was persuaded against my better judgement, to take-off and fly east towards Barbados and check the weather at first hand at altitude. As it happened the storm passed westwards at a greater speed than predicted, and with a powerful tail wind we made Puerto Rico in record time. However I frankly hated myself in allowing Clancy to persuade me to fly that day against my better judgement. That had never happened previously and I was never going to allow it to happen again. From San Juan Puerto Rico we boarded an Eastern Airline's scheduled flight to San Antonio in Texas, and I was still seething inside when Clancy and I took our seats in the forward section of the aircraft. As we taxied out for take-off I turned towards him and gripped him by his shoulder placing my eyes close to his, and said "Don't you ever do that to me again." He smiled at me indulgently like a small boy who has had his own way, but I knew now, only too well, that he could not control his violent mood swings, and that here I had a very sick boy masquerading as a man. Twenty-five years later when I looked up the details of that flight in my log book, I found I had annotated it with just one word—'Mad'!

The visit to Texas, as far as I could make out, was to buy a new Swearingen Metro aircraft, and to arrange my training on the type with Flight Safety, the renowned flight training organisation in the States. Here I met for the first time Bruce Chuber, the Vice President of International Sales for Swearingen Aircraft Corporation. Here was a man constructed in the John Wayne mould, big, self confident, yet immensely funny and assertive. We became good friends, and some years later we were to work closely together both in Berlin and the Caribbean. In his time he had many flying adventures delivering Cessna aircraft to outlandish airfields in South America. He had amazing luck on one occasion when delivering a single engined aircraft across 2,000 miles or so of Pacific Ocean to Honolulu, a crazy thing to do in any event. Nearly the end of his journey he lost his way in bad weather, but providentially put his aircraft down in one piece on an uninhabited island, one in the Hawaii chain. Later the authorities picked up his beacon signals and were able to pin point his position and rescue him. Several weeks later I re-visited San Antonio for my planned course, and spent two weeks on the aircraft simulator and in ground school by day, and visiting the night spots in the evening with Bruce. San Antonio itself is a beautiful city, and the highlight of my stay was a visit to the Alamo, where I saw the dragon flag of Wales proudly flying, representing the Welshmen who died there, defending the fort against the overwhelming Mexican forces of General Santa Ana in 1836. Clearly I hadn't been the first Welshman to visit the Alamo, but unlike some of my resident forebears I had no reason to remain there that long, and soon departed once more through Miami to Grenada suitably enamoured with my ninety-eight percent pass-mark on the course. Clancy had been busy in my absence, and had located suitable premises as my office half way along the road to St. George's, the island capital. He had also acquired for me, an American secretary who unfortunately found spelling and typing somewhat difficult. Judy however was a vastly entertaining person and within a matter of days had summed up the dreaded Clancy. We spent many hours discussing this strange phenomenon and work on the airline documents became of secondary importance. My next flight was to Barbados once more, to carry all the pictures from the Clancy home, which had been mysteriously smashed. I yet again began to fear for the safety of the other occupants of that household, but their decision to stay or flee was not one I could make, or render an opinion on, as it would woe betide me or anybody else, who would intervene between man and wife. It was at this stage, that I discovered that she had fled the island on the day of my arrival hoping to catch a flight from Barbados and return to the UK. The story of her father passing through Barbados had clearly been a fabrication.

Now I began to feel rather desperate, and began to send out my curriculum vitae to a number of companies in Europe, hoping for salvation from the crazy situation in which I found myself. Had I been alone the decision would have been easy, but my home back in Wales had been rented out for a year, and having my family with me, I now decided that the only ploy available to me was to play for time, and be patient, not my strongest suit I must say. I had of course, not decided on working in the West Indies without taking some precautions, and had telephoned the Foreign Office on a number of occasions regarding the stability or otherwise of the area. The most I got in answer to my requests was the remark, 'that the natives are friendly'! Additionally requests to the old wing commander at Luton

Airport, for information on the character and financial viability of Mr Clancy had also drawn a blank response. But what is life without risk, and it is always better to travel hopefully, than never travel at all. I had fallen in love with the island of Grenada with its sun soaked unpolluted beaches. It was just one of the many beautiful islands that stretched down from Puerto Rico and the Virgin Islands to the South American continent. For both sailor and airman it was at least for most of the year, much of a paradise where green seas beat at rust coloured reefs, and leggy palms fringed legendary beaches. The children in their beautiful school uniforms and the young ones in their knee pants and school caps were a pleasure to behold. No parent's cars to take them to school in the morning, yet in groups they would happily walk miles to their destination, a marked contrast, I thought, to the UK today. Yet into this paradise, politics had thrust its ugly head in the shape of Grenada's Prime Minister Sir Eric Gairy (notice the knighthood bestowed by a British Government), who had a predilection for woman's clothes and a fervent belief in flying saucers. Grenada at that time was the second smallest member of the United Nations, but by no means the least talkative. Before his last visit to the UN in New York, he had filled a boat with all the weapons he thought were on the island, confident in so doing, that he would avoid a coup d'etat. Unknown to him however, a great number of arms had been infiltrated into the country during his many absences. It was on one of these occasions that the so-called New Jewel Movement under its leader Maurice Bishop, announced over the radio that its new people's Revolutionary Army had taken possession of the country with Bishop as the new Prime Minister. With Gairy abroad and all his Ministers in gaol the new Marxist regime took control. This was the country I had been told by a Foreign Office official where 'the natives are friendly'. It was this Marxist Government that Clancy had to negotiate with to establish a national airline for Grenada. Later, much later in fact, I discovered that he had spent half a million United States dollars to prepare the ground for the new airline. Indeed the routes I had planned for him from Grenada to Caracas, Puerto Rico and Barbados were at the point of finalisation when the Revolutionary Government sent the proposals to Havana and that was the end of that! The atmosphere on the island had become quite feverish with troops everywhere. The island radio announced daily on all the military triumphs, including the capture in a heroic action of the local post office by two soldiers and a dog. I still occupied my little office with my American secretary and the new regime had little effect on our day to day lives, and my children attended school in St. Georges in the normal way. Near Christmas I received a call from Scotty Thompson, the managing director of Inter Island Airways, who had acted as a line check captain during my flights to many of the Islands. "John, you probably don't know that I am leaving this job to set up a new operation based on St. Lucia. Consequently we are looking for a new managing director, and I had completely forgotten you were available and here on the Island." I readily affirmed my interest and agreed to go with him to Antigua to meet the Chairman of LIAT (Leeward Island Air Transport), the parent company of Inter Island Airways. I imposed only one condition that he would approach Clancy and inform him that I had been asked to take the job, and this he agreed to do. Much to my surprise Clancy offered no objection to this, and even allowed me to use the Aerostar to fly to Antigua for my interview. Dev Archer was the genial and very likeable chairman and chief executive of LIAT at that time, and he greeted me warmly. During the interview he asked me why I had applied for the position. I corrected him, pointing out I had been approached by Captain Thompson. He then offered me the position immediately without further discussion. I did however, ask him for a week's grace before I accepted or rejected his offer as I wished to discuss the offer with my family and relations. Secretly I hoped that one of my job applications would be successful, thus at least providing me with a choice. Mr Archer agreed to this request and I promised to contact him within the next week. At the end of that period I had heard nothing from my applications and consequently signed up for a two year stint as managing director of Inter Island Airways, still however based in Grenada.

LIAT had been established in 1956, with BWIA (British West Indian Airlines) providing most of the equity capital, primarily for LIAT to operate services in to the smaller islands, and to act as a feeder service for the main airline. The company had grown significantly by the time of my arrival, when it was using Hawker Siddely 748 (HS748) aircraft, and the ubiquitous Britten Norman (BN2) aircraft. In 1971 Court Line of Luton UK had purchased seventy-five percent of the holding, the remainder being held by the various Governments in the Caribbean. When Court Line collapsed in 1974, it took emergency aid from the UK and local governments to keep it going. A former director of Court Line told me an amusing story about a creditor's meeting held in Antigua. The Official Receiver had turned to the erstwhile financial director of the company and told him that he had his Note of Guarantee for the sum of $500,000 (five hundred thousand US Dollars). This director (a Welshman as it proved), asked to see the note whereupon it was pushed across the table to him, whilst the other directors looked on. Having read the note slowly and calmly, he put it in his mouth and ate it, much to the amazement of his fellow directors and the chagrin of the Official Receiver. Thus in a stroke he removed all the physical evidence of the debt. I have no doubt as to the veracity of this story, as it is was told me by a director who had been present at that very meeting. It merely goes to prove, what I had known from a young age, that the Welsh are a very clever lot! Today that Welshman continues to live in magnificent splendour in Miami, and his digestive system remains in fine fettle.

As a last favour to Clancy, I agreed to fly his Aerostar aircraft to Pompano Beach in Florida where it was required for major maintenance. Although I had received a rough ride by just being in his company, there had been compensatory benefits. He had paid me regularly without demur, and I had benefited as a pilot by flying into new airports like Caracas, San Juan Puerto Rico, Trinidad, Barbados and St. Kitts etc. an experience which would stand me in good stead in my new job. My flight to Pompano Beach became very interesting as I routed via San Juan, then by way of South Caicos Island to Fort Lauderdale Executive Airport, where I would clear customs. Finally a short hop to Pompano Beach, the end of my journey. I had read many stories of the mysterious happenings in the so-called Bermuda Triangle and my track would pass through its western edge. I had climbed to 18,000 feet in beautiful weather after leaving South Caicos and soon noticed that the sea and sky seemed to merge in an indeterminate cream like colour, although it was still possible to see the various Cays and islets below. For almost an hour I failed to contact Miami Centre on the radio despite trying a number of frequencies. Sitting alone with the sun beating down on the canopy, I suddenly looked at the empty seat next to me and knew that my father was there alongside. He had died only months before my arrival in the West Indies, but the sensation of his presence was undeniably strong. I talked to him at length about our lives together back in Wales, and as I did a warm feeling and reassurance spread through my very being. Never in my 10,000 hours of flying had I experienced any extra sensory feelings of this kind, yet here I was a rational human being talking in measured terms to an empty seat. Minutes later my call to Miami was answered, and no, they had not received my previous radio calls. A week later, after I returned from Pompano Beach, I received a telephone call from the chief engineer working on the aircraft there. It appeared that the tail of the aircraft had been riddled with salt corrosion and he could not understand why the whole tail section had not failed during my flight. I sat quietly in a corner of the airport and mused as to who measured the fate of one man against another. Yet again I had been lucky, or had it been fate or my dad's presence which had contrived to keep the aircraft flying in one piece to its final destination?

CHAPTER 13

AMOUNG THE REVOLUTIONARIES

By the late 1960s Grenada, nominally still a British dependency, was in the hands of one Eric Gairy, who later was knighted by the Queen, as already described. He enjoyed dressing up as a woman and was a womaniser to boot! Also a firm believer in flying saucers he later made many speeches on the subject at the United Nations in New York. By 1973 Gairy had applied for Grenada's independence, the first island in the Caribbean Associated States so to do. The opposition to Gairy in the early days had been slight, but two young Grenadian lawyers soon changed all that. Maurice Bishop had taken Silk at Lincoln's Inn in London, and when in 1970 he returned from London he 'teamed-up' with another lawyer Kendrick Radix to start the New Jewel Movement, standing for 'Joint Endeavour for Welfare Education and Liberation'. In 1976 at the first post independence election a challenge was offered to Gairy's rule, and six seats were won to Gairy's nine. Bishop and Bernard Coard, later to become Bishop's deputy, were among the six. Evidence now existed; that Communism was being spread throughout the eastern Caribbean by Cuban intelligence agents, in an area always considered by the USA as an American lake. At that stage however, Jimmy Carter, the then President of the United States, saw little to fear and consequently no action was taken. The 'Mongoose Gang', who was in effect 'Gairy's Heavies', had terrorised the opposition since its inception, and Maurice Bishop's father had been murdered by them. His picture on thousands of leaflets, were stuck to trees all over the island, where they remained well after my arrival. Finally the Gairy Government was overthrown by armed force on the 12th of March 1979, when the People's Revolutionary Government took over. Less than five months later I had arrived in the island with the Foreign Office words still ringing in my ears 'Don't worry the natives are friendly'. Within weeks of the New Jewel Movement taking over the Government, heavy armaments began flooding in from Cuba. The weapons, even to my unpractised eye, were pretty sophisticated and largely Russian in origin. Machine gun posts had been set-up throughout the area and an anti-aircraft position had been put in place at Pearl's Civil Airport. The official propaganda was resolutely anti-American and in some respects anti-white also, although myself and family were always treated with respect and in a friendly fashion.

On the 18th of January 1980, I completed my instrument rating and base check successfully, flying between Antigua and Guadeloupe in a LIAT aircraft. The next day I went to work, completing ten landings at Carricou, Union Island, St. Vincent and St. Lucia before returning to Grenada. This appeared to be the general 'milk-run' of the company, flying northwards to St. Lucia before the return flights to Grenada. There are two defining weather periods in the Caribbean Islands, the wet and the dry seasons. The seasonal temperatures varied between 25°C to 32°C, but the humidity ranged up to 90 percent in the wet season and was quite horrendous. The cockpit was like an oven, your shirt a damp cloth in seconds with sweat running in rivulets down every part of the body, quickly rotting away your belt and trousers. It was paradise to reach 2,000 feet where it was relatively cool, but with flight sectors rarely exceeding thirty minutes this respite was only temporary, before the descent commenced once more into the oven-like conditions.

My family now moved from the south of the island to the north coast, sitting just above a most beautiful beach with splendid views north up the Grenadine islands. Huge concrete blocks had been placed just offshore, thereby creating a most wonderful and natural salt-water swimming pool several hundred yards long and about twenty yards wide, and no more than four feet in depth. The huge blocks of stone ensured completely safe swimming in an idyllic sea temperature ranging from 75 to 85 degrees Fahrenheit. The sea around of course had its fair proportion of sharks, and quite often whilst flying along the multitude of islands they could be seen swimming in droves in the beautifully clear water. There was no organised Air Sea Rescue in the islands and my greatest fear was having to land in the water for whatever reason. A short time after I finished my contract with LIAT, a company Twin Otter Aircraft with sixteen passengers aboard ditched in the sea just south of Hewanorra Airport on the south coast of St. Lucia. Neither the aircraft or any of its passengers were ever seen again, a subject on which, as one of the world's heavy sinkers, I was never keen to dwell. My young son, Gavin, and daughter, Sian, were now attending school in Sauteurs on the north coast of Grenada, but here unlike the expatriate school for white children in the south, all the children were of West Indian origin. In one of the earliest days of my children's attendance at the school, a small boy from a local village was seen rubbing his upper arm with a rope end. The more he rubbed the more he cried, until eventually the teacher noticed, and asked him why he was doing that, he replied that he was trying to get down to the white! It appears my children were the first white children he had ever seen in his life, and with the sea, sun and salt of the island they were almost pure blond in colour. It has to be said that during our two years or more of residency on the island we as a family were treated wonderfully well by the Grenadians, and for most of our stay any threats to our safety were more imagined than real.

As the managing director of the locally based airline it was clear that sooner or later I would come into contact with the leaders of the Revolutionary Government (The New Jewel Movement). It happened one morning when I arrived at the airport to fly the schedule up the islands. Carriacou was the first stop, an island belonging to Grenada just fifteen minutes flying time north. Annette, one of my delightful traffic staff, seemed to be somewhat upset and stressed that morning, and as soon as I arrived in the building she cried out, "Cap, the Prime Minister and the Army have already boarded and are waiting", and this despite the fact that it was still thirty minutes before the scheduled departure time. I looked in the aircraft, exchanged the normal courtesies, and saw that every seat was taken by a soldier with the Prime Minister sitting alongside General Hudson in the second row. What I then saw appalled me, for every soldier had a submachine gun across his knees, and in an instance I saw that the safety catches were in the firing position. I looked directly at Mr Bishop and said, "I'm sorry, sir, but the guns will have to be carried in the baggage hold and not in the aircraft." I had already visualised the aircraft rocked in turbulence and an idle finger tightening on the trigger and spraying us all with bullets. There was a few seconds of silence. 'My God,' I thought, 'what have I done, he may just order me out behind a building and have the soldiers shoot me,' and I was amazed at my own temerity, or was it stupidity. Every head in the aircraft turned towards the Prime Minister in a silence which seemed positively sinister. It was seconds later, but appeared many minutes, before Mr Bishop nodded his head in agreement. I collected all the guns with the safety catches now on and securely stowed them in the rear of the aircraft out of harm's way. Fifteen minutes later the wheels of the aircraft touched the concrete runway at Carriacou. To my amazement and without any regard for their safety the soldiers began leaping out of the aircraft during the landing roll. They ran alongside the aircraft as it slowed ripping out the guns from the rear compartment and handing them out to willing hands. Clearly the revolution had not been as successful as they claimed, and they were still concerned with subversives in their midst. Fortunately that morning there were none present and no gunfight ensued. When I grew to know the Prime Minister better I realised that he was a decent man, if not a shy one. He once asked me, what were my views on Margaret Thatcher, the then Prime Minister of the UK, and her government. I professed little love for that administration, which seemed to please him, as his request to them for an armoured car of some sort had been refused.

The island had now become quite a dangerous place with arms from Cuba flooding in at an increasing rate. Young children of fifteen years or more were now armed with Russian or Cuban revolvers or rifles. In their enthusiasm many Wyatt Earps were created, and some managed to shoot themselves in their more delicate parts. I did witness a young Grenadian on the harbour wall in St. George's, throw his submachine gun down into his small boat, with the safety catch off, the gun suddenly sprayed bullets about haphazardly. The young boy soldier watched in horror as the boat, with a gentle 'glug glug', disappeared into the depths of the harbour taking his gun with it. I had received an invitation from Comrade Unison Whiteman, who was the Minister for Tourism, to attend a reception at the Horse Shoe Bay Hotel near St. George's, the date Friday 27th June 1980. As I was unsure of the directions to the hotel, I asked a young Len McCleish, a Grenadian taxi driver, and a good friend of mine to drive me there in my car. Len loved driving the old Volkswagen Beetle and having him along that evening saved my life. It was getting dark as we left the reception and drove along the main road into St. George's. Almost at once we met the first roadblock manned by members of the Revolutionary Army, armed to the teeth with a variety of weapons including Kalashnikov rifles (AK47, capable of firing 600 rounds per minute). A second and a third roadblock quickly followed as we climbed out of St. George's northwards across the island.

As the managing director of the local airline I was generally well known to the militia, unfortunately to many of the youngsters now carrying guns I was merely another 'white man'. Len now suddenly stopped the car on a deserted stretch of the mountain road. "What's up Len?" I asked. "Look Cap," he replied, "there's bush." On the centre of the road there was a small thin branch of a tree, which I would have driven over had I been alone. "Come on Len," I cried, "let's go." "No! No! Cap we will have to wait here." Impatiently, I sat for two or three minutes for no apparent reason, then out of the darkness about a dozen figures emerged, and approached the car from both sides of the road. In the local Grenadian patois Len exchanged words with the leader of the group, but we were both forced to step out of the car to be searched. I stood spread-eagled against the car while a young girl of about seventeen years searched me for weapons, her hands probing between my legs and buttocks, a task which she seemed to enjoy. Apparently satisfied, she then opened the glove compartment in the car and took out a small cardboard box, which contained a part of a car shock absorber, which was a round solid metal ball. When she grasped this, she suddenly screamed and dropped it on the road clearly believing it to be a hand grenade. This young girl clearly had received no weapons training, as hand grenades are not willy nilly dropped around, safety-pin in or out. Len and I were now aware that the Grenadians were playing war games that night, so the remainder of the journey was slow and tedious. In all, we were held up at gunpoint eleven times, and without the presence of Len in the car I am convinced that I would never have made it safely back to my family.

My next near death experience did not involve the People's Revolutionary Army. My wife and I had been invited to dinner at the home of a Government minister, and for the first and last time on the island, we left our two young children at home in the care of a very trustworthy Grenadian child minder. In order to reach the destination, we journeyed along an unfamiliar road culminating in a long shallow hill. At the bottom I saw strewn on the road some of the now familiar 'bush'. The roads in Grenada tended to be full of pot holes so my speed generally was between 20 and 30 mph. As I approached the bush I slowed further, remembering my previous experience, although I was aware that there were no war games this night. The only alternative road was a dark narrow track on my left, which seemed only to lead to a stone farmhouse. I pressed on rather slowly and cautiously and suddenly found to my horror that the road in front had completely disappeared. What had been a narrow bridge had collapsed into a mountain ravine some fifty feet below. I braked as hard as I could and the car came to rest with the front offside wheel hanging in space over the precipice. The nearside front wheel was resting on a foot's width of remaining road. My wife started to open the passenger door to get out clearly without realising that had she done so, the ensuing balance would have sent the car with me in it toppling onto the rocks in the ravine below. I crawled across the wife to the open door with her hanging grimly around my waist until we were both clear. Then in typical female manner, she remembered that she had left her handbag on the back seat of the vehicle, so the contortions continued as I stretched to retrieve it. We made our way to the nearest farmhouse, in deep shock, when we considered the implications for our two young children had we perished. Having explained our plight to the locals it took less than ten minutes for a crowd to appear and pull the car to safety. When we reached our destination the Minister and his guests sympathised with us, and told us that all the local people knew of the collapsed bridge. Unfortunately this example of the 'jungle telegraph' was one to which most of the white people were not connected.

In general Grenada was not a dangerous place, unless of course you showed yourself implacably hostile to the new Government. My family and I was treated with a great friendliness by the local people, and mixed with them more often than not, preferring them in most cases to some of the white expatriates living in the area. I was however alarmed at the great influx of arms pouring into the island from Cuba. I used an intermediary to pass on this information to the British Consulate in Barbados, but what action was taken, if any, was not conveyed to me. The Americans were now clearly concerned by the airport construction at Point Salines on the south end of the island. Apart from arms, Cuban doctors, teachers and dentists all arrived in addition to the many construction workers. Huge trucks driven by Cubans arrived on the already damaged Grenadian roads, creating huge delight among the mass of locals, who liked nothing better than to clamber aboard, and stand there smiling on everybody as they swayed their way across the island. In complete contrast to the local work ethic, the Cubans would toil away in the heat, while the Grenadians were happy to sit under the palm trees and watch contentedly. However, this smallest nation in the western hemisphere with great economic problems, had by this time, created a standing army of two thousand men and a militia of almost eight thousand.

The British had taken over this island like many others in the Caribbean during the seventeenth and eighteenth centuries. The had provided a civil service, a police force and a modicum of education for the locals, but on the whole the Brits kept themselves largely to themselves, in the houses, clubs and yachts. They however depended on the locals to provide the labour, and supply the goods, which were then transported back to Britain. It was now the Cubans who supplied the schools with books, teachers and training. My dentist was a Cuban, who was quite brilliant, and was both fluent in Spanish and English. The Grenadians on the whole still lived in their little huts on stilts, with their fresh water supply obtained from a communal tap, where every morning would stand a queue of women waiting their turn to fill their buckets and pans. The men on the other hand seemed to do little work of any description, at least, little that I ever saw during my stay. Each morning as I drove slowly to the airport at about 0600 hours,

I always passed a man stretched out on a fallen branch, his hat pulled down over his eyes. Probably recognising the sound of my Volkswagen, he would unfailingly shout out, "Good morning, Cap," as I passed by. When I returned some eight hours later he would still be there and greet me in the same manner, his position on the branch unchanged. He only had to reach up and grasp a readily available banana to sustain himself during the day, so no great effort was needed there! Gangs of women were employed on a continual basis to fill in the many potholes in the roads. Most mornings I would drive past a very fat Grenadian lady balancing a board on her head. This board carried a large amount of tar, which she had made for her road repairing work. As I passed slowly by with all the windows open, (my only air conditioning), she would speak out in a rhetorical fashion, "White man Cap", without as much as a look in my direction. Friendliness could indeed take many forms and invitations to Grenadian homes were quite frequent. One evening I had left my car in a garage and begun the short walk home, as I did, I fell into step alongside a young Grenadian girl carrying a young baby. I ventured the usual compliments as to the beauty of the baby, but I was shaken by her automatic response. She looked at me and said, "Would you like to make one with me, Cap?" Looking at my watch I replied quickly, that I had to take a flight out that afternoon and therefore couldn't spare the time. Her remark was not made, because she thought I was any more attractive or wealthy than the next guy. Her main desire was to give birth to a baby with a whiter skin than other babies and certainly whiter than herself. Maybe this was a historical built-in desire of the West Indian, clearly misconceived, as to the perceived superiority of the white man, and of course the recent curse of slavery. Indeed there remained on the islands many relics of slavery. Manacles adorned the walls of many buildings where slaves had been tied up at night like animals. For some West Indians the epoch of slavery lived on in their hearts, and one of my pilots living in St. Lucia positively hated me, simply because I was white.

Fortunately he was the one exception to the rule, and I found out that if you treated them fairly and well, they reciprocated in kind. I have often wondered how I would have reacted had our roles been reversed. With much less grace, I felt sure!

It was of interest also to compare the living standards and way of life in those islands once controlled under the British Crown and their French counterparts. The British West Indies were never made citizens of the British Empire, whereas the French dependencies of Martinique and Guadeloupe were considered outposts of France and every person living there became a citizen of that country. A policeman in Lyon may well have been of West Indian birth, and a Frenchman born in France may well have filled a similar role in the West Indies. By this time of course St. Lucia, Grenada, St Vincent as well as Barbados and Trinidad had become independent states, but the contrast with the French islands was all too evident, with their people living in high-rise apartment blocks and driving their cars on freeways (motorways).

My wife normally drove the children to school every morning to the village of Sauteurs, but on some mornings Tim, a smart seventeen year old Grenadian, would appear at the house early and volunteer for the job. He was a good looking, intelligent boy, who had aspirations to become an airline pilot. Many evenings I would sit with him at home and discuss the various aspects of the civil aviation business. Then I would teach him basic air navigation, the use of the pilot's computer, meteorology and other sundry subjects. He quickly grasped the basics of these subjects and I felt that he should be sponsored by the Government to join a pilot's school in the States or the UK. With this in mind I decided to raise this subject with Mr Bishop, the Prime Minister, when I saw him next. Before I could do this however, the terrible news broke. It appeared that Tim had been in a car with three other people, one of whom in the opinion of the New Jewel Movement was a subversive, in other words anti-Marxist. Their car was stopped at night on a lonely road, and all the occupants in the car, including Tim, brutally murdered. Tim was found with seventeen bullet wounds, one for each year of his life as it happened, emphasising that the militia wanted no prisoners and certainly no witnesses. I saw two bodies that morning on my way to the airport, but I was waved angrily, or impatiently, on by the heavily armed soldiers before I could stop and identify Tim's body. At this time there appeared to be a purge against any real, or perceived, opponents of the regime. Young Joe, just nineteen, worked for me at Pearls Airport, as a baggage handler, but his brother considered a subversive had already been 'locked up' in the prison at St. George's. Young Joe had become quite paranoid, and expected imprisonment, or worse, at an early date. He now sought my help to escape the island and fly to the USA, where he already had relations in New York. Tourism had almost halved under the new regime and I had impressed it upon the Government to operate extra flights to the island. With this in mind, I used my powers of persuasion to help them purchase their own aircraft for this purpose, which Inter Island Airways would operate on their behalf. The Embraer Bandeirante was the aircraft I had in mind, and somewhat to my surprise they accepted my proposals and the deal was done! This involved a further trip for me and some of my pilots to the Embraer facilities in San Jose dos Campos in Brazil for training. I then made the suggestion that young Joe also make the trip to be trained as an aircraft mechanic. In this way an exit-visa was obtained, and I sent Joe off to Barbados to join a connecting flight to Miami and thence Rio de Janeiro. I advised ham to carry a white set of overalls and a hammer, so that whilst in transit at Miami Airport he could pose as an aircraft worker and pass through security. This ruse worked and eventually Joe reached New York and to my knowledge remains there to this day.

The initial months with the company passed peacefully enough. I passed any requests or orders verbally by personally flying to all the islands where my staff were stationed as the postal and telephone services left much to be desired. We did have short wave radios at our offices, but the reception particularly in the wet season was also abysmal. After a while at the job I suddenly found that many of my orders had not registered, or had been quietly ignored, and life continued in the same old way. In Grenada I had two lovely girls in passenger reception. I called them in my office one day and had them to stand side by side facing me. First I spoke to Annette, "Tell me Annette, did you carry out the tasks I listed last week?" "Yes Cap," she replied, smiling at me. "Did you do the work yourself Annette?" "Well, no Cap. I asked Cheryl to do it." I then turned to Cheryl, who was also smiling broadly at me, and said, "Cheryl did Annette ask you to carry out the work?" "No Cap," she said, still happily smiling. I continued the same line of questioning for a few more minutes without a glimmer of success, so like a good manager, I decided to quit whilst on top. Generally however, I learned to trust my employees and found them capable of hard work, and therefore it was no surprise to find that the airline had made a small profit at the end of the financial year, at a time when the parent company had made considerable losses. To my amazement I soon discovered that very few of my employees had ever left the island of their birth, so had little idea of the problems facing their colleagues elsewhere on the route system. I therefor arranged for staff to fly on our scheduled services to other islands, and spend a week working there. This ploy was enjoyed by everybody, and without doubt improved company efficiency. However, as most islands were classed as separate states problems inevitably rose over immigration rights and work permits. At first I completely ignored the laws of the day, but political pressure was brought to bear and it was inevitable that in the end I was forced to return to the status quo however not before a great deal of good had been done. A few years later I visited some of the islands whilst on a demonstration tour with a new aircraft. I was received with 'open arms' and great friendliness and even my former pilot colleague in St.

Lucia, who had no love for the whites, greeted me like an old buddy, but then of course I was no longer his boss.

Flying the scheduled routes could be very boring in the dry season, and sometimes very frightening during the wet season. Despite my exhalted position as managing director, I still found in necessary to fly a minimum three or four days a week and sometimes more if one of my pilots was sick or absent for any reason. A duty period usually involved 8 to 12 landings and sometimes more. My flying log book indicates that in December 1980 I made 85 landings in the course of eight days and on one occasion actually completed 18 landings on one day. The UK Ministry of Aviation law on flying duty periods carried little weight here, and the company still operated under the then defunct 1964 Air Navigation Order, and even that was interpreted rather loosely. The daily schedule ran from Grenada to Carriacou, then on to Canaan or Mustique, Union Island, then by way of St. Vincent to Hewanorra Airport on the southern coast of St. Lucia. Finally a short hop up and around the northern tip of the island to Vigie Airport and the capital Castries. The company also operated daily flights from St. Lucia to the French island of Martinique and a weekly positioning flight to Antigua for maintenance. Perhaps it wasn't so surprising that until my arrival the airline had operated without a published timetable, and I never once saw one published by the parent company either. Perhaps that was the reason LIAT standing for Leeward Island Air Transport was amusingly referred to as 'leave island any time'! I therefore produced a timetable for Inter Island Airways in the American Commuter style, which pleased my chairman no end, the format being eventually copied by the parent company.

It was now left to me to organise our schedule departure to Brazil for myself, two of my pilots and also the Director of Civil Aviation for the West Indies and his wife. The presence of the Director was an essential part of my plan, which will soon become apparent. As I had previously attended the training course in Brazil with Air Wales my presence there was in essence to control the mob and re-acquaint myself with the Bandeirante aircraft. More importantly however, it was to ensure the aircraft was approved by the Director of Civil Aviation (DCA) and placed on the West Indian register without problems arising. I knew some of the Directors of Embraer from my previous visit and assured them that for us to achieve the desired ends, it would be very necessary to charm and entertain the DCA and his wife. I had also persuaded the DCA to bring to Brazil all his stamps of approval. This he did with good grace, and he and his wife were lavished with goodies and entertainment during their stay. The day our training ended and as the DCA emerged grinning from the Embraer Boardroom I grabbed him and led him to an office where all our licences and forms were laid out awaiting the appropriate stamps of approval. Like a lamb he carried out these duties with a certain aplomb. It had been a superb example of discrete blackmail, without which weeks might have elapsed before his administration got their act together, and the aircraft utilised on the company's schedules.

The night before I has left the West Indies for Rio in Brazil, I night stopped at the Holiday Inn in Barbados. The English cricket team was also in residence, and as I sat with one of my pilots in the hotel lounge I spied Geoffrey Boycott, the English opening batsman, walking across to the bar alone. Never having met him I called out, "Hey Geoff over here." He came across and for the next hour or so we talked cricket. "It was more congenial talking to you," he said, "than that bunch down the hall," pointing to the rest of the team. Apart from himself, he said, it was only Gower with his natural ability who could bat at the highest level. Furthermore, he explained, that if he got out early against, the West Indian quickies, the dressing room on his return would be in a state of funk. He described Michael Holding as a black beetle on his run in to the wicket, and by far the most dangerous of bowlers. He asked me if I played, and I was pleased to tell him that at one time I had been attached to the Glamorgan County cricket staff, that is before my RAF service took me away. Establishing that I had a young son, he said that he would give me a copy of his book, entitled I believe 'The Boycott Book of Cricket'! What a decent guy I thought to myself, as he left the lounge to fetch me a copy. When he returned he suitably autographed and dated the book made out to my son Gavin. He then said, "And that will be fourteen pounds ninety nine pence." I looked at him to see if he was serious or not—he was! I duly paid up, and when I left I spent a few minutes pondering on Mr Boycott in particular and Yorkshire men in general. I had heard that they were really Scotsmen with all the generosity knocked out of them, but was nevertheless pleased that I had met him. I learned later that he had bought a copy of his book from the hotel shop and the presented it to me for payment. What a chap!

I took the Bandeirante VP-LCM off the ground at San Jose dos Campos in Brazil at 0330 hours on the morning of the 19th March 1981 bound for Grenada. The early departure was made simply to avoid the huge weather build-ups that could occur in the heat of the afternoon. My first landing was made at Brasilia, the capital of the country. Flying over the city was a totally new experience with its geometric setting and very wide boulevards, much wider than any city I had ever seen before. The next landing took place in a large jungle clearing at Carolina. Here we were beset by a throng of young Brazilian children. I sat on the aircraft steps about to eat the sandwiches in the lunch box, when I observed the look on their faces. Clearly they were very hungry so I brought out all the food on the aircraft and watched them demolish it in next to no time. The next landing was at Belem near the mouth of the Amazon River on the equator. Here it was stifling hot (32°C) with a high degree of humidity (90 percent) and I felt in a very bad way, carrying influenza and a chest infection, which had really bugged me for days. We night stopped near the airport, in a hotel where the air conditioning had failed. Sleeping was almost an impossibility and

I was soaked in a continual bath of perspiration, no doubt assisted by the paracetamol tablets I had taken. The following morning I was airborne at 1040 hours en-route for Zanderij Airport, at Paramaribo the capital city of Suriname. The weather was excellent and I levelled the aircraft at 10,000 feet. It took me almost 15 minutes to cross the mouth of the Amazon River, where I watched the yellow effluent from the river stain the sea surface almost ten miles from the shore. The remainder of the flight took place over a solid green mass of Amazonian jungle as far as the eye could see, and as I gazed at this wide expanse of green I fervently prayed that I would not have to make a forced landing here. Even if we had survived, I very much doubted that we would ever have been found. Zanderij Airport was almost deserted as we landed at 1350 hours and by 1530, having refuelled, we were once more on our way, this time direct to Pearls Airport, Grenada. The coastal rout along the north eastern coast of Guyana took us past the lovely named towns of Timehri and Charity, before crossing Trinidad toward Grenada. The whole flight had taken almost thirteen and a half hours, and a huge crowd had been directed by the Government to attend our arrival, with Government Ministers and a band in attendance. By this time I was almost 'out on my feet', but I could not refuse the Ministers when they requested I take them on a pleasure flight around the island. When we reached Point Salines, where the now airport was being constructed, I pealed off from 3,000 feet and dived flat out across the new airfield, followed by a hard pull-up on the control column, which must have caused some stomach pains in the back of the aircraft. When I landed back at Pearls the Ministers were as excited as children, having seen and flown in their own aircraft, and despite the mild aerobatics complimented me on my flying. I spent the next couple days recuperating in bed with a temperature of over 100°.

It was at this time also that the dreaded asthma returned to haunt me. Most nights I would be forced to leave my bed and sit head down between my knees in the toilet, where I found breathing a little easier. Grenada is well known as the Spice Island, and it was the blooms and their perfumes, that caused the allergic reaction. When I got airborne around 2,000 feet or more, my chest would relent, and clear of the allergies I felt a return to normality. However, the task of dressing in the morning, and driving to the airport, now became tasks almost beyond me as I struggled to breathe, but fortunately, help from a strange source was at hand. Every Sunday the beach tended to attract a group of the locals, and I generally joined them in a game of cricket. I stood down one day owing to my breathing difficulties, and had to explain to my Rasta friends the details of my health problems, "Cap," one said, "I will visit your home tomorrow and bring you some bush that will cure you." The next day I received a bucket full of 'bush', which I would only describe as weeds, which had to be boiled and distilled. I drank three cups of the evil looking liquid and waited for an improvement to my breathing. The following day strange disturbances began in my stomach and bowels, the like of which I had never previously experienced. For three days I had diarrhoea of the worst kind and was never able to stay more than a few yards from the nearest toilet, with flying being a complete impossibility. The net result of the medication, cleared out my inside, left me as weak as a lamb, and with a profound distrust of any further Rasta cures. Finally I was forced to admit myself for a few days into hospital in Barbados, where in a sterile environment, plus oxygen and the usual diet of tablets, I was soon up and about, and running around the hospital grounds making myself a nuisance to the nurses. Later I found out that the Rastas had fed me with marijuana or 'ganga' as they called it, which grew wild in Grenada and was quite legal. It seemed that this medicine was a cure for all their mental and physical problems!

December 1980 was the hardest month, in flying terms that, I had ever undertaken in my aviation career. The previous April I had completed 137 landings in a 28 day period, but in December this rose to 147 landings.

The complicated approaches to some of the runways did not make things any easier, and flying down the side of mountainous terrain was quite commonplace. Air Traffic Control at times was inept and at other times completely non-existent. Flying northwards to Union Island one morning in torrential rain I made the customary call to air traffic. Despite a number of calls, I received no answer so in poor conditions I continued my approach and landed safely. I taxied alongside the stilted hut, which passed as an Airport Terminal, and there I saw the Air Traffic Controller sheltering from the rain. He had merely to cross the runway to enter the Control Tower and commence his duties. I cried out, "why the hell aren't you in the Tower doing your job?" "Oh Cap," he said, "I would have got my head wet, if I had done that thing!" My further remarks were unprintable, but then, I had only been in the West Indies a few months, and I still had a lot to learn! I soon realised that the West Indian had a natural abhorrence to getting their heads wet, and children on their way to school and caught in a shower would run for cover and squeal like pigs.

I had taken off from St. Vincent on a day when unusually the volcano on the northern side of the island was completely clear of cloud. My dear mother in law was on board that morning returning to St. Lucia for her flight back to the UK. This was an opportunity I couldn't resist so on reaching 4,000 feet the volcano beckoned. That morning I had a few tourists on board so for the first and last time whilst in the West Indies I flew very steep turns within the boundary lip of the volcano with the cameras clicking incessantly. The steam was rising from the pools of bubbling larva and the coloured pictures when they arrived a few weeks later were most impressive. Some days later the weather again was superb, and I was on the last of my morning flights from the island of Carriacou to Grenada. Level at 2,000 feet and somewhat bored by the too beautiful conditions, I decided to have some fun with the passengers. The aircraft was full and in the second row sat a very fat negress of at least sixteen stones in weight, who had compressed the tiny lady sitting next to her in almost half a seat space. I pushed the control column quickly forwards and then backwards, and then looking back could see the smiles that suddenly appeared. I repeated the procedure and noted that the fat lady was really bubbling with her rolls of fat bouncing up and down. A final time had the whole aircraft in hysterics with rolling eyes and screaming laughter. I told the passengers that the movements were due to still-air turbulence, which was obvious rubbish, but by this time the passengers were too happy to care. After landing I sat in the cockpit completing the post flight documentation, when Annette came up and said, "Cap, you know the very fat lady who sat in the second row, well she's just delivered a baby on the floor of the Terminal Building," a slight pause and then, "I thought you ought to know." Annette was not aware of my antics in the air but undoubtedly these had assisted in the almost instant delivery of the child on arrival at the airport, the first time in my life I had assisted in a birth. Anywhere in Europe I would have been informed that I had a pregnant woman on board, but in the West Indies such matters seemed just 'run of the mill'.

I remember almost too well the advent of the hurricane seasons in the West Indies as the family's arrival had coincided with hurricane David, the remains of which I had followed in the Aerostar to Puerto Rico. The following day I flew directly over the storm as a passenger in an Eastern Airlines 727 en-route to San Antonio in Texas. Later I saw the front page of the magazine 'Newsweek', and was amazed to see the extent of the hurricane from a satellite photograph, with it completely filling the Gulf of Mexico. A year later, almost to the day, I was on a routine flight to Grenada on a day in the most perfect of weather conditions imaginable. From aloft I could see the bottom of the ocean and the large variety of fish swimming there. I was aware of course that hurricane Allen was moving westwards from the coast of Africa directly towards us. I had seen the satellite photographs relayed to Air Traffic Control in Barbados and it was clear that the hurricane was tracking along the latitude 10° north, directly in line with Grenada. As I flew I heard a French pilot in an Air Martinique aircraft remark that he had seen no birds flying that day, followed by the words, "They must know something we don't!" In the history of hurricanes in the West Indies never once had one struck Trinidad, which is approximately 100 nautical miles south east of Grenada. Nobody I had ever met had been able to explain this phenomenon to me, but it certainly was true. My intention therefore was to arrange for all the company aircraft to fly to Grenada, and if the hurricane continued on its present course to fly onwards directly to Port of Spain Trinidad. I phoned the wife on arrival and informed her of my plan, in order that she could ready herself and the children for a quick getaway. I drove along the rutted road in record time, and quickly loaded the car. I was in the process of locking the front door when my telephone rang. It was Flight Operations in Antigua now informing me that the hurricane had changed path to a more northerly direction and was now at 12° north on direct track to strike St. Lucia. That night all my crews stayed at my home, with the aircraft all tied down for security at Pearls Airport. Later the southern edge of the hurricane passed overhead and we all sat on chairs looking northwards through our extensive glass patio doors. It was a picture show never to be forgotten. The rain descended in torrents and small rivers ran out of the house gutters, but the pyrotechnics must have resembled the artillery barrage prior to the battle of the Somme in World War I. The sky was wrenched by a fury rarely seen, the roofs rattled to the thunder and the continuous lightening illuminated the sea well to the north. It was awesome! I thought of my colleagues further up the islands who were taking the full force of the storm, the core of which passed between the islands of St. Vincent and St. Lucia. In the calm of the next few days, I flew along the east coast of St. Vincent, which had been completely devastated, with hundreds of trees felled, looking like so many matchsticks from the air. St. Lucia too, was smashed and my office constructed in the mid nineteenth century by the British Army looked like a blitzed building, its steal roof having been torn to shreds. Grenada had only suffered lightly, but even then the fury of the storm could be measured by the fact that the Pearls Airport sign, which must have weighed at least half a ton, was found fifty miles north on the island of Carriacou.

The Revolutionary Government had now become almost totally dependent on aid from the Soviet Bloc, particularly Cuba. Having free access to Pearls Airport I soon became quite friendly with Cuban pilots, who allowed me to clamber over their Russian built aircraft and even examine their cargoes which were largely military in nature. Despite this assistance however, the Grenadian infrastructure was clearly deteriorating, but it was the failure of the electricity supply that affected us more than anything else. Almost every night the lights would fail for up to three or four hours and we relied heavily on our stock of candles, by which we were able to read the three week old British newspapers. Once the lights failed it took literally seconds for the cockroaches to appear, and by the time the candles were lit we were constantly entertained by our five kittens demonstrating their curtain climbing powers in pursuit of these agile interlopers. Chicken legs were in common supply on the island, but some of the local islanders developed a preference for eating cats, a habit which I found profoundly disturbing. The electricity supply, or lack of it, had devastating effects on the food in the supermarkets, where the air-conditioning would cease to operate for hours on end. Fortunately, I only suffered food poisoning on one occasion, and that in Antigua following a company celebration. The locals had clearly built up a resistance or tolerance to most of their indigenous bugs, but visitors like me had no such immunity. I saw a television set just once during my stay, but we were indeed blessed by having a small portable radio, which served us well. I looped an extended aerial over the rafters in our lounge and thereby was able to listen in comfort to the BBC and the Voice of America. The local station was Radio Antilles, which played on hour of classical music every Sunday evening. The presenter of this programme had a posh voice and sounded very much like Sir Trevor McDonald of ITN in the UK. He would first give précis details of the composer and then the piece about to be played. In our dim candle lit lounge he talked this night about Tchaikovsky and the 1812 overture. We sat back, to listen, and then over the airways came the strict tempo music of Victor Sylvester and his Ballroom Orchestra. I thought, after our few minutes of laughter, that the presenter would realise his mistake, take the record off, and apologise for his error. I was wrong on all scores, and the record played on to its bitter end, which sent us again into wild paroxysms of laughter. From that moment on, his programmes became compulsive listening every Sunday evening.

During the latter part of 1982, a sense of oppression, even depression, became very much in evidence on the small island, and even the locals seemed to smile that less often. It was during this period on one early morning around 0500 hours that my telephone rang and woke me with a start. It was the Minister for Homeland Security, who informed me that he wanted me to fly over the island to look for some subversives who were in hiding. Whether it was because I was half asleep or whether perhaps I objected to the tone and the bullying techniques of the regime, I do not know, but I positively refused to carry out his order. I informed him that I was employed by LIAT, who paid my salary, and not by the Revolutionary Government. Further, I said that permission to use the civil aircraft for military purposes could only be granted by the chairman of the company. Lastly, I told him that if he were successful in these demands then he should ask a homespun Grenadian pilot to fly the plane. He took my reply in good spirit and later one of my local pilots flew an aircraft on this task, and nearly lost his life in the process, when machine gun bullets took-out one of the engines and narrowly missed him. Maybe the minister thought as a visitor and nearing the end of my contract I was expendable, but the situation alarmed me sufficiently to request a meeting with my chairman, Dev Archer in Antigua, in order to voice my concerns. Days later when I was in St. Lucia my wife and children were subjected to a hail of bullets near the house, an event which decided me to send them back to the UK as soon as possible. Dev Archer was his usual charming self and did his best to allay my fears. I insisted however that I would be taking my family back to the UK for Christmas (my first leave in two years), and that they would remain there when I returned alone to complete my contract. He agreed to all this, and then came the bombshell. He smiled at me and then asked me would I like to take his seat behind his desk. At first I failed to grasp his meaning, then suddenly it dawned, he was offering me the chairmanship and chief executive position of the parent company. He enumerated my qualities as a leader, and my popularity with the staff and also the ambition to make a success at the job. I had great respect for this man, but shocked him by saying, "But Mr Archer you have forgotten the most important fact." "What is that?" he asked. "Mr Archer I am white and your employees around the islands (over 600 of them at the time), would never accept and work for a white man as their chief." Archer looked completely stunned, and I realised then that he had looked at me, and not seen the colour of my skin. It was the greatest compliment that any man could pay another, and the one I greatly treasure above all others. A few weeks later my family and I flew from St. Lucia to Miami then on to Orlando where we enjoyed the delights of Disney World and our re-emergence into the free Western culture. A few weeks later, totally refreshed, we flew home to Wales. I alone returned to Grenada to complete my contract, but now I spent more time in Barbados and St. Lucia and flew the schedules from there. However I ended my flying as I had started, on the Britten Norman Islander VP-LAD flying up and down the islands saying my good byes to my staff. I had learned a great deal of life, and my love of the islands and its people will always, remain with me. The two and a half years had been a wonderful experience for the family and me. I knew instinctively that Grenada and its move to Marxism would end in bloodshed, but fortunately that did not occur until later that year, when I was based in Miami facing an entirely different set of problems.

CHAPTER 14

VICELESS IN MIAMI

During my almost two and a half years in the West Indies, I found that I had completed in excess of two thousand landings, so it was no wonder that my appetite for flying had taken a sharp down turn. My health, too, had had suffered and I felt completely washed out! I returned to the UK with the firm intention of taking a long rest at home with the family free from the stresses and responsibilities of work. This however was not to be, and within a week I received a telephone call from David Oldfield, the Vice President of Barnett Bank at Miami Airport, "Hi John," he said, "I'm sitting here with an investor who wishes to start an airline based at St. Croix in the American Virgin Islands. Would you be interested in setting up the operation and running it?" Within two days I was sitting with the two people in question over a coffee at Miami Airport. The investor, a large South American named Paul Hera, who spoke better Spanish than English, did not impress me at all, but at least he was friendly and congenial. David Oldfield had been born in the Dominican Republic of a British father, who had domiciled himself there after World War II, and who had sold aircraft for the De Havilland company of the UK. From my first meeting with Paul I had developed firm doubts about his authenticity, his main interests fluctuating from the type of girls we would hire, to the uniforms they would wear. David clearly realised that we needed an American of some stature on the Board of Directors, and one day having briefed me beforehand took me to the Omni Mall in the city to meet Dame Jean Loach, who had received the title of Dame from our Queen for her many dedicated services world-wide on behalf of various charities. She had also travelled widely on behalf of the City of Miami selling its attributes as a public relations officer. I summed her up very quickly, as a bright tough and friendly lady who would not suffer fools gladly. Her life story was quite fascinating, impressive enough to warrant a new Hollywood film 'Call me Madam Mark 2'. In fact she had been the protégé of Pearl Mesta, the original 'Hostess with the Mostest', in the film 'Call me Madam', a part played with much vigour by the incredibly voiced Ethel Merman, and the musical score by Irving Berlin, his last big success. President Eisenhower had sent Dame Jean on an American goodwill mission to Moscow, where she had met President Bulganin. Later she was to have her own television show in Detroit which lasted for ten years, and she subsequently represented show-biz stars as well as governments and various business firms. Her office walls were covered by pictures of various kings, queens and Hollywood stars all personally signed to her with love or gratitude. She was still a single lady when I met her, and confided in me that she had recently turned down the offer of marriage to a Scottish aristocrat, laughingly admitting that she just loathed Scot's Porridge Oats. By this time I had established a close rapport with the lady who now in turn began to voice doubts about Paul. For a person who had once organised magnificent parties at the White House for visiting dignitaries, she now turned her attention to raising finance for the new airline. I in turn approached a variety of aircraft manufacturing companies to supply us with the most appropriate aircraft for our route system, and it was Embraer of Brazil who made the first positive move in our direction. A Bandeirante aircraft soon arrived, and on the 1st May 1982 I was able to make a demonstration flight from Miami International

Airport. I remember this flight well as I was able to fly low along the famous Miami Beach waterfront and wave at the astonished bathers. In the meantime Dame Jean had enticed a mega-rich Middle Eastern prince to stump-up the millions of dollars necessary for the new operation. The one stipulation being that the complete transaction remained a close secret. Dame Jean would be a front for the investment chiefly for political reasons, and I flew down to St. Croix to make preparations for a base there. Sadly however Paul proved the weak link in the organisation and this soon became apparent when he named the prince as the origin of the funding to a third party, probably to exaggerate events, and the part he played in them. Consequently the finance offer was withdrawn and the operation, such as it was at the time, had to be closed down. For Paul however, worse was to follow. Some weeks later after I had returned to the UK, David rang me to say that Paul had been murdered in Miami by a person or persons unknown. No motive was apparent, but it appeared that many of his financial debts were outstanding and when he wouldn't or couldn't pay, the inevitable happened. Dame Jean and I had established a fine relationship, and before I left Miami she invited me out for dinner at the restaurant in the Omni hotel. Here she was well known, and flashed her wealth in the most refined manner. Her diamonds and rubies on ears, wrists and fingers were small but bountiful, and she proved the most charming of companions. A regular visitor to her condominium was an elderly gentleman who was clearly in love with her. He was a violin player of quite exceptional talent. That evening sitting in exquisite surroundings he stood in front of us, and played the haunting refrain of 'Play Fiddle Play', as a serenade to his love. As one who plays the piano and knew that piece of music I was completely entranced. Later he told me that he had composed that very song way back in 1933, his name Emery Deutsh. Today, whenever I play that piece of music I am always reminded of that wonderful occasion in Miami.

Back home in Wales I was kept busy attending to more mundane family matters when I received a telephone call from my old colleague from Brymon and Air Wales days, Terry Fox. He had tickets for the Farnborough Air Show Trade days, and would I like to go? As he volunteered to drive me there, I couldn't really refuse the offer; little knowing that it would lead me once more into further adventures abroad. My first port of call on arrival at the show was the Fairchild Aircraft Corporation's chalet. My visits to San Antonio, Texas had been many whilst I had been working in the West Indies, and I had become very friendly with Bruce Chuber, who was still the company's Vice President of International Sales. The last time I had seen Bruce was during his visit to see me in Grenada, when he had spent a few days holidaying with my family. Quite a lady's man was Bruce, a large and confident Texan. He and I had stood and watched topless Grenadian girls leaping off a river bridge into the waters below, happy in the fact that we were there to admire them. He soon appeared from the chalet and grinning from ear to ear, ushered us both inside, booked us in for lunch and poured the drinks. After lunch Terry left to visit another company and Bruce and I exchanged yarns mostly about Grenada. I always retained a vision of him standing in the doorway of my office at Pearls Airport, remarking that he hadn't realised that 'Africa was on America's doorstep'. He asked me what I was up to at the present time and when I answered resting he said, "Well I'm shortly going to introduce you to your new boss." I was somewhat startled at that, but then Bruce was always full of surprises. An hour later a tall slim good-looking chap walked in and I was introduced to Gabriel, a Colombian from Bogota. He was clearly well off and already held a series of aircraft sales franchises, among which were Embraer, Dornier, Beech and Fairchild. Quite brazenly Bruce introduced me to Gabriel as his Groupo Miami's new Caribbean Manager. Groupo Miami had offices in Bogota and at Brickhill Avenue in Miami. The remainder of the conversation remains hazy, but it appears that I agreed in principle to the terms offered, with my new base to be Miami, Florida. The offer of course was totally unexpected and I felt rather pleased with myself, as it had been an ambition of mine for some time to become involved in airline sales. I had previously been involved with the sale and purchase of a number of aircraft, but never before, had I been involved in a company with such wide sales interests such as Groupo Miami. Brickhill Avenue was the acknowledged Wall Street of Miami, and my only doubt about the assignment concerned my family. After much debate it was decided that they would remain in Wales in order that the children could continue their schooling uninterrupted, although I have to say it was a tough choice to make. However we seized every opportunity to fly the Atlantic and be with one another, and collectively I believe we completed twenty-six Atlantic crossings. The reason for my decision was the belief that Miami was not an entirely safe place to be, and I had no desire to place my family at risk once more, as they had been in Grenada. I never carried a gun in Grenada, but I had certainly considered it, and my companion at night was a stout mahogany stick resting handily at the side of my bed. In all my time in Miami, however, I never felt threatened or needed a weapon of any description, but there certainly was violence in the city and there were certain areas best avoided, and generally I did just that.

I arrived back in Miami on Thanksgiving Day in 1982. Having chosen a bad day to arrive nobody was there to greet me at the airport. Consequently I took the courtesy bus to a hotel I knew on North West 36 Street and settled in at my new surroundings. I took an Avis hire car on a two-week rental basis, while I expected to search around for a flat or condominium of some description. It was 7th December, the anniversary of Peal Harbour when I left the freeway on my way to the office. I arrived at an intersection, where I swear there were at least eight lanes of converging traffic. I stopped at the lights and as soon as the green light appeared accelerated across the intersection, turning into what I considered to be the correct lane. At that precise moment my car was struck in the rear and on my near side with considerable force, which catapulted me along the road for about thirty yards or so. 'Oh my God' I thought, 'now somebody will come up with a gun and shoot me.' I clambered out shocked but unhurt, and looked at the missile that had hit me. The car I recognised as an Italian one, and a very expensive, one which now its near side ripped apart along its length. Then the man stepped out and what a man! He looked about eight feet tall at that moment, but even in retrospect he stood closer to seven than six. To my alarm he screamed out, "My car! My car! look at my lovely car!" This was followed by a slight pause, then another scream and the words, "It's the third car I've smashed this week, what will the wife say?" I listened to this soliloquy, cowering behind a concrete pillar, and was very glad when at that moment a police care drove up and a lady cop stepped out. Unfortunately she seemed averse to foreigners, and clearly attributed the accident to me, but found difficulty proving that assertion, when she saw that it was my car that had been struck in the rear. She was a real tough cookie, who would have found a real niche in the Waffen SS, but fortunately for me she seemed to be in great demand, allowing me to get off quite lightly in the end, promising only to exchange car documents with the tall Italian American. Some days later I paid him a visit in his furniture factory, by which time the raging volcano had cooled down, and he behaved as gentle as a lamb. He spied the Rolex watch I was wearing and asked me whether it was for sale. Well just the day before I had bought eight of them (all fakes of course), for the princely sum of forty dollars. Taking the accident into account and extending a certain degree of goodwill, I sold him the one on my wrist for two hundred dollars, I have to say that we both appeared pleased with the deal!

When Saturday arrived I found myself at a loose end, so I motored over to Miami University in the vain hope that perhaps a soccer or rugby match might be in progress. Crossing the campus towards the playing fields, I heard the loud and raucous tones of a coach bellowing out instructions, and all this in an unmistakable Welsh accent. I wondered across the pitch at half time, and after he had finished his team pep talk, introduced myself. David Clements was from Newport in Monmouthshire and worked in Miami as an import and export agent for another Welshman Rolant Huws a millionaire who was normally domiciled in Barranquilla on the north coast of Columbia, where he lived in splendour on a 10,000 acre estate. Rolant regularly imported and exported goods between Columbia and Miami, and on that Saturday evening would be in Miami, so I was invited to the Clements' household for dinner to meet him. David picked me up at my hotel later, and drove me to his home in Coral Gables. In the course of conversation over the dinner table, Rolant became very excited when he heard that I had been responsible for the start up of Air Wales in 1979. His father apparently had been a fervent Welsh Nationalist in the 1920s and I got the distinct impression that Rolant shared many of the same instincts. The very fact I had returned to Wales to start a national airline for the country as a sense of duty, impressed him immensely. Later I discovered that he was spending considerable amounts of money on a design project to build a barrage across the Severn Estuary, to generate electricity for South Wales and West of England. Typically the authorities decided to build a second bridge instead, ignoring the generation of electricity in a completely environmentally friendly way. It appeared that Rolant and I seemed to agree on most matters, and as the evening wore on he suddenly turned to me and suggested that I needed a good home in Miami, and that I was welcome to use his condominium in Coconut Grove. It appeared he spent little time in town and normally rented it out at $1,800 per month, but for me it was free of charge. 'Oh that more people were like him,' I thought.

The next day complete with my few worldly goods I took up residence in the absolute splendour of Coconut Grove, probably the most desirable area in Miami. It had everything, with bars, restaurants, shops, a theatre and Roosevelt Park with its specially designed jogging tracks. It was here that I saw sights which were unbelievable in a UK context. A very fat negress would jog along at about one mile per hour, her end wobbling uncontrollably from side to side. Fit young joggers of both sexes and all shades of colours would zoom past completely ignoring this phenomenon. In the UK she would have been the butt of many people's jokes, but not in Miami. Perhaps the funniest sight was one guy in his shorts, wearing a head set clearly tuned in to heavy metal music, being pulled around the park on his roller skates by four Pointer dogs. Yet again nobody seemed to notice or care. In Miami you sure strutted your stuff as if you were on your own separate planet. Well-muscled guys and splendidly attractive women of all ages, could be seen running and hanging inverted from exercise bars along the tracks each fully engrossed in their own fitness regimes. In a climate like this it was all too easy to get yourself fit and I became a regular performer on the Roosevelt Park circuit. My condominium was real Hollywood style with wonderfully spacious accommodation and a balcony on the sixteenth floor, overlooking the city. At night I could gaze out on the millions of lights, and remember my childhood and the diet of American films in which Miami frequently appeared and really felt that I belonged here, not just in Miami but in the USA. I regretted then not having trained as a pilot in the States, as almost certainly I would have found a reason to stay. Fate however had decreed otherwise.

I had thought that Rolant's offer of free accommodation extended for a few weeks only, and I continued to search the newspaper columns to find alternative accommodation. Well, weeks stretched to months and ultimately two years. Rolant would visit for a few days and disappear just as quickly. He refused my many offers of payment, and when my family visited the city they were overwhelmed by the luxuriousness of it all. Certainly, it provided us with an unimaginable lifestyle far removed from anything we had experienced elsewhere. I seriously considered again bringing the family over on a permanent basis, but in talks with the police and the company lawyer I learned violence was at times very close to the surface, and perhaps it was wiser to let matters as they were. The condominium had its own security guards and the area was surrounded by high wire fences and security cameras, which tended to create a siege mentality, but after a period of residence this became an inevitable and acceptable part of everyday life.

I had been employed by Groupo Miami as the Sales Manager for the Caribbean, and this involved contact with all the regional Governments, Air Guard, Coast Guard, airlines and air taxi companies in the area. My first job was to ensure that the decision making people in the aviation field, in this wide expanse, quickly became aware of Groupo Miami and its services. I had arrived in Miami during a period of recession in America, and consequently, although certain companies might want our aircraft, funding the purchase was likely to prove extremely difficult. The Caribbean is considered by the Americans as their 'lake' and when American sneezes the Caribbean countries catch a cold as they are inevitably a part of the American economic area. However, I certainly had some in-built advantages having already worked in the Caribbean for over two years, and had a wide variety of contacts in the political and aviation fields. I was also aware from my previous dealings, that selling involved a certain amount of bribery, and in this case the West Indies was no different from any other part of the world. My initial purpose was to sell two types of aircraft, namely the Saab Fairchild 34 seat commuter aircraft (later the Saab 340), and the Swearingien Metro a fast pressurised 19 seat aircraft. Both produced in San Antonio, Texas. In order to do this I planned to organise a tour of the Caribbean in the Metro, and induced Bruce Chuber to accompany me, although he needed little persuasion. Mike Ashley would act as pilot in command of the aircraft with Bruce and myself helping out as required. My chief responsibility was to arrange the contacts, make the representations and sell the aircraft.

We took off from Fort Lauderdale Executive Airport at1640 hours on the 7th February 1983 on a beautiful afternoon. As we climbed through 2,000 feet for 25,000 feet (Flight Level 25 in airline parlance) I spied a wind surfer about two miles off shore skimming the waves blissfully unaware of a phenomena clearly visible to me of a group of sharks following in his wake, their shadows clearly evident in the clear blue water. Mercifully we then climbed through a cloud layer and the picture was quickly lost to view. The first landing was made at St. Thomas, where the aircraft was demonstrated to Air Virgin Islands quickly followed by a short visit to St. Croix, and then directly onwards to Barbados. Here we had some fun before landing, and flew a complete circuit of the island at about 100 feet, buzzing a few swimmers at the same time. We stayed on the island for three nights in great comfort at the Southern Palms Hotel, which, conveniently sited on a beach, allowed us to combine business with pleasure. The next day we flew to Port of Spain, Trinidad where I addressed the officers of the Coast Guard and the military establishment again demonstrating the aircraft. Back in Barbados I briefed Mr Yearwood, the Chairman of Caribbean Airways and that night we were all entertained by Tony Wilson (the Britten Norman representative), at his home. I was delighted that his piano was still serviceable and not devoured by woodworm which is so often the case in such climates, so I was able to play on into the early hours of the morning. Next day we stopped off at St. Lucia where I met up with some of my old colleagues from Inter Island, followed by aircraft demonstrations to the airlines in the French islands of Martinique and Guadeloupe, then on to Antigua where I had the pleasure of flying some of the directors of LIAT, my former employer. Our last port of call in the Caribbean was Puerto Rico where we stayed at the Palace Hotel, a favourite haunt of mine in previous years. Here I met an old acquaintance, one Juan Villafane, who owned one of the oldest FAA (Federal Aviation Agency) approved maintenance organisations on the island. I had chosen this company to be the maintenance base for any aircraft I sold in the Caribbean area. Finally we demonstrated the aircraft to Prinair the largest commuter airline on the island. On 18th February we returned to Miami after a four and a half hour flight. It had been a gruelling two weeks and we had covered a great deal of territory. Although I was desperately tired my diary indicates that on the following day I jogged five miles, so clearly I wasn't as tired as I thought. Gabriel appeared pleased with my efforts and the report of the tour, and positive results soon followed. A number of regional airlines were now seriously interested in purchasing one or more of our aircraft. Perhaps this wasn't too surprising as I had agreed with them some considerable commissions on sale, which were to be paid directly into certain private off-shore accounts. The problems which were to follow primarily involved the funding of the purchases, in what was now a severe economic downturn.

Crown Air, an airline in Puerto Rico, had become a prime target of mine, and with Quinn, a young American who was the Chief Executive, I spent a great deal of time cementing a relationship which I hoped would prove beneficial to the cause. One night as we climbed the steps into the casino, he suddenly stumbled and cursed as he re-adjusted a fastener around his ankle. When I looked down I saw that the fastener was a part of a holster which carried a loaded automatic pistol. I questioned his need to carry a weapon, and was astonished when he told me that in his six months on the island already two attempts had been made on his life. Certainly some strange events were afoot, and I eventually discovered that the money behind Crown wasn't exactly kosher, and the more I delved, the less satisfactory it all seemed. In fact, the longer I examined the finances and ownership of many airlines particularly, on the American islands, the more questionable it all became. Furthermore, few of these companies seemed able to construct a sound business plan, sound enough that is to present to the financial institutions on the mainland. Inevitably I was forced into this work myself and some weeks after sending off the first, I received a call from the Centerre Bank in St. Louis. It was from one of the bank's Vice-presidents, who opened the conversation with, "Hi John, your business plan is doable." This was the first time I had heard this expression, as it was completely unknown to the banking circles in the UK. From that day the word 'doable' became a permanent addition to my sales patter.

The office staff at Brickhill Avenue was a cosmopolitan group of people. My secretary, Marisol, was a beautiful Cuban exile, with a temper that had to be witnessed to be believed. Her parents plus their three daughters had been driven out of Cuba by Fidel Castro, and had arrived in Miami in the clothes they stood in. Dad had taken on three jobs simultaneously, and went about educating his daughters. The eldest had qualified for her medical degree, and worked as a doctor at the Bethesda Hospital in Washington. The second daughter became a concert pianist, and Marisol the youngest eventually gained her doctorate in Law—what a family! Gerda was our senior secretary and office boss, extremely efficient and fluent in English, Dutch and Spanish. Conrad was the company lawyer and an expert in aviation law, and the President of the company was Gabriel, a native of Columbia. He had attended university at Heidelberg in Germany and spoke five languages fluently. His father had been at one time the Colombian ambassador in Nixon's Washington and his uncle Pablo the ambassador to Brezhnev's Moscow. An astonishing group of people who certainly contributed a great deal to this Welshman's education.

I had discovered that Gabriel also lived in the same building in Coconut Grove, his condominium being on the twelfth floor, four floors below me. I had managed to keep this a secret from him, aided and abetted by the office staff simply because of his hectic social life into which I would have been quickly drawn. This came to an end one day when he asked me to drive him home as his car was being serviced. I drove him directly into the underground garage and unthinkingly entered my card into the machine which controlled the barrier. "How did you get a card for this garage?" he asked with some surprise. When I told him I had lived in the same building for some six months he burst into loud laughter and questioned the legitimacy of my birth. After that I was at his beck and call with invitations to dinner, parties, barbecues etc. On one occasion he asked me to make up a foursome with his wife and her friend Ursula who was down from New York. I cried off this engagement and managed to convince him that I was already committed elsewhere. That evening I slunk out of the building and completed my jogging session around Roosevelt Park. I had just entered the foyer on my return when Gabriel plus his wife and Ursula stepped out of the lift. Was I shocked, for there stood a smiling Ursula Andress in all her glory, the famous star of the very first James Bond movie 'Dr No'. Gabriel introduced me, but standing there in a sweaty vest and shorts was not the best moment in my life. I promised myself to listen very carefully to any of Gabriel's invitations in future. When I flew with him to Bogota some days later, I saw another completely different side of his character, which left an unpleasant taste in my mouth! We were both jostled by the crowd on leaving the airport and when a poor baggage porter stepped in his way Gabriel just turned on him, swore and kicked him. I had seen nothing like this since my time in Tripoli, North Africa years before and once more it saddened and sickened me.

My next visit was to Jamaica, this time to demonstrate the Metro to Trans Jamaican Airlines. This company was largely government owned, and my main point of contact was Dr Hervey, the government's chief economic advisor, who was directly responsible to the Prime Minister, Michael Manley, of the People's National Party (PNP). A few days later I flew Dr Hervey back to Miami with me as he had a dental appointment in Coconut Grove. It is truly amazing what one has to do to sell aircraft and here my knowledge of British soccer helped. Dr Hervey was a Hungarian national and had been a spectator at Wembley in November 1953 when England had been thrashed by six goals to three by the then Olympic champions, Hungary. As I had viewed that game on a fifteen inch black and white television I was able to agree with him that England had been outpaced, outmanoeuvred and outclassed by a magnificent exposition of football skills. I also remembered that England had played a return match in Budapest a month or so later and lost by the huge margin of seven goals to one. Dr Hervey positively beamed at my description of the games and my description of the magical Magyars. My sales patter had certainly been enhanced, and by the time I had deposited him at the door of the dental clinic, I knew I had sold him an aircraft or two. It was a well known fact at that time that Jamaica just did not have the necessary currency in United States dollars to complete the transaction, and their offer when it came was a barter deal exchanging bauxite for our aircraft. Jamaica was at that time the world's third largest producer of bauxite, that clay like mineral which is the chief source of aluminium, but to arrange the deal involved participation in the Futures and Commodities markets, and involved me in a number of visits to New York. Despite all my efforts, however, no agreement could be reached on the volumes and price of the commodity. There was as already mentioned, a period of recession if not depression in the area, and despite many further meetings at Kingston and at the Jack Tar Hotel in Montego Bay we were unable to close the deal. 'C'est la vie'!

A new airline in formation was Sky Burst of Puerto Rico, but with their main offices in New York, they had already indicated their preference to purchase Bandeirante aircraft from Embraer and I set out to reverse that decision and sell them Fairchild Metros. I arranged a meeting with their main board of directors and agreed in advance, to repay them all the deposits they had made to Embraer for their aircraft, and suggested also that there were some additional 'rich pickings' in the offing. I flew with

Eastern Airlines to La Guardia Field, New York, and took a cab ride down Fifth Avenue to the offices of Sky Burst Inc. My arrival was unpropitious as at the top of the stairs I was frisked for weapons by two 'heavies', who could well have been described by PG Woodhouse as "plug uglies'! David Brume was the Chairman of the company, a balding middle aged Jew. In fact I seemed to have entered a small Jewish fraternity, and as I had often been called a Welsh Jew, initially I felt quite at home. We sat drinking coffee around a rather large boardroom table and I explained the plot to exchange our six aircraft for the Embraer types, whilst at the same time enriching them to a considerable degree. Their language was quite foul, and most of their jokes were directed at me and my limey and English ancestry. I protested vehemently at this rank injustice, proclaiming my Welsh background, which I declared was infinitely better than being a bunch of 'bloody Manhattan Rabbis'. This caused huge merriment and the laughter was even shared by the hitherto glum looking heavies standing by the door, and I knew then that they had been 'winding me up' for whatever reason. Seemingly I had passed their test and out came the drinks and our relationship deepened and became quite convivial. Brume had arranged to take his holidays at the Contemporary Resort Hotel at Disney World in Florida, at which time I expected him to put pen to paper and sign the aircraft contracts. The meeting was arranged for Friday 13th May, and whereas I was not particularly superstitious, that day proved particularly disastrous. Brume and his associates plus their female companions were drunk, indeed very drunk, and remained so during our visit, so Gabriel who had accompanied me to Orlando left empty handed. A few weeks later I heard that Brume had fled the country only slightly ahead of his creditors, and Sky Burst remained forever 'Burst".

My next venture was to take place in the Dominican Republic, first at Puerto Plata and then on to Herra and finally La Romana. We flew the Government officials in a series of flights. Despite the success of these flights our passengers seemed more interested in the trinkets we handed out like the small model aircraft and Fairchild baseball caps. In fact they behaved like small kids given an afternoon off from school. Yet again we discovered a government without funds to develop their infrastructure, who were on the whole dependant on 'hand-outs' from the United States, so yet again we returned empty handed to Miami! In fact by that time I was convinced that nobody in the Caribbean Governments had heard of the word 'ethics', and were either broke or on the take! Clearly this was not fair to some, but by that stage my views were particularly jaundiced.

My family had now arrived in town and we took a holiday together touring the 'flesh pots' of Florida and Georgia. Back in Miami Gavin, my son, and I visited the Elizabeth Virrick gym for boxing, which had been created to keep the kids off the streets and out of crime. At the gym we met a fine bunch of people dedicated to helping the less fortunate, including a former trainer of the renowned Mohammed Ali. When they discovered I was from Wales the name Tommy Farr arose in conversation. For them Tommy had been one of the toughest fighters ever to climb into the boxing ring, and when I told them that my father and mother had known the great man I was treated like a favourite son. Now I felt it was a good time for my young son to learn the so-called art of self-defence. They even provided a personal trainer for him, although he was only nine years of age, and nightly put him through his paces. The apartment block was well equipped with its own gymnasium, where all the family worked out, plus the customary swimming pool and tennis courts. Dr Jeff was my usual tennis opponent, and our games were always seriously competitive. Neither of us liked losing, and after the game the loser would pay for the pizzas and cokes. Juan Domique was a more casual player, with a charming disposition win or lose. Sometimes he would entertain me after a game in one of the more expensive restaurants in the Grove, and talk of his family in South America. A few weeks after our last game I flew to London on business and spent a few days there before returning. When I entered the foyer of the apartment block I was told by the security guard that I had missed all the fun during my absence. It appears that the Miami police had entered the building unannounced, gone directly to the 13th floor and broken down the door to Juan's apartment. According to eyewitnesses the place was awash with drugs of one sort of another. Juan's intelligence in the drugs business had been quite extraordinary as he seemed to know when and where the money and the drug suppliers would meet. He would then mysteriously appear, and murder both parties then collect the money and the drugs. Apparently by the time I arrived back in town it was alleged he had already killed eight victims. I felt rather pleased that I hadn't beaten him at tennis too often. A charming man indeed!

It was Thursday 20th October 1983 when I left my condominium and walked across the landing to knock on Dr Jeff's door to arrange a tennis match that evening. A copy of the 'Miami Herald' newspaper lay on the floor and I idly picked it up to hand it to Jeff when he answered the bell. I stood in deep shock as I read the headlines, 'Grenadian Prime Minister Slain'. Maurice Bishop and some of his followers, many of whom I knew quite well, had been murdered by revolutionary troops under the direction of his former deputy, Bernard Coard, and the leader of the army, General Hudson Austin, who declared that the country was under martial law and was being run by a Revolutionary Military Council. In late 1983 an internecine struggle had broken out with Coard leading a group of leftwing extremists, whom Fidel Castro called 'the Pol Pot Group'. This was the group who had turned on their colleagues and murdered them. Among them were officials with whom I had been friendly and frequently flown during my stay in Grenada. My diary listed Norris Bain, Fitz Roy Bain, Unison Whiteman and Vincent Noel among others. Two others I knew had already been imprisoned in goat pens at the Richmond Hill prison, which stands high above the capital, St George's. This in effect had saved their lives, as almost certainly they would have accompanied Bishop on that fateful day. In the meantime the USA had refrained from intervening, but had watched with some alarm as the Cubans had constructed the new 9,000 foot runway at Point Salines, which was an ideal refuelling stop for flights to Africa. Perhaps it was Maurice Bishop's murder that was the turning point, as shortly afterwards the US 82nd Airborne Division parachuted into the island and by 27th October the island was freed of insurrection. I felt a personal sorrow for Bishop. We had met on a number occasions and I felt he was a kind and decent man whom I respected. Like his father before him, he had paid the ultimate price for what they hoped would be a better Grenada. Can anyone in life hold dear a greater aspiration than to try to better the lives of their own countrymen? Bernard Coard and his comrades were imprisoned for life at the Richmond Hill prison. Some have been released, but Coard remains there to this day.

A few weeks later back in Wales I stood near the bonfire in my own little village during the 5th November celebrations. I looked at the happy faces of my family and the children standing around. How I loved being with them once more, fully realising how transient our life on this planet really was. Perhaps only today was real, and that the secret of life could only be expressed and enjoyed in what we have and do now? Shortly after Christmas I found myself flying a desk once more in Miami. In my absence Ocean Air, the largest regional airline in Puerto Rico, had gone out of business and the future for aircraft sales in the area looked decidedly slimmer. I had grown to love Miami in particular and the United States in general. Here they were not locked into the past, were innovative and forward looking, and I realised that a person like me, with ideas and drive, could achieve much in this land, and furthermore be appreciated. I certainly 'came to life', as soon as I passed through Miami Airport on arrival, and well remember the words of the song 'this land was made for you and me'. Well it was certainly made for me, but again fate intervened to change the course of my future.

Fate, that is, in the shape of my old chum Terry Fox, my one time colleague from Brymon and Air Wales. Terry was one of those people who had that particular ability to persuade people into following a course of action they normally wouldn't wish to pursue. However as he always considered me to be his mentor, I suppose the same criticism could be applied to me. From time to time I wondered whether I ever controlled my own destiny, or was it some magical force which directed me. I was often reminded of a verse from the Rubaiyat of Omar Khayyam.

> *'Tis all a chequer-board of nights and days where destiny with men for pieces plays: hither and thither moves and mates and slays, and one by one back in the closet lays.'*

Well I hadn't yet arrived at the 'slain or the closet bit', but the rest seemed quite true!

Terry it appeared had a customer at Gatwick Airport with a requirement for two of our aircraft. Unfortunately the UK was outside our franchise area for aircraft sales, and it took some days before I arrived at a solution to this problem. In the meantime we had sold a couple of aircraft to a German customer based at Tegel Airport Berlin. They had unfortunately defaulted on their schedule of payments and Conrad and I were sent as trouble shooters to sort out their difficulties. During our stay in Berlin we took the opportunity to cross the wall at 'Check-point Charlie', and visit the Russian sector of East Berlin. Here the contrast with West Berlin was profound. Although the people looked poorer, they also appeared to be more purposeful and fitter than their countrymen in the decadent West exemplified by the young with their long unkempt hair and dirty jeans. In the early twentieth century Berlin had been the second-largest city in Europe, but had been largely destroyed in World War II. In 1961 the East Germans had constructed the Berlin Wall and I remember Conrad saying as we both stood on an observation platform overlooking the wall, that it would never come down in our lifetime. Yet it came down, just six years later on the reunification of Germany in 1990. The highlight for me however was my visit to the Olympic Stadium, which was constructed for the 1936 Olympic Games, and made famous by that wonderful film 'Olympische Spiele' in 1936. Leni Riefenstahl, the German film director, had made this and a number of other propaganda films for Adolf Hitler including 'Triumph of the Will' in 1934, another masterpiece. When I entered the stadium I looked across and saw the same box where Adolf had given the Nazi salute in 1936. I walked across and tried the door to the box and found it unlocked. Now my fantasies took over. I looked around carefully to check nobody was in sight, then I took up the same position as Hitler had in 1936 and gave the Nazi salute to the empty stadium and tried to imagine the power and personality of the man who had started the greatest war in the history of mankind.

Having now sorted out the airline problems in Berlin my next stop was Gatwick Airport in the UK. I had made a suggestion to Gabriel that we use the couple of million in US dollars we had as a built in commission in the aircraft, and convert this into shares in the new UK airline, thereby allowing us to place two of our aircraft with that company. It was a novel way of circumnavigating the franchise problem and brought me considerable praise from Gabriel and his fellow directors. We had been told by the chairman of the new company that an agreement had already been reached with British Caledonian Airways and that the new company would be approved by them as a new feeder airline receiving their full support in maintenance, ticketing interline service etc. Unfortunately on closer examination we found that none of these agreements were in contractual form, and it really meant starting again from first principles. The original Chief Executive was now paid off and, unfortunately for me, I was appointed the new managing director of the company, a position I didn't really want and had never sought. It also meant that my position as sales manager for the Caribbean had clearly been forfeited. This did not please me one iota, but by conjuring up the plot I had been neatly hoisted by my own petard. I stayed long enough to discover that British Caledonian was in big trouble themselves and had little time to be accommodating, the game becoming a political charade. In characteristic forthright fashion I explained my views to Gabriel and apologised for placing the company in the position it found itself. I then strongly suggested that he replace me as managing director with a new face and perhaps somebody with some new ideas. An American was then appointed to lead the company, unfortunately with little success, and the whole business was closed down shortly afterwards. I had wonderful memories of my time with Groupo Miami, and whereas I hadn't proved the most successful of sales managers, in mitigation I could plead that my time there coincided with a huge downturn in the American economy. For all that, it had been the most exciting and stimulating time of my life to date!

CHAPTER 15

IN SEARCH OF A HERO

I had returned from Miami in the middle of a British winter, the cold weather exacerbating the time change problems. I sat on the floor of my lounge, my back against the radiator, a hot drink in my hand, when suddenly the image of Roy Milton, my schoolboy hero, appeared in front of me. He was just as real as he had been when he entered my classroom a short time before he disappeared on operations in1944. Yet amazingly, I had not consciously thought about him during the intervening years. I had made a promise to my mother as a schoolboy that one day I would find out what had happened to Roy and write about it. Even Roy's own family had little idea of his fate, and I was determined to put that right. The problem confronting me however was how to begin to investigate an event then forty years old, of a crashed RAF bomber somewhere in Europe and the fate of its seven crew members.

My first call was to Royal Air Force Records at Gloucester, who informed me that I needed the Milton's family permission to obtain the personal details on Roy's file. I drafted a suitable letter and had it signed by Roy's younger sister. I next obtained the names of his crew, and was advised to send a letter to each of them, which to protect confidentiality would have to be forwarded via the RAF Records Office to their last known addresses as on file in 1944. This I knew was a long shot but no alternative method readily came to mind. A week later, early on a Sunday morning, my telephone rang and I was introduced to the voice of Flying Officer Fred Thompson, the Wireless Operator in Roy's crew, who had chanced to live in the same address since 1939. The details of the crew and their last operation together now began to fall in place, and we agreed to meet at a London hotel, where I interviewed him at length. Soon I was armed with two hours of taped conversation and I promised to contact him again once I had visited Beuren in Germany the scene of the crashed bomber. However I had first to return to the USA and decided that my quest for Roy's story would begin there. This proved to be a long journey and one which would involve travel to Nova Scotia, Canada, the southern states of the USA, Germany and many parts of the UK. During this time the pieces of the puzzle gradually unfolded. The story began like this:—

> Roy had been called up on July 14th 1941 to the Royal Air Force Volunteer Reserve (RAFVR) and like many others reported to Number One Aircrew Reception Centre at Lords Cricket Ground in London. He was billeted at a flat in St. John's Wood, fed at the canteen in London Zoo and was fitted out with all the usual impedimenta necessary for war. A series of lectures on the RAF followed, interspersed with injections (jabs) against all known and seemingly unknown diseases. The recruits were marched daily civilian style through the streets of St. John's Wood and Regent's Park. The posting to Number Seven Initial Training Wing in Newquay Cornwall on August 2nd was something of a relief as it was one step nearer his cherished desire to fly aeroplanes. But for the next six weeks the students endured never ending square-bashing, physical education, lectures on the theory of flight, basic Morse Code and again lectures on the

wartime RAF. Roy now learned that his flying training was to take place in the USA a very exciting prospect. Following a week's embarkation leave he was posted to the RAF station at Wilmslow near Manchester where he awaited his trans-Atlantic convoy. On Saturday September 27th 1941 he wrote the following letter to his mother.

Dear Ma,

I expect this will be my last letter from this country for a while. We've had some information today and may be going anytime now. I was supposed to be going out tonight but I changed my pass for tomorrow night (Sunday) so that I could go to chapel. We've just been told that there's no passes tomorrow night so I'm unlucky.

You can write to me at the address at the bottom. It may be a week or two before I get the letter. We'll be staying there for a few days when we land. So if you write straight away the letter will arrive the same time as me. No more news now—don't worry—I'm OK and looking forward to the trip.

Love
Roy

They were soon to arrive at Liverpool Docks where they boarded the 'Highland Princess', a meat ship converted to a troop ship, bound for Canada and Halifax Nova Scotia. Just after 1000 hours on Monday October 9th the ship approached the Canadian mainland and docked at 1500 hours. That night Roy stood on the boat deck and watched the lights of Halifax, a thrilling site after the blackout at home. Each recruit was then paid 10 Canadian dollars and at midnight entrained for Toronto.

Roy awoke next morning, October 10th, and looked out at some beautiful countryside. The scenery was a mass of colour as the train raced through Adamsville, Rogersville and Newcastle all in New Brunswick. Ten o'clock the next morning the train arrived at Toronto after a journey of approximately 1300 miles through Nova Scotia, New Brunswick, Quebec and Ontario. They were housed in barracks at the Exhibition Hall in Toronto and despite tiredness went on the town that night and were amazed to find that the shops were still open at ten o'clock. In preparation for their move south into the United States all the cadets were now fitted out in grey flannel suits as America's strict neutrality policy meant that RAF uniforms could not be worn. A long train journey once more lay ahead to Montgomery in Alabama where they hoped at last to begin their flying training. Britain and the USA had reached an agreement to train would be pilots in the southern states of the US where good weather would ensure almost uninterrupted flying training. The 'Arnold Scheme' under which Roy was about to train was set up by American General Henry (Hap) Arnold, who after World War II ended became the first five star General of the independent US Airforce. But when this scheme was first visualised, it passed Congress by a two vote majority only. The scheme allowed RAF recruits to be officially discharged from their RAF service to give them civilian status. At Toronto they had to apply to the US Immigration Service for visas to obtain entry to that country, which were only valid for the period it took for the recruits to gain their wings. These arrangements therefore, made it legally possible for America to train British pilots while still remaining neutral.

The first three courses in the Arnold Scheme had gone direct from Toronto to their primary flying schools, but this transition had proved a very difficult one with the change in food, weather, US Army Airforce discipline, language and the many different meanings of language. Consequently the new arrivals including Roy went to Maxwell Field Montgomery for a period of orientation, not a common word in British usage at that time.

They now began to learn American rifle drill, were called Kaydets but were allowed to march British style. They met many American officers who were far more informal than their British counterparts and were regarded as great fellows by the cadets. Yet another new word 'callisthenics' entered their vocabulary known to them as Physical Training. The weather was hot by British standards and the American style tropical khaki uniforms were well suited to the existing climatic conditions. Finally graduation parade at Maxwell took place on the last day of October 1941. The class now officially 42E was able to enjoy 'Open Post', meaning time off duty usually away from the camp. The next few days were spent in leisurely fashion and on Thursday November 4th class 42E handed in their rifles and spent the afternoon packing kitbags and suitcases ready for departure the next morning. Flying training it seemed was finally about to begin.

Reveille sounded at 0400 hours the next morning Wednesday November 5th, and by 0615 hours the cadets were bound for Souther Field Americus in Georgia. Souther Field (pronounced Suther) was one of six primary flying schools in the Arnold scheme all civilian operated. However the cadets had been informed at Maxwell that only two basic flying schools were available for the next course which made it inevitable that a high percentage of cadets would be eliminated. This did nothing to improve morale, although the possibility existed for some 'washed-out' cadets to return to Canada and re-muster into other aircrew categories. Course 42A for example had 263 cadets eliminated from the course for one reason or another, not necessarily linked to flying aptitude. Cadets could be 'washed-out' for a variety of infringements such as low flying, not saluting a dim and distant officer, imprecision when folding bed blankets and an excess of demerits etc. The new arrivals at Souther soon learned that the Field had considerable prestige as a training airfield for it was here that Charles A Lindbergh had learned to fly in 1923, an ironic coincidence given Lindbergh's current opposition to the provision of assistance to Britain! Outside Souther Field today one can read the Lindbergh memorial which states “I had not soloed up to the time I bought my Jenny at Americus”, signed Charles Lindbergh.

"I had not soloed up to the time I bought my Jenny at Americus."

LINDBERGH MEMORIAL DEDICATION CEREMONY AND AIR SHOW

Saturday, December 30, 1978

Souther Field, Americus, Georgia

Souther Field in fact was named in honour of Major Henry Souther, a pioneer in the development of aircraft engines and a close associate of General Billy Mitchell, a leading advocate of the use of large offensive bomber operations. The Primary Course was to last ten weeks, followed by the Basic and Advanced Stages. The combined stages amounted to something over 200 flying hours when the cadet would be awarded his 'wings'. During Roy's period at Souther almost one third of all cadets were 'washed-out'. The training aircraft was the PT17A Stearman with a 220 horsepower Continental engine, and on Monday November 10th Roy had his first flight, thoroughly enjoying the experience. The course was punctuated by flight checks and for this purpose two American Army Air Force instructors were permanently attached to the staff. The normal day on all the courses were split between ground classroom lessons and flying, with Sunday a welcome rest day.

Sunday December 7th 1941 was a memorable day in world history because of the Japanese attack on Pearl Harbour and on the 11th of the same month Germany and Italy declared war on America. From this date onwards the cadets could now wear the RAF uniforms openly, and the reaction by ordinary Americans was quite fantastic. They were showered with invitations to diners, dances, swimming parties and church social events. They enjoyed delicacies previously unknown to them like watermelons, "grits", iced tea and corn-on-the-cob. They also enjoyed the company of "emancipated" American girls and were often picked up by them, driving their own cars. Strange as it appears now, the cadets virtually without exception had never driven a car and certainly never owned one. In fact they learned to fly a plane long before driving a car! For many cadets however that day sadly would never come. Roy developed a close relationship with the daughter of a local family and letters passed between them for a considerable time after he left the States. After his young and formative years in the economically stricken Rhondda in Wales, America was proving a revelation, and he had fallen in love with the expansive American way of life. His great ambition to return to America after the war, and establish a life for himself as a pilot in the Civil Airline Industry. Having successfully passed through the Primary Stage, the cadets, Roy among them, boarded their buses for the short ride to Macon also in the state of Georgia. Basic flight training was about to begin, but this time under the disciplined regime of the United States Air Force. The day was January 10th 1942. Here at Cochrane Field Macon he flew Vultee Valiants the BT13As, a low winged monoplane with a 440 horsepower engine, and learned to use air to ground radio and spent many hours under the hood of the Link Trainer practising instrument flying. The failure rate at this stage was estimated at ten percent including fatalities. Success at this stage led Roy onto the final and Advanced Stage of training essential to gain his 'wings' standard. This he did at Dothan, Alabama flying the AT6A Harvard low wing aircraft, satisfactorily graduating to gain his wings and become a qualified pilot. Success brought him the American Silver Pilots' Wings in a ceremony at Dothan Field, and later at Monckton in Canada he received his coveted RAF wings. He had done well to survive all the flying, the ground training and examinations, but also the strict American discipline so different in many ways from our own e.g. 'Hazing' where it was quite normal to "shop" ones classmates to authority for any offence. This American habit went against the grain with the British Students but the Americans accepted this code without complaint. The 'wash-out' figures in the Arnold scheme from the three flying stages was roughly forty percent, which was almost identical to those of the US Army Air Force.

The Arnold scheme started in June 1941 produced nearly 4,500 pilots for the RAF and ended in February 1943. Public records at Kew in Surrey indicate that the American schools in total combined to train 14,000 pilots 1,700 Navigators and almost 700 Wireless Operators / Air Gunners. This was a wonderful contribution made by America to the War effort and one which has largely gone unrecognised in the United Kingdom. When Roy returned to the UK he was first posted to RAF Harlaxton near Grantham in Lincolnshire where he learned to fly Oxford twin engined aircraft with 12(P) A.F.U. and acclimatised to British weather conditions. His next posting was to 22 O.T.U. (Operational Training Unit) at Wellsbourne Mountford, five miles East of Stratford-upon-Avon where he joined the course on the Wellington (Wimpy) Bomber on which he would begin his operational tour of operations. Following his leave he probably felt surprised to be posted to 427 Squadron which was a part of 6 GROUP Royal Canadian Airforce based at Croft Airfield, five miles south of Darlington in County Durham. It is from this airfield he flew the Wellington on his first six operations over occupied Europe, before his squadron, and he converted to fly the Halifax bomber at Topcliffe Airfield near Thirsk in Yorkshire. The squadron had been stood down on the 1st May 1943, transferred its equipment to 432 squadron at Skipton, and posted five trained crews to the new unit as a nucleus. Upon arriving at the new station, Leeming, the squadron personnel were much impressed by the change from a satellite station like Croft, to a permanent long established station like Leeming, which rests alongside the A1 road just seven miles southwest of the town of Northallerton. Victoria Day, 24th May, was celebrated by a ceremony at which Metro Goldwyn Mayer, the film company, adopted the Lion squadron. The director of MGM Great Britain presented an inscribed bronze lion to the squadron, and eventually each member of the squadron received a lion medal, entitling them to free admission to any cinema showing a MGM film, an extremely popular gesture. The MGM company's film stars had agreed to adopt individual aircraft, which would bear his or her name, and a draw was held to determine which crew would get which star. Lana Turner was the most sought after, closely followed by Greer Garson and Hedy Lamar. Naturally the ceremony was recorded on film to be shown at cinemas all round the world (today that film rests in the MGM studio vaults in Hollywood). The Prime Minister, Winston Churchill, had visited North Africa in 1943, and had been presented with a pair of lion cubs, which he had placed in the care of Regent's Park Zoo. 427 squadron requested that it adopted one of these cubs, called Mareth. Minister Churchill wrote the following note to the squadron in answer.

> I was very pleased to hear on my return to this country that the Lion Squadron of the Royal Canadian Air Force has made the suggestion that the squadron should adopt 'Mareth' one of the lion cubs at the zoo.
>
> With every good wishes for the success of the squadron.
>
> Yours faithfully
> (Signed) Winston Churchill

An adoption ceremony was subsequently held in November at the zoo, and was recorded by MGM and the BBC.

By the summer of 1943 the German Night Fighter force had become extremely dangerous and the losses to Bomber Command grew alarmingly high. Between November 1943 and March 1944 over 1000 aircraft of the Command had been shot down, the majority by night fighters. In January 1944 alone, 427 Squadron lost almost fourteen percent of its aircraft, and this was by no means the largest percentage loss among the squadrons. It was indeed ironic that at that very time, when the Command was being hammered at night, the American fighter squadrons were winning the day battle over Germany with the ubiquitous Mustang fighter aircraft. It seems astonishing to think now that RAF Fighter Command at that time sat largely on their hands, when their comrades in Bomber Command were being butchered. Fighter Command intruder flights over German night fighter airfields were late and few and far between, certainly when measured in terms of the number of sorties flown and aircraft available.

By late 1943 Roy had now flown missions to the Ruhr Valley many times including Duisberg, Dortmund, Essen and Cologne. He missed the Hamburg raids due to severe sinusitis which hospitalised him for the period. The Battle of Berlin had now begun and he visited the 'Big City' (as it was known to the aircrews), four times as well as completing attacks on Frankfurt, Milan, Nuremberg and Peenemunde (the V Bomb experimental works) on the Baltic coast. He had completed twenty-six operations and had risen to deputy flight commander of 'B' flight. At that time only three pilots in ten survived the complete tour of operations of thirty. The odds on survival were further exacerbated by the worst weather Europe had experienced in one hundred years, and many crews were seriously contemplating their chances of survival.

On Friday 25th February 1944 the target for the night was Augsburg in southeast Germany. Augsburg was the home of the Messerschmitt and MAN factories. The latter constructed diesel engines for the U-boat arm. The two bomber streams crossed into Europe via France and Holland and withdrew using the same route. It would be Roy's third operation in the faster and better Halifax III aircraft registration ZLW759. The squadron was happy with their new aircraft and considered that now they had an equal chance of survival compared with squadrons equipped with the Lancaster. That night 594 aircraft, 461 Lancasters, 123 Halifaxes and 10 Mosquitoes, took part in a raid that had for only the second time been split into waves as an attempt to reduce casualties. As it was a long flight, 427 Squadron sent only their nine most experienced crews as a part of the second wave. Roy's Halifax rolled down the Leeming runway on take-off at 2130 hours local time in absolute freezing conditions. A weather COL sat astride the route (i.e. a weather system situated between two high and two low-pressure systems), and at 22,000 feet there was no cloud and little wind. From the Dutch coast the black painted Halifax flew under a panoply of stars, past Aachen and towards its next turning point just North of Lake Constance. At Augsburg the temperature on the ground was—18°C and even the River Lech had frozen over.

The Germans were not sleeping however, and the aircrew of III Nachtjaggruppe (III NJG4) (Night Fighter Group) had been following the progress of the bomber stream drawn by a ghostly hand on their ground-glass situation map. By 2315 hours German time the Messerschmitt 110s at Juvincourt airfield had taken-off to intercept the bomber stream. Staffelkapitan Hans-Karl Kamp was a German night fighter ace already having seventeen night kills to his credit. He was alerted by his radar operator, Franz Stein, shortly after 2400 hours local time of a likely target at approximately five kilometres distance. He gradually closed the range staying below the target until he spotted the bomber visually silhouetted against the light night sky and easily betrayed by the flames emitting from its four engine exhausts. He climbed slowly and eased underneath what he could now clearly recognise as a Halifax bomber. The Luftwaffe's standard method of attacking RAF bombers at night was from below and behind known as the "Von Unten Hinten" method. From this position the fighter merely raised its nose at the point of firing and allowed the bomber to fly through the burst from its cannon and machine guns usually with fatal consequences. Inside the bomber Fred Thompson, the wireless operator, had just finished pushing out the last of the bundles of "window" down the chute ("window" were strips of course black paper with thin aluminium foil stuck on one side). "Window" had been shown earlier in the year to swamp German Radar set by generating false echoes, rendering them virtually useless. Stein's radar however, the latest development of the SN2 radar, could easily discern the target through these false echoes. Thompson was just settling back in his seat when he felt a searing pain in his right leg where almost twenty pieces of shrapnel had entered. The aircraft lurched and then dived to the left. Thompson, who was sitting directly under the pilot's position, struggled to his feet and stood alongside Roy who was now fighting to control his fatally damaged aircraft. Both the port engines had been shot out of action as was the intercom, but the aircraft had not caught fire. Roy pointed at the escape hatch in the nose and Thompson soon had it removed and then dived out into the night expecting the remainder of the crew to follow. Minutes later he floated down into a field of snow near the village of Beuren in the Hochwald. Back in the aircraft Roy realised he would not be returning to Leeming that night now decided to land the aircraft on one of the many snow covered fields below. Visibility was excellent and his crew remained on board confident in Roy's ability to pull off a safe landing. Eyewitnesses first heard the noise of the stricken aircraft descending, and then saw it describing a left-hand circuit. It was at this point that fate intervened with devastating consequences. At below two hundred feet above ground level the port wing suddenly burst into flame. Five members of the crew now baled out, but they had left it too late and their parachutes were found only partially opened when they struck the ground. As Roy lined up the aircraft to land, the petrol tanks exploded throwing Roy forward through the cockpit and into the snow some distance away killing him instantly. The rear gunner for whatever reason had remained in his turret and was found dead at the scene of the crash. Hans-Karl Kamp flew back to base his eighteenth victim confirmed. He had been born in Essen on the 19th January 1918. He was soon promoted to the rank of Major and sent to command III/JG300 on the 5th December 1944. He was already the holder of the DK (German Cross in Gold) and was earmarked in the near future to receive the Knight's Cross (Ritterkreuz) from Adolf Hitler. This event never took place however as Kamp was himself killed over the city of Hanover on the 31st December 1944 by which time he had shot down 23 RAF bombers.

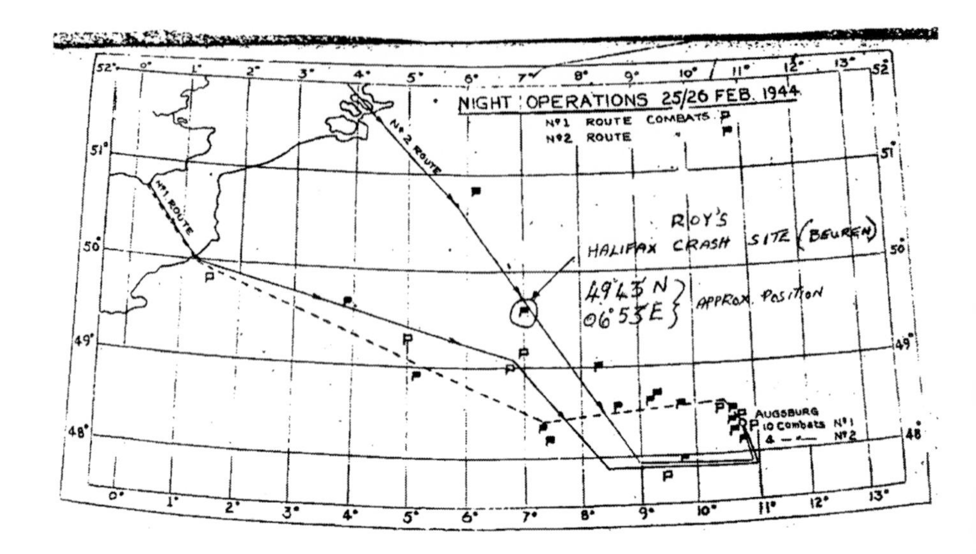

It was 0530 when my telephone rang with my early morning call. By 0600 I had checked-out in the vast foyer of the Intercontinental Hotel in West Berlin. The Pan American flight to Frankfurt was due to depart at 0730 and I had elected to catch the airport bus to Tegel Airport from the hotel entrance. A white mass of fog hung over Berlin. Buderpestrasse was cold wet and deserted, and I sat in the bus, a solitary figure for the journey to the airport. My mind was buzzing with thoughts of my impending visit to Beuren. Since I first heard of it I had imagined it to be a picturesque village high in the hills east of Trier. The crash site loomed large in my thinking and my imagination had painted the picture. The previous night in my room I had watched the giant Mercedes Benz sign revolving and illuminating the night sky above the Kortfurstendamm. Roy had flown here in these skies above Berlin seeing only the flashes and reflections of the bomb and flak explosions, highlighted against the cloud and probing searchlights. I could visualise him sitting there, crouched in the small cockpit amidst the fire and fury, desperately longing for the moment when the Bomb Aimer cried out “Bombs Gone”, so that they could leave this accursed city. Four times he had flown his Halifax aircraft here and four times he had made it back home safely.

Tegel was busy with its early morning departing businessmen. But on this day they weren't going anywhere in a hurry, the fog saw to that. The Pan American coffee tasted good, and after several cups had passed my lips the fog lifted. Shortly afterwards, the Pan Am 727 aircraft did the same and cruised effortlessly down the airway to Frankfurt. The Luxair Fokker Friendship connecting flight to Luxembourg looked a trifle sad and forlorn as it stood outside the departure lounge at Frankfurt Airport. Its appearance was matched by its aerodynamic qualities as it groaned to its cruising height of 12,000 feet. Clearly Luxair was not at its best this morning and this was confirmed when what passed as "lunch" was served! To escape the noise of the cabin (I was sitting in the front seat between the propellers) I soon found myself sitting up front behind the captain in the cockpit, after a few friendly words with the stewardess. Here at least it was serene and pleasant as we flew across the snow covered land of West Germany. We soon approached the higher ground of the beautiful Hunsruck country. Beuren in the Hockwald lay some miles South of our track, and forty years almost to the day, the snow had lain on these same fields on that fateful night in February 1944. Soon we descended into Luxembourg Airport and after landing I thanked the Captain for allowing me into his private domain, and then clambered out into the weak afternoon sun.

Some hours later I turned the hired Ford Escort onto an easterly heading, which would eventually bring me to the German frontier near Trier. The road was largely clear of other traffic and my progress was fast, despite the snow. My thoughts raced ahead to Beuren. Who would know what I was talking about? Would anybody remember the night in question? I couldn't speak German, so what the hell was I doing here anyway! I should have been back in Miami enjoying the sun, not rushing around Europe with its foul winter weather. I stopped the car at a garage just west of Trier to buy a road map, and a little later I crossed the Moselle River and negotiated Trier losing my way en-route. By this time I was both tired and hungry, and my thoughts were anywhere but on the road ahead. I guessed that Beuren would be too small a village to boast of any suitable hostelry, so decided to night stop at the town of Hermeskeil just seven kilometres away. It had been here that Thompson had been taken to hospital after the crash and therefore a suitable place to commence my investigations. It now appeared that I had taken an indirect scenic route running alternatively along high hills and into deep valleys. Not an easy place, I thought, to force land an aircraft particularly at night. Pretty villages like Pluwig and Kell came and went, but my navigation failed me not, and a signpost soon indicated that Hermeskeil lay directly ahead. It was still light as I drove the Ford up the long hill, which seemed to be the main shopping area of the town. Seeing no hotel, I retraced my steps and eventually saw a large rectangular building standing back off the road. This turned out to be the Hotel Wiemers, which proved to be a better hotel than its outward appearance indicated.

I checked into my room in record time, threw my one bag on the bed and was gone. It was dark now but the snow lightened up the surrounding countryside. Beuren soon appeared on a road sign and a long straight run-in soon saw me at the centre of the village. I tried this and that road looking questioningly at each field in turn as the possible crash site. Parking the car I put my imagination to rest and re-entered the real world. I stood near the Spar Store and watched a few people enter and leave. Nobody inspired me sufficiently to attempt an introduction with my ludicrous German until a dark haired pleasant looking girl approached, but she knew less English than I did German! By this time fatigue was rapidly overtaking me so I returned to the hotel for an excellent and much needed meal. I sat in my bedroom that night totally unsure of my course of action. Why had I come all this way? How could I talk to these people about events forty years ago! Who could I speak to and would they be able to understand English? I recorded my thoughts and the events of the day on my tape recorder, and felt very tired and totally disillusioned. Perhaps the morrow would be better, and I owed it to Roy to continue. With these thoughts, I took to my bed and slept the sleep of the dead.

It was as if God had touched me in the night as at breakfast next morning I knew exactly what course of action to follow, and gone were the doubts of the night. Clearly my mood had been conditioned by fatigue and a lack of food. I decided to start with a visit to the local Rathaus, something similar to our local council. Surely someone there would speak English and be able to help me.

The morning was cold and misty as I drove the Ford Escort and climbed the long hill of Hermerskeil. Near the traffic lights at the top I found the Rathaus. I walked through the slush until I found a side entrance to what proved to be a travel agency, and here a couple of locals were talking to the solitary attendant. They all turned and smiled at me in welcome and as one said "Guten Morgen". I replied, "Guten Morgen", praying they wouldn't continue the conversation, I slunk into a corner and busied myself with some books until the customers left, then I turned to the attendant. "Do you speak English?" I asked hopefully. He addressed me in perfect English and introduced himself as Ludger Schattel. I began hesitantly, "Well forty years ago a RAF Halifax bomber crashed near Beuren, would you have any information here on that crash?" He looked at me as if this was the sort of question he was asked every day. "One moment," he said as he picked up the telephone and spent the next few minutes deep in conversation. "There is a person coming to see you in a few minutes who might be able to help you", said Ludger. Clearly here was an intelligent young man who soon became interested in my story of Roy Milton.

The door suddenly opened and Ludger's colleague appeared clutching a sheaf of papers. "Here are the available documents relating to the aircraft crash", he said. I must have looked completely dumfounded and he smiled reassuringly as he handed me the papers. I looked at the heading which read 'Meldung über den Luftkampf in der nacht vom 25 zum 26 Februar 1944um 0.15 Udr Südöstlich des Ortes Beuren Landkreis Trier'. Translated it said:—"Report of Air Battle on the night of 25th/26th February 1944 at 0.15 hours, southeast the locality of Beuren in the administrative region of Trier". It was difficult to believe it, but here it was all three pages of it. It was now clear that Ludger had become very excited by the story, and he quickly provided local ordinance survey maps of the area around Beuren in the Hochwald region, to pinpoint the crash site. Now he offered his services as my interpreter and soon he was on the phone to the ex-Burgomeister of Beuren. An animated conversation took place and Ludger and I agreed to meet after lunch at my hotel when he would drive me to Beuren. I returned to my hotel in a state of shock, what people these Germans were I thought, how was it that they ever lost the war? My council at home couldn't tell you what had happened the previous year let alone events forty years back!!

Promptly at two o'clock, Ludger arrived outside my hotel with a screech of brakes, strangely this day was St. David's Day exactly forty years and five days after the events of 1944. I had visualised the scene so often as a kid, and now I was to experience the reality. What were these people like? Would any of them remember the night? Would any eyewitnesses still be living in the village? Perhaps they had all died or moved to another village or town in Germany. Well at last I was finally going to find out. The car slowed as we entered the small square in Beuren. A crowd of people stood there and I said to Ludger, "What's going on here today?" He smiled at me, "They are all waiting to greet you," he said disarmingly. As I stepped out of the car the people stared at me, not with any hostility, but intensely with a great sense of curiosity. Nevertheless I felt greatly unnerved, 'My God', I thought, may be they think I was on board the aircraft that night. 'No of course not', that couldn't be, but the atmosphere was electric and heavy with suspense. I was soon sitting comfortably in the home of the ex-Burgomeister at a table heavily laden with bread of various types, meats, fruits and Moselle wine. The welcome was genuinely warm and in many ways re-assuring but my feelings of strangeness would not go away. I set-up my tape recorder on a small table and started asking questions for Ludger to translate. But even as I faced these friendly people former enemies of my country, my thoughts drifted back to the war years and the dark dangerous skies above Europe. My daydream was short but very clear, and the events stood out as if I was watching a film.

I came to with a start. I was still sitting in the warm and comfortable house in Beuren, the questions and answers all being recorded on my small tape recorder. Suddenly the room door opened and a middle-aged lady half entered and stared at me. She spoke eloquently in German and Ludger rapidly translated. She said, "I have waited for you to come, I knew you would, and I have something from the crash I have kept for you". Then as suddenly as she appeared she disappeared. I felt the hairs on the back of my neck stand up. The atmosphere in the room was simply electric, the likes of which I had never experienced in my life before. Yesterday I knew nobody, had nothing, and yet today I was surrounded by people of goodwill, most of whom it appeared had witnessed the events of that night in 1944. The lady soon re-appeared and handed me a supermarket plastic bag with the "Spar" logo. The room fell into a deep silence as I struggled to undo the simple knot, my hands trembling with emotion. It was a RAF officer's cap, but what was more important it belonged to Roy and inside the leather border he had written in ink his name 'MILTON J.R.G.'. It took a little time for me to recover my composure and then the story was explained to me.

The people of the village had stood outside listening in awe to the thunder of the bomber stream as it passed overhead en-route to Augsburg. Now a noise of a stricken aircraft took centre stage as it descended in an arc out of the night sky. The drama deepened when they saw a parachute descending and land in a field adjacent to the village. This of course was the badly injured Thompson. Herr Becker and another member of the home guard left their homes suitably armed and captured Thompson, who in deep shock was in no condition to escape or put-up any resistance. In the meantime the Halifax had exploded on landing and the young Matilda Becker frightened for her father had left the house on the edge of the village with her sister to search for him. As she approached the road dividing the fields she came across the dead body of Roy spread-eagled on his back lying in the deep snow. She saw his officer's cap nearby picked it up and hid it at home, convinced that one day somebody would come to the village who knew the dead airman. So it was Matilda Becker, now Hemmes, who was the middle-aged lady who presented the cap to me that day in Beuren. The Becker family took in Fred Thompson that night, tended to his wounds and made up a bed for him in their living room. They did not report him to the military authorities, instead Frau Becker contacted her friend Captain Dengler, a retired Wehrmacht officer and a holder of the Knight's Cross, and explained the situation. He in turn resisted both the Luftwaffe and SS authorities' attempts to convey Thompson directly to a prisoner of war camp. In the morning Dengler picked up Thompson and conveyed him to the civilian hospital in Hermeskeil where he remained until he recovered from his wounds. Undoubtedly it was Dengler's Knight's Cross that allowed this course of events to take place as in Germany even Generals salute any ranks however lowly, if they were the holder of a coveted decoration.

Fred Thompson recovered from his wounds and was taken by train to Eastern Germany and captivity in Oflag Luft 3. After liberation in 1945 he returned home to the same address and to the same job. I related to him the story of my visit to Beuren and impressed upon him to make a return visit, but this time not by parachute. He took his wife along with him the following summer and was treated like royalty by the villagers. Although

I was invited, I was in the West Indies at the time and unable to accept. For Thompson however it proved to be the most exciting and wonderful moment of his later years. Perhaps my research and efforts had reaped a fine dividend after all!

I said goodbye to the Becker family promising to return the next morning prior to my departure for Luxembourg. To create in words my feelings at that moment would be impossible, but I knew instinctively that I had to return to the crash site alone that evening. Following dinner I drove slowly back to Beuren, the night was quite light due to the absence of cloud and the snow covered landscape. Strange I thought that this night was so much like that February night forty years earlier. I parked the car at the side of the road and walked to the spot where Fräu Becker had made the indentations in the snow to mark the spot where Roy's body had fallen. Across the field I visualised the crashed Halifax bomber. I saw the intervening years as through a kaleidoscope. Roy in his short trousers pushing his father's wheelbarrow full of vegetables from their allotment. Standing tall proud and handsome, talking with Miss Caldicott, our English Teacher who had taught him years before. I remembered the cooing noises of the girls and Miss Caldicott's words of rebuke. I remembered kicking the boy next to me and boasting that this was Roy Milton a pilot from my street, this act bringing a sharp admonition from Miss Caldicott and an even greater grin from Roy. Lastly I saw him that week in February 1944 a Saturday morning with the rain falling heavily. Dressed in my football gear I had walked in the front room many times that morning to check the weather in the vain hope that the rain would stop. Suddenly at the bottom of the street, I saw Roy, hatless in a white raincoat bent forward against the wind and rain. I watched him until he disappeared into his mother's house at number 15. I felt a great sense of sadness and foreboding and rushed into the kitchen where my mother was preparing lunch. I blurted out, "Mam I have just seen Roy and I will never see him again." My mother looked at me strangely, as I was not in the habit of making such philosophical pronouncements, "Don't be silly dear," she said, "of course you will."

The thoughts tumbled through my mind in an incoherent fashion. I knelt in the snow feeling Roy's presence. I looked up towards the northwest towards home and the direction he had come that night and my tears stained the snow. Roy and I were indivisible, a part of the same village fabric separated only by a quirk of age a few extra revolutions of planet earth. I wept for him and for his crew, I wept too for his parents who had through hardship and poverty given him the very best that they could offer. I cursed the futility of war and I prayed for us all for the blindness, stupidity and wickedness of all the things we do against one another. I thought of his previous aircraft, Sierra Sue, which he had flown ten times to German targets. Sierra Sue had died with another crew over Berlin one month earlier in January 1944. The words of the war song now came to mind, "Sierra Sue I'm sad and lonely," and as images of our childhood flashed before me I knew that Roy and I were both sad and lonely and that our little valley was lonely too!

Note:—Today on the Honours Board of Tonypandy Grammar School (now known as the Community College), second from the top is the name J.R.G. Milton. Just a name to today's children but a hero nevertheless. He remains 21 years of age.

CHAPTER 16

THE END OF THE BEGINNING

I had walked for at least two hours in search of the crashed RAF aircraft. Everybody had talked about it, but I alone of our gang went out to search for it. Perhaps the RAF had got there first and carted away the wreck, and I scoured the mountainside above Gilfach in vain, until darkness fell, and I returned home sadly disappointed. My father was an engineer in the local hospital, and being aware of my interest in aeroplanes, would from time to time bring home pieces of flying uniforms, like the pilot's brevet and badges of rank, from aircraft crash victims obtained from the hospital morgue. In a macabre way, my chums and I would sniff at these items of uniform, like some sort of demented bloodhounds, when the smell of petrol and burned fabric would be all too evident, propelling our imaginations into the reality of the air war. My mother, in her wisdom, now decided that I should go away to boarding school, subject of course to my passing the entrance examination. Never one to do things by half, I therefore found myself sitting two different eleven plus examinations, the first of these for the county, and the second one for the local grammar schools. It was the county examination in which I needed to do well, because it was on this that my place in the boarding school depended. Fortunately I managed thirtieth position, and second among that year's boarder intake. It had been a pyrrhic victory however, as the geographical position of the school, low down in the Vale of Glamorgan, increased my susceptibility to the multitude of allergies which afflicted my breathing, and thus causing me severe asthma. Then, of course, there were no modern day type inhalers available, so I seemed to spend half my time in the sick bay, attended by matron and the school doctor. To the present day I have found myself in a war of attrition with asthma, a war which through my sporting endeavours and achieved levels of fitness, I was largely able to contain, and sometimes conquer for long periods of time. In later years, when confronted with aircrew medicals and medical history forms, I unblushingly lied, telling myself that it was up to the medics to declare me unfit—they never did! As a consequence, my flying career spanned over thirty years and 10,000 hours of accident free flying.

I slept in 'top dorm', as it was called, which housed about twelve first form boarders, they were a generally decent lot, but inevitably there was one exception. He was a boy named Rowe, much larger than the rest of us, who continually boasted of his superior English ancestry, and the fact that an uncle of his had once played rugby for England. Despite my delicate state of health, I was regarded as a bit of a tear-away, and had already created a reputation for defying the school rules, particularly at night. I now decided to take on Rowe, but as I needed all the advantages open to me. I waited until he was in bed one night in a horizontal position before I leapt on him and belaboured him with my pillow. He was stronger than I suspected however, and soon clambered to his feet, and hit me so hard I flew backwards, off the end of his bed, landing flat on my back on the dormitory floor. The noise was terrific as the others in the dormitory now joined in the 'free for all'. The house master was very angry that night, and we all suffered 'ten of the best' with a leather slipper across our bottoms. For the next hour I squirmed with pain, halfway between tears and laughter, and if it that wasn't enough the next day's news was worse.

The school had been built early in the seventeenth century, and when I hit the dormitory floor a portion of the middle dormitory ceiling, below, had crashed down narrowly missing some of its occupants. The combination of my poor health and nocturnal activities now culminated in a meeting of the head and my parents, who had been summoned to the school. The formal reason for my departure was never stated, but my father was fond of repeating a statement made by the head, the day I left. "John," he said, "is a born leader of men, but would he please lead them somewhere else!" My days at boarding school were therefore over, and I now looked forward to attending the local grammar school, closer to home.

At Tonypandy grammar school, my new headmaster proved to be a big fat balding figure, with apparently little humour, known to us all as 'Bomber'. He clearly had little time for children who had attended, what he must have considered to be, a privileged institution. Consequently, he completely ignored my eleven plus credentials and led me to the dungeon of aspirations in the shape of form 1D, the lowest category of human intelligence in the school at that time. Here I soon developed an almost filial affection for some of the inmates; namely Maurice, of the thick glasses and spotty face, and (you have to believe this) Mutt, the butt of all the headmaster's jokes, and Geoff, who although small in stature had an immense appetite for fighting. He would fight anybody for no apparent reason at any time. Finally there was little John, who was a poor hunchback kid with a voice like an angel. We five, for whatever reason, became very good friends, and generally sat at the back of the classroom, and did as little work as possible. In the first term examinations, I achieved a position of 33rd out of the class of 36, improving to 28th by the end of the second term. By this time my poor mother had been driven to near despair, and soon drove me in the same direction by hiring-in a local school teacher to put me back on track. Vernon Jones turned out to be a good chap, and one I grew to like, so perhaps it was no surprise when at the next set of examinations I reached second in the form. This however meant that I had to leave the congenial company of my friends and move-up one form to the 'C' stream. I also missed the beautiful Sylvia Williams, our form mistress, she of the beautiful black tresses, lovely face and voluptuous body. She would often stand at the back of the form, next to my desk, and hypnotise me with the swaying of her hips and the tightness of her skirt over her belly, and all this at a time when my sex hormones had not reached the 'gearing-up stage', so to speak. However, she did much to alert me to the possibilities, in preparation for the future. One thing you can say for sure about lust, is that it showed up early in my development! Sylvia was much admired in the school, particularly by the male members, and was undoubtedly another reason why the 'D' from held such a magical attraction for me. That year I invited young John, of the golden voice, to join my family over the Christmas holidays, an event which proved a great success, with John joyfully singing to my accompaniment on the piano. In the afternoon we went to the fairground on de Winton field, and in the evening saw 'The Man Who Came to Dinner', at the Empire Theatre, Tonypandy, starring the prim Bette Davis as a cool, but harassed, secretary, and her boss the garrulous and witty Monte Woolley. Young John unfortunately had a limited life span, and today, when I watch the video of that film, I am forever reminded of the joy which registered on his face, on a day I knew I would always remember. The school had developed a system of 'late-class'. This was designed for pupils who arrived late for school, either for the morning or afternoon sessions. As I always went home for lunch, it was inevitable, with my dilatory habits, that I would be late back for the first afternoon lesson, with the result I tented to be a regular member of the 'late-class' fraternity. Here, more often than not, I would be reunited with Mutt, Geoff and little John. We would be kept in a class from four o'clock to five o'clock, staring at the supervising teacher, and doing little else. This boredom would be punctuated however, by a visit from 'Bomber', the head, usually carrying a large tray of 'left-overs' from school lunch. Most of the time it was bread pudding slices, which he would sell to his captive audience at two pence a slice. Here for the first time also he showed a streak of benevolence and humanity, which I barely suspected. Seeing Mutt and little John, he would smile and then make a little joke about his two regulars, and provide them with free slices. This of course was wartime, when food rationing was in effect and kids from poorer homes often went hungry for long periods.

With the promptings of Vernon, I quickly passed through the 'C' and 'B' forms to the 'E' form (meaning express), where the brighter and more esteemed children sat for their school leaving certificate, one year earlier than the rest. However, having missed half the syllabus, it was no surprise to me that I failed to pass the said examination at the end of that year. The following year, now in form '5E', I put that right by passing in six subjects, but achieving little distinction in the process. An inner voice had by this time convinced me that my future lay in aviation, more particular as a pilot, but nobody existed, either among my teachers or family, who could advise me on the career I sought. I clearly couldn't discuss my plans with my parents, as my mother in particular considered flying, in any shape or form, totally abhorrent, and of course very dangerous, and there were few secrets between her and my father. Fortunately, I had been born with the twin characteristics of obstinacy and imagination. My mind and soul were therefore transported at regular intervals into far-off worlds, free of the humdrum of daily life and grind. I was ready to commence such a journey then, and despite many disappointments along the way eventually achieved the desired goal. It was a path strewn with many obstacles, not least my health, but the very by-product of these problems had built in me a steely determination to succeed, and in that I had a notable family act to follow, in the shape of my great uncle Henry. He had begun working in the local Maerdy colliery in South Wales at the tender age of twelve years, not a wholly unusual experience for boys in the late nineteenth century. On Christmas Eve 1895 his father, working as under manager in the same mine, had been blown to pieces in an underground explosion. Henry then was just seventeen years old, and therefore became the sole breadwinner in a family consisting of his mother, four boys and two young girls. Twice a week after his colliery shift he would walk across the mountain from Maerdy to Aberdare, before the road was built, where he eventually completed his mining qualifications becoming, by the age of twenty-nine, a colliery manager. In the late 1920s, he achieved the position of general manager of the Cambrian Combine (a group of collieries), which by 1935 employed over 25,000 men. In 1910 he was decorated with the King Edward Medal for heroism underground. This was presented to him by King George V in a ceremony at Buckingham Palace. He became an author in 1919 with the publication of his book in Welsh called, 'Aelwyd Ac Heol Fy Ngwlad', (literally translated as 'Home and Road of My Country'). In 1928 Foyles of London published his poem 'Y Camp', ('The Feat'). Before his death in 1935 he had become the chairman of the Monmouthshire and South Wales Coal Owners Association, a meteoric rise in his fortunes. Sadly his first four children died at a young age, but his fifth son, John Victor Evans, won a place at Oxford University, and as a first-rate speaker served as treasurer, then secretary and finally president of the Oxford Union in the Lent term of 1922, possibly the first, and only, Welshman to achieve that unique distinction. I merely hoped that my genetic make-up was similar to that of my great uncle, who proved a wonderful example, and a hard act to follow.

LIST OF MEMBERS

WHO HAVE SERVED ON THE STANDING COMMITTEE.

Michaelmas Term, 1921, to Easter Term, 1922.

MICHAELMAS TERM, 1921.

Mr. K. M. LINDSAY, Worcester, *President.*

Mr. C. B. Ramage, Pembroke, *Ex-President.*
Rev. Dr. Carlyle, University, *Senior Treasurer.*
Mr. A. D. Lindsay, M.A., Balliol, *Senior Librarian.*
Mr. J. S. Collis, Balliol, *Junior Treasurer.*
Mr. J. B. Herbert, Ch. Ch., *Junior Librarian.*
Mr. E. Marjoribanks, Ch. Ch., *Secretary.*
Mr. R. M. Carson, Oriel.
Mr. J. G. Morgan, St. John's.
Mr. G. W. Wrangham, Balliol.
Mr. A. R. Woolley, Wadham.
Mr. R. C. C. J. Binney, Balliol.

LENT TERM, 1922.

Mr. J. VICTOR EVANS, St. John's, *President.*

Mr. K. M. Lindsay, Worcester, *Ex-President.*
Rev. Dr. Carlyle, University, *Senior Treasurer.*
Mr. A. D. Lindsay, M.A., Balliol, *Senior Librarian.*
Mr. R. M. Carson, Oriel, *Junior Treasurer.*
Mr. E. Marjoribanks, Ch. Ch., *Junior Librarian.*
Mr. J. G. Morgan, St. John's, *Secretary.*
Mr. J. D. Woodruff, New College.
Mr. R. C. C. J. Binney, Balliol.
Mr. A. R. Woolley, Wadham.
Mr. S. Tetley, Keble.
Mr. A. G. Bagnall, St. John's.

During the next eight years, first in college and then as a teacher in East Sussex, I took every opportunity to take to the air. I acquired my first private pilot's licence at Cardiff, with that fine man and instructor John Bennett. Then I flew at Biggin Hill, in Kent, with Tiny Marshall and Peter Chinn of the Surrey and Kent Flying Club and finally with Cecil Pashley, the renowned flying instructor, at Shoreham Airport near Brighton. Pashley was probably the most experienced flying instructor in the county, with well over 20,000 instructional hours to his credit in a forty plus years career. I had been told that he had flown over 10,000 hours in Tiger Moths alone, and at one time had actually instructed Albert Ball, the World War I flying ace. He alone, it was said, kept Shoreham Airport alive and in being, and today, in his honour, the approach road to the airport is called Cecil Pashley Way. Undoubtedly, he was one of the great heroes of civil aviation in the United Kingdom, and deserves to be remembered. Some years later, I was to fly with Tubby Dash, the chief flying instructor at the Newtonards Flying Club, in Northern Island. I met Tubby when I had to renew my instructor's rating, at a time when I was flying with Emerald Airways at Belfast International Airport. Most evenings he would end up drunk, after flying was over. One night, in such a state, he had left the club, tripped up and broken his leg. When I arrived to fly with him, his leg was encased in plaster-of-Paris, so in a respectful way I asked whether he was fit to fly. His answer was unprintable, but we became quite good friends, and at dinner at his home one evening he proudly showed me the copper urn suitably etched with the famous name, James Mollison. He described how he had been asked to fly the ashes of his friend and empty them over Bantry Bay, in Ireland. Not having done this type of thing before the inevitable happened, when the ashes flew back into the cockpit filling his ears, eyes and nostrils. That evening most of Mollison's ashes went down the plug hole of his bath at home. In the 1920s and 30s of course, Mollison had made the world famous flight from Australia to the UK in eight days and nineteen hours.

In 1932 he had made the first crossing east to west of the Atlantic, later married the famous aviatrix Amy Johnson, and in 1933 was awarded the Britannia Trophy. Another great character I had met on my travels was Joe Viatkin, already mentioned in Chapter Seven. He once confided in me that when he walked across a hanger floor he was apt to loiter, touch the aircraft and often talk to it. I was extremely relieved to hear this, as it was my habit also. It was almost as if we believed that an aircraft was anything but an inanimate object. Joe, never given to using two words when one would do, confided in me one day, in a grave secretive way, that during World War II he had to test fly a rebuilt Wellington bomber before it was returned to a squadron. During the flight he and the co-pilot had heard the voices of the former crewmembers shouting in fear. It transpired that they had been killed in the aircraft, and although the pilot had managed to land he too had subsequently died of his wounds. Later on a bombing raid over Germany the aircraft had been shot down and all its crew killed.

By 1961, having acquired my professional pilot's licence after much work and many disappointments, I now turned my attention to the opposite sex, with a zest bordering on mania, almost as if I had been hot-wired for it, completely discounting the inevitable and sloppy consequences. Perhaps this was due to the restrictive opportunities of my youth, coupled with the fact that I had undergone almost five years of teaching in a regime of strict conformity. I had certain opportunities of course, and one with a very attractive brunette, a teacher from another school in the same town had seemed to offer the greatest promise. In my flat one night, having plied her with drink, I placed my hand behind her back in order to lower the side of the settee down to a horizontal position. My finger then became wedged in the wooden hinge and as she lay back in expectation, the increased weight of her body nearly removed my finger. Unfortunately she mistook my muffled screams of agony for passion, and it was some time before she recognised that my finger had been partially amputated. With my ardour suitably cooled, I promised myself to take greater care in future. Now however in company with Paul Weeks and Stan Edwards, I followed a completely hedonistic path that first led me to lose my first airline job. Now they do say that making love can boost the heart, relieve pain and keep you healthy, but the reverse seemed to be happening to me. I was clearly seeking a different sort of stimuli and a direction to follow, but all my attempts to do so were proving abortive. Late night parties seemed to follow one another with an almost monotonous regularity. Angela was a nice attractive Cambrian hostess, and it was her passion for Paul that threatened to break up our gang of three. Every night, after her flying duties had been completed, she would appear in the club and make a bee-line for Paul, isolate him in a corner and act in a 'lovey-dovey' sort of way—quite sickening really! He in turn stared at her like a stoat threatened by a snake, longing to escape, but not knowing how. After weeks of this behaviour she appeared one evening positively beaming, collared Paul and showed him their engagement ring, which she had just purchased. Paul's face took on the hue of a sick and endangered animal, and I realised that now that it was time for all good men to help end this charade once and for all. However, when the end came it happened in a completely unscripted fashion. Stan and I had picked-up some nurses from the Royal Infirmary, Cardiff, and drove to Angela's celebratory party at her flat in Cathedral Road. When we arrived the party was in full swing, and I noted, through an alcoholic haze, that Angela had already grabbed Paul and hoisted him off to the far recesses of the room away from any other female predators. Stan and I resumed our drinking, and I devoted special attention to the blond nurse I had brought along. She appeared to be rather special, and my devious mind was already planning ahead to ensnare her into some of my future adventures. As the evening wore on, I noticed a large painting that hung from the wall depicting a French knight with a sword, in all his finery, sitting astride a large, and noble, stallion. It looked tasteful and certainly matched the colours of the room, which by this time was swarming with people. Stan and I were now both pretty much 'tanked-up', and a look across at Paul showed that he was similarly 'loaded'. The music now demanded that I join in the dancing with my unique Fred Astaire style, seize the blond and sweep her up into a rhythm, when our senses would soar. These grand joyous moments can only be enjoyed of course when the couple is in perfect harmony, but after a few steps I noticed that the lady had somehow disappeared from view. Now my solo dance-act had taken on an instinctive style, and it appeared that everybody else had left the floor to watch in admiration. I also noticed, for the first time, that I was still holding a near full brandy glass. I had completed a second, and superb fast pirouette, when the brandy, conforming to the laws of physics, surrendered to the centrifugal force applied, and flew across the room splattering the wall and its lovely picture. At that point inertia took over and I collapsed on the nearest chair to rest. I was recovering my natural poise, when Angela screamed so loudly, I leapt to my feet, and like everybody else in the room, turned in the direction of her gaze. "The picture, look at my lovely picture," she screamed repeatedly. It was simply unbelievable. The French nobleman in the picture was gradually sliding off the horse's back, and worse still the horse's legs were buckling and growing shorter. It was like a very slow motion picture, as the horse's legs grew shorter by the minute and the rider slipped evermore off its back. The room was in uproar with Angela's continued screaming, Stan was convulsed with laughter on the settee, with Paul trying to console her and look serious, but nevertheless also shaking with laughter. The brandy from my glass had obviously dissolved the oil in the painting. The enormity of my actions hit home, and brought on the usual symptoms in such circumstances of fight or flee. In this case I fled, doing my Fred Astaire act down the stairs, ending up in a heap but apparently unhurt at the bottom, and with Angela's screams still ringing in my ears, ran the first half mile in record time. I slept very badly that night, with a recurrent dream of pursuit by riders, half on and half off very short-legged horses. The upshot of the evening's events however, had helped in the break-up of Paul and Angela. After all who would want to be engaged to a chap who had friends like Stan and me!

Eventually it was through partying interspersed with the odd bit of flying at the club that led the way to a more permanent and satisfying lifestyle. We all had enjoyed another great party, which had only ended when we had tumbled into bed at 0530 hours. It had been a triumph of the will, to leave the comfort and security of the bed and its attendant warm and yielding female flesh. The day had barely begun, was empty, wet and still dark, but at least he rain had now stopped. I looked at my watch; it was only 0730 hours. I shuddered in the cold, my eyes half closed and drew my coat tightly around me, as Paul and I entered the car and began the drive to the airport, without as much as a coffee to sustain us. However, it wasn't as if the ensuing charter that morning would challenge a man, as it only involved flying for fifteen minutes across the Bristol Channel to Weston-Super-Mare. The passengers were councillors from the nearby town of Barry, who were in the process of investigating the feasibility of building a Billy Butlin holiday camp on the hill just to the east of the fairground on Barry Island. At Weston they were to be picked-up by Butlin representatives and driven to Minehead, where they would examine the workings of an existing Butlin camp. We were to take the councillors, among whom was one of the Forte family, in two light aircraft, Paul in the Piper Tripacer and me in the older, and somewhat battered, Auster. I swung the aircraft into a climbing turn, which I thought was accomplished with a certain panache, and focused my attention on Paul's Tripacer, already a dot in the distance. My eyes were certainly troubling me, and the saying 'pee holes in the snow' suddenly came into mind, which brought on a fit of the giggles. This was brought to an abrupt stop, when I found the councillor sitting alongside staring at me in some alarm. Paul was already on the ground, watching as I came into land. I apparently rounded out the aircraft much to high above the runway, and Paul told me later that he had crossed himself, expecting the wings to end up back in Wales. I only remember a distant 'sinking feeling' as the aircraft contrived to waffle earthwards. Fortunately the strong rubber bungees of the undercarriage and the thick grass cushioned my arrival. I politely declined the invitation to accompany our passengers to Minehead, although Paul, clearly in better shape than me, did. I tottered over to a spot of long grass near the control tower, stretched out and fell into a much-needed sleep. Seven hours later I awoke totally refreshed, used the toilet in the control tower to wash and brush-up, just in time to meet the passengers when they returned a little later. Monty Stevens, the airfield manager, had spotted me earlier and shouted out, "If you take off after five o'clock, you do so at your own risk. The airfield is closed and I'm going home". Well there was nothing new in that, as it seemed to be the norm when and where we operated, rather than the exception. Later that evening Paul and I sat in the clubhouse at Cardiff Airport, and then as things tend to happen in life casually and in a serendipitous way I said, "Why must we always fly for others, why don't we operate for ourselves?" It was this remark following an arduous day that led us to form Cormorant Aviation, which proved to be my entry into the 'Business of Aviation'. Four regional airlines were to follow, plus two jet operations, all the result of my febrile imagination and self belief. These operations collectively generated almost two thousand jobs, a statistic, which has always given me an enduring feeling of pride and satisfaction.

It was the late evening of Thursday 18th September 1997, as I sat and watched the television, results of the Wales Devolution Referendum. Previously in 1979, 79.9 percent of the people had voted against the proposition, but now something better was expected. That evening the accession seemed to hang in the balance and when the TV commentator announced that Cardiff had just voted against. I switched off the television set in disgust and went to bed. The following morning I couldn't tune in to Radio 4, which was usual habit, and instead switched on the TV to Teletext, leaving the sound off. The very first thing I saw was that Wales had voted for devolution. With this I leapt out of my chair like a dolphin out of water, full of excitement at the result. This at least would show the world that Wales did have some pride, and I remembered the shame I had felt in Mexico in 1979, when the Swedish owner of the store I was in, turned to me and said, "What sort of people are you in Wales?" having seen the devolution result in a Mexican newspaper. The 1997 result however, resulted in a narrow 'yes' vote, by 50.3 percent, to a 49.7 percent 'no' vote. It had been a close run thing, but a victory nevertheless. Living outside Wales meant that I had no opportunity to vote, but I felt strongly that I should contribute in some way to the new feeling of optimism, which surely would sweep through the land. For four days I prowled around the house like a caged tiger, but by lunchtime on the fifth day I had arrived at my decision. I would return to Wales to set-up a National Airline, as I had in 1978, but only if I would be able to re-acquire the name 'Air Wales'. This might appear to be somewhat pretentious ambition on my part, but I felt confident in the outcome. However, the Germans say, "Man denkt, Godd lenkt", 'Man makes plans, God decides'. In 1979 'Air Wales', the company, had been purchased by Air UK and I felt that retrieving the name would prove difficult, if not impossible. However, on the fifth day, after just one telephone call, I was able to retrieve the name, and that for a mere one hundred pounds. Now fate intervened to ensure that my dream of a new National Airline for Wales would once again become a reality.

Family business now found me temporally staying in a small village in mid-west Wales. It was one morning in the local antique shop that I met a young aviation photographer, who was seeking a World War II flying jacket. Whilst helping him locate one, the conversation turned to the airfields which abound in west Wales. In this way I discovered that

Winston Thomas, an old chum from the previous Air Wales days, was now the lessor of Pembrey airfield near Llanelli. A few days later I visited Pembrey, and discussed with him the idea of a new Air Wales. The idea was received with great enthusiasm, and Winston felt that raising the finance for the project from local sources would not prove too difficult. Within a two week period I found myself addressing a meeting of potential investors at the Marriott Hotel, Swansea, when after a four hour speech I was able to persuade half of those present to financially support the new company. From the positions of Chairman and then Managing Director, I nursed the new airline through the formative two to three years of its existence, before resigning to assist the new Winchester based British Light Aircraft Company to locate its production facility in Wales under its Chairman, Brian Kyme. Despite moving all the jigs and tooling to Wales and storing them at their own cost, it took the Assembly fifteen months to refuse grant aid for a production plant, which would have employed up to four hundred and fifty workers. In the same time frame, a further application, at a much lower level of grant aid for an aircraft assembly plant employing two hundred people, was also rejected. This decision with its procrastination, timidness and lack of vision clearly indicated that while the Assembly were very good at opaque discourse, and issue fudging, they were certainly past masters at risk aversion. The BLAC has subsequently been embraced with open arms by the Romanians, where Aerostar SA has now agreed to build the aircraft parts and ship them to the UK, where they will be assembled and sold from their new base in the south west of England. I had realised from the beginning that returning to Wales as a Welshman to set-up a business would be very difficult. The old saying that 'a prophet is without honour in his own land', sprang to mind. I didn't expect flags to be waved, or bunting in the streets, but I did expect a letter from an Assembly member, a Member of Parliament, or a member of the European Parliament, congratulating and welcoming the re-appearance of

Air Wales. It came as rather a shock that not one such communication was ever received. The truth is that Air Wales received more support in 1978 from the various bodies in Wales than its successor twenty years later, after devolution and the creation of the National Assembly.

My disappointment at the apathy in Wales was soon alleviated by yet another visit to the United States. I sat fascinated by the little aeroplane attached to a map on the forward bulkhead of the cabin, a few seats in front of me. Driven by the Global Positioning System (GPS), I saw the aircraft climb out of Amsterdam Airport and set course for the States. About one hour later I watched it cross north Wales near Anglesea, a position confirmed by the captain on the aircraft intercom, informing the passengers that we were about to commence our crossing of the North Atlantic. As a pilot of many years, it still seemed like magic, watching the aircraft I was sitting in, move inexorably across the map. I was somehow taken back in time, when as a small child, I had sat enthralled, sitting behind Santa Claus as he flew his own aircraft over the roof tops of the city, delivering his Christmas presents, and all this in a Cardiff store. More recently I has watched the ship's progress, with a similar use of GPS, leave Harwich harbour and sail up the North Sea to its Gothenburg destination. The Boeing 747-400 had a full passenger load, and as we approached Kennedy Airport New York, I watched the display aircraft fly along Long Island Sound, and line up to land on the runway in use. The landing itself was as imperceptibly soft as a female's touch, and I marvelled at it, as did many of the other passengers, who burst into spontaneous clapping.

The date was Sunday the 9th September 2001, and I stood at one of the many bus stops waiting for the first hotel courtesy bus to arrive. As usual I hadn't booked a hotel room in advance, and that evening found myself at the Marriott Hotel in Queens. My ultimate destination was Buffalo in New York state, but the time of my arrival there was fluid, as I intended spending a few days in Manhattan, either on my journey out or on my return. The clerk at the hotel check-in apologised to me that she had no vacancies for that evening, alternatively she suggested that there were rooms available in the Marriott in downtown Manhattan, but if I was prepared to wait a while, the possibility existed of a room cancellation. I felt particularly weary after my journey, so I took a seat in the lounge and poured myself a coffee and read a Sunday newspaper. After a short while I became restless and once more approached the check-in, this time to arrange a ride downtown. She then confirmed that a cancellation had just occurred and a room was now available. Later I booked a flight with Jet Blue Airlines leaving Kennedy next morning, 10th September for Buffalo. As the half empty Airbus 320 climbed out over New York, the weather was misty with some low cloud and I could see the city only in part. What a difference to the weather the following morning, when the inhabitants were greeted with a perfect cloud free day in glorious sunshine. That morning, the 11th of September, America received the biggest shock since the attack on Pearl Harbour in 1941, when two rogue airliners smashed into the Twin Towers of the World Trade Centre. Being close in New York state, I could see the shock on the faces of ordinary Americans, as they themselves had never previously faced an attack on their shores like this in modern times, and yet again I reflected on my own good fortune; a quirk of fate that somehow I had just missed being in Manhattan that very morning.

My four days in Ellicottville with Bill Northrup and Century Jet south of Buffalo were well spent in almost ceaseless sunshine. What was truly amazing was the complete absence of aircraft, and jet contrails in the sky. There was an all-pervading quietness, like the lull before the storm. Was this an omen of a further more ghastly attack? Fortunately all these feelings were misplaced, as I now planned my return to New York. All the civil airlines were on stand-down, so I decided to take the Amtrak train service and return in a more leisurely, but slower style. The route took me through the towns of Rochester, Syracuse, and Utica to Albany and then down the

Hudson Valley to New York's Grand Central station. Sitting comfortably in the train I spied the interesting name of Poughkeepsie on the map (the name of a Native American tribe), and just north of it the name of Hyde Park, in Duchess County, a place I had wanted to visit for many years. Six hours or more after leaving Buffalo I left the train at Poughkeepsie and asked the cab driver to drop me off at the nearest hotel or motel to Hyde Park. I was highly pleased that directly opposite the estate was a motel with vacancies, and as soon as I checked-in and dropped my bag, I was crossing the fields towards the home of my long time political hero, one Franklin Delano Roosevelt, in my view the greatest man of the twentieth century. The house was named Springwood, and he had been born there on 30th January 1882, the land and house standing on the eastern bank overlooking the Hudson River. As a child my father's father, often spoke of FDR (as he was called), in my presence, extolling his virtues as a great man, and everything I had studied and read in my lifetime only confirmed that opinion. My pace quickened and my excitement grew as I walked around the great man's house, museum and library, being somewhat surprised at the lack of any security, particularly as it was late in the evening and only days after the attack on New York. The next day I accompanied the guide around Springwood, spent hours buying books in the shop and studying artefacts in the museum. I stood apparently alone, later that day downstairs in the museum with just a ceremonial rope separating me from Roosevelt's specially built car with its hand controls. On the nearby wall was a large picture of him in the same car with his black Scottish setter, Falla, along side. Now I had the overwhelming urge to step over the rope and sit in the car as the great man had so often done in years past. In that split second of doubt before action, a security guard materialised out of thin air and walked towards me. I tried hard to persuade him to allow me this one favour, but in vain. Such things were just not permissible, so I contented myself by sitting on the bench on the south lawn, much as Eleanor and

FDR had done many times. He had won four terms (a record) as America's President, yet strangely had never won Duchess County, his home patch. All this he accomplished whilst having been struck down at the age of forty (in the summer of 1921), with poliomyelitis. From that moment a man who emanated animation and vitality, had to crawl around his home, or be pushed like a baby in a wheelchair. He trained to walk with leg braces, he himself designed, but only then with another's support. He had a stubborn refusal to be pitied and inevitably presented a bright confident face to the world. A cripple then, who had successfully brought America through the greatest depression in world history, saved the country from the threat of Communism, and then stayed on as the main driving force to defeat world Fascism. I spent three days absorbing the atmosphere at Hyde Park, and I knew that the world we lived in today in Franklin Roosevelt's world. It manifestly is not the world of Adolf Hitler, whose one thousand year Reich lasted a mere twelve years. Neither is it the world of Joseph Stalin, whose communist regime eventually imploded before our eyes. Nor is it the world of Winston Churchill, who glorified Kingship and Empire, concepts now largely out dated and vanished into history. On my final evening I stood alone in the Rose Garden, where Franklin, his wife, Eleanor, and his two dogs are buried. There I paid homage to a man of the loftiest ideals, who faced life with great courage and good humour, surely the final and true test of any man. In April 1945 a future President of the United States, Lyndon Johnson, said of him, "He was the only person I ever knew, anywhere, who was never afraid. God, how he could take it for us all!"

I closed my eyes in the darkness cabin of the Boeing 747 as it crossed the Atlantic at its cruising level of 34,000 feet. In a half-sleep, my mind travelled back to my early days of flying in the 1950s and 60s, closer in many ways to the flying of the 1930s, than the new millennium. Many of my former colleagues had now folded their wings, and some indeed had had their wings folded for them, forever! I had travelled far from my valley home, and travel is fatal to prejudice, bigotry and narrow-mindedness, as Mark Twain once reminded us. Yes I was glad that I lived and flew when I did, when the enrichment of my knowledge had been quickened by the necessity of the moment. Now I looked forward to the next challenge with its attendant risks, in the firm belief that only a person who risks is really free. The colours of the sky were now emerging as the sun rose in the east and I instinctively knew that this was not the end, in fact it was not even the beginning of the end, but for me it was certainly, the end of the beginning!

The Viscount Alanbrooke.
104 Naunton Lane,
Cheltenham,
Glos.

11. May 82.

Dear John.

Here at last the long awaited book. Please accept this copy as a token of my respect to you as a Historian, Family-man, Pilot and Adventurer!

Heaven knows where you are now, but maybe you will be back at Glyncornel sometime soon to find this. I suspect you have probably found your way to the Falklands?

Give my regards to the family.

Yours sincerely

Victor

The mining valley of the Rhondda in Wales is not the natural breeding ground for pilots in peacetime. John H Evans however, was a successful and notable exception to the rule. Although nourished in the Welsh non-conformist tradition, his was always a buccaneering spirit allied to a questing mind. Drawn to flying by his memories of a World War II bomber pilot, his adventures spread from Belem to Berlin; Ramsgate to Rio, the Scillies to San Antonio and Tangier to Toronto.

Inadvertently he became involved with the Mafia, was approached to help in the escape of a 'Great Train Robber' and aroused the wraths of the Libyans, when he rescued a beautiful blonde from Tripoli. He was flown over 10,000 hours and carried such notables as John Lennon and Yoko Ono, Prime Minister of Grenada.

His entrepreneurial spirit helped to start three UK regional airlines and two jet operations creating almost 2,000 UK jobs in the process. Clearly a 'character', in his book one can well detect his enjoyment of life, his eye for the main chance-business and ladies alike! Indeed his lack of pomposity and disregard for authority, coupled with a natural humour is typical of the man and is brilliantly encapsulated in this book. Yet his search for his bomber pilot schoolboy hero displays a great sensitivity in this most poignant of passages. Aviation is an international business allowing participants to make contact and develop personal relationships with many cultures and people across the world. It is therefore quite remarkable that John H Evans stands out on this stage and is recognized for his knowledge, vision and will to succeed.

In this book his very individual and imaginative style of narration captures the reader's attention from start to finish, and once started is difficult to put down.

So 'fasten your seatbelt' as you are taken on a roller-coaster ride of your emotions!

Lightning Source UK Ltd.
Milton Keynes UK
UKOW04f0626180615

253708UK00004B/131/P

9 781465 359667